Charles
Nodier
Pilot of Romanticism

Charles
Nodier
Pilot of Romanticism

A. RICHARD OLIVER

 Syracuse University Press   1964

This work has been published
with the assistance of a
Ford Foundation grant.

LIBRARY OF CONGRESS
CATALOG CARD: 64-8670

Manufactured in the United States of America
by The Heffernan Press of Worcester, Mass.,
and bound by Vail-Ballou Press, Binghamton, N. Y.

To STANLEY PARGELLIS,
historian, humanist, and for
long years the genial curator
of the Newberry Library, this
book is respectfully inscribed.

Preface

ASIDE FROM *La Fée aux miettes* and a few short stories, the vast bulk of Charles Nodier's literary output has all been forgotten.

If Nodier had been a composer instead of an author, he might have fared better in the eyes of posterity. The recurrent figures, the theme with variations, the repeated prose rhythms, all indicate a musical gift of the highest order. The elusive champion of the fantastic, the *féerique*, the *merveilleux*, of the truth "as it is given my nature to see it," would have been invincible in tone. Instead he was the helpless target of all the fact-gatherers simply because they were not geared to understand his complex musical statement, which demands a generally fixed overall form containing shifting patterns of detail within.

French critics complain that Nodier wrote for half a century, yet one cannot point to a single masterpiece of his invention. The fact is that Nodier's masterpiece is not one work, not a novel, nor an essay, nor a short story, but a problem which runs like a thread through them all: through the early novels ("I must be loved") coloring his illegitimate birth and fictionalizing his early years; through the articles, essays, prefaces, and stories, which promise an earth-shattering revelation which never comes; and finally, through the puzzling mystification of the later novels, *Trilby*, *La Fée aux miettes* and, most baffling of all, *Le Roi de Bohème*.

The constant search for love in dreams, the escape in dreaming, the preference for dream over reality ("enjoyment is good, but dreaming is better"), the new theory of love ("something myself, yet greater than I") are all manifestations of a thwarted love which find their home key in the impossible love plots of *Trilby*, *La Fée aux miettes*, *Francesco Colonna*, *Jean Sbogar*, and many more.

But Nodier was tormented on another score: that of literary creation. "Let us make ancient verses on new subjects." He quoted André Chénier as having once said that, long before romanticism had come into its own. Yet, try as he might, he could not meet the implications of that challenge. Though he was old enough to be a precursor, all his artistic innovations of a romantic sort ended in frustrating failure: his meager poetic output was overshadowed by that of Victor Hugo; the fantastic short story was preempted by Hoffmann twenty years after Nodier introduced the genre in *Une Heure ou la vision* (1806). So he had to be content with a secondary role in the romantic movement, that of guide or mentor. Since he could not *do,* he must perforce guide the faltering first steps of the young movement with his advice and criticism. This he accomplished, if not always with the loving care of a father, at least with the sympathetic hand of the teacher.

Because of all this, Nodier's compelling though elusive figure demanded a biography that would take into account the exaggerated praise of his contemporaries and the equally unmerited scorn of later writers, to weld all into a new appraisal of his exciting work and personality.

I must assume full responsibility for all the passages translated from French into English except for one paragraph from Madame de Stael's *Germany* (London, Murray, 1813), quoted in Chapter III. (See note 5.)

My thanks are due to M. Jean Mennessier-Nodier for many interesting details about his great-great-grandfather known only to him, to M. Jean Pommier for opening the treasures of the Bibliothèque de Louvenjoul to my use, to Professor P. G. Castex for putting into my hands an unpublished dissertation for the *doctorat d'état* by E. Duban on Nodier's youth, and to Mlle Anne Marie Laffitte, who helped me locate Nodier's letters in the files of the French Academy. M. Franz Calot was very kind to receive me in the Arsenal Library and show me many Nodier manuscripts. Nor must I forget the courteous service of the Archives Nationales, the Bibliothèque Nationale, the Bibliothèque Mazarine and the Bibliothèque de la Sorbonne. I should like to acknowledge my indebtedness to the staff of the Library of Dole, which houses the manuscript notes of August Dusillet on Nodier's lectures there in 1808, and to the archivists of the Doubs and Jura departments. And finally,

I wish to express my special thanks to M. Jacques Mironneau, curator of the Besançon Library, who placed before me the many fugitive pieces of Nodier and Weiss held there, as well as to M. France Dobrovoljc of the Library at Ljubljana.

A. RICHARD OLIVER

Washington, Pennsylvania
Fall, 1964

Contents

I

A Child of the Revolution

(1780-1804)

*We were the orphans
of liberty disinherited
by Napoleon.*

NODIER, *Clémentine*

ANYONE living in Besançon in the late eighteenth century was aware of the emergence of a child prodigy who took part regularly in the deliberations of the Friends of the Constitution of that city. Not much older than the Revolution he supported, Charles Nodier was the only son of Antoine Nodier, a respected citizen who had rather late in life abandoned a successful teaching career to take up the profession of law. This change in the older Nodier's ambitions necessitated a move to the city of Besançon where in due course Charles was able to come into close contact with the rising revolutionary tide that swept the provincial city. The ease with which he discussed problems of state endeared him to the local citizenry, who soon came to look upon him as a boy wonder. Perhaps the emotional climate of those days fostered an admiration of new ideas in the very young, in any case, Charles enjoyed immensely his reputation as an *enfant célèbre*.

The Nodier family originated in the eastern part of France bordering on Switzerland known as La Franche-Comté. From 1032 an appendage of the Holy Roman Empire, the province became a quasi-independent ducal entity in 1382, first in the domain of the Capetian line of Valois-Burgundy and later under the House of Hapsburg with Margaret of Austria. The almost four hundred years of relative political freedom were brought to an end by Louis XIV, who annexed the little duchy to the kingdom of France after the peace of Nimegen in 1678. Even then there were Nodiers in the area around the capital city of Besançon, in the towns of Arbois and Ornans, in the villages of Aumont, Colonne, Grozon and Pupilien, who had themselves buried face down in protest to the rape of their land by the French invader.

The first Nodier to come to public notice was Charles' paternal grandfather Joseph, a stonemason, *maître-maçon,* also called an *entrepreneur* and popularly known as "the architect," who, having been summoned in 1776 to the Château du Pin near Lons-le-Saulnier to carry out repairs of one of the dungeon towers, lost his footing and plunged to his death on the flagstones below. The old stonemason was ninety-two at the time of the accident, having been born at Ornans in 1684. His second wife, Anne Claude Coton, had borne him seven children, four of whom survived: two sons, Antoine Melchior, May 20, 1738, the father of the writer, and Antoine François Xavier, September 24, 1747; and two daughters, Charlotte Françoise, 1741, and Elisabeth, 1744. The latter, having been seduced by a court lawyer, André Pajot, became the mother in turn of another distinguished member of the family, the Lieutenant-General Count Claude Pierre Pajot, February 3, 1772, who later changed his name to Pajol. As an officer under Napoleon, he won fame at the battles of Austerlitz and Jena and defeated Bagration at Ochmiana. Retired in 1816 for his opposition to the Restoration, he placed himself at the head of the insurgents who hastened Charles X's exile in 1830. During the July Monarchy he commanded the first division and was made governor of Paris. After the July Revolution, Charles was to appeal to this influential cousin to help him retain his post as librarian of the Arsenal.

Both of Joseph's sons were exceptional students who maintained an active interest in letters. The youngest, Charles' uncle, entered the gendarmerie at Lunéville. He was in command of the gendarmerie at Bourg when a band of highway robbers was apprehended and executed there, an event later utilized by Nodier in his *Souvenirs de la Révolution*. His taste for literature, more than any ties of family relationship, endeared him to his nephew.

Following the pattern set for bourgeois families in the eighteenth century in France, the first-born son of the architect was probably intended for the priesthood, for he entered the Congregation of the *Oratoire*. After brilliant studies with this order, Antoine Melchior taught Latin and rhetoric in the principal *collèges* the Congregation controlled in Besançon, Lyons, and Salins. In Lyons he had as colleagues such outstanding professors as Lasserre, author of an excellent treatise on rhetoric, and Delisle de Salle, the philosopher of nature. On one of these assignments he met Mathieu Oudet, an acquaintance he was to develop later when that gentleman became Fouché's secretary. Around 1763-65 Antoine was sent to the Collège Royal de Salins, an assignment he did not relish, or perhaps he had had enough of teaching and decided to study law. Toward 1768 he quit the Congregation to become a member of the *cour de parlement de Besançon*. The bar association of the capital city in the Doubs department boasted at that epoch many brilliant attorneys of the calibre of Courvoisier, Druout, and Grasse, so that Nodier, who was better known as a distinguished professor and man of learning than for his ability to plead, was never given any important cases. There are also signs that the ex-Oratorian was not pleased with his new profession, and would probably have remained a mediocre lawyer for the rest of his life if the Revolution had not brought him into prominence.

In 1778 Antoine engaged as housekeeper Suzanne Pâris of Granges-Longin, commune of Grozon, near Poligny, a large, bustling girl with dark complexion in her early twenties. He soon found himself obliged to marry the pregnant girl. Since she had no education and no dowry she was poorly received by Antoine's mother, who for long years would not give her consent to the match. However, the couple lived secretly as man and wife in Besançon and their two children, Charles (1780) and Elise (1784) were born out of wedlock. When Charles was an infant, Suzanne lived at Poligny with him while Antoine stayed in Besançon to look after his practice. On weekends and on holidays the lawyer would join his wife and his dear little *Fanfan*. The French have a habit of doubling the last syllable of a given name to create a term of endearment; thus Henri gives the nickname of *Riri*. Charles, who was referred to by the couple as *l'enfant*, soon became *Fanfan*. Both children were finally legitimized when the couple was legally married on September 12, 1791, two weeks after Antoine was elected presiding magistrate of the criminal tribunal the Revolution had set up in the Doubs department. Veuve Nodier was finally persuaded to give her consent now that her son had become a public figure, but she refused to come to the wedding. How seriously Antoine viewed the regularizing of his marital status may be judged by the fact that he presided in court that very same day.

A fervent and enthusiastic supporter of the oncoming Revolution and an active member of the Jacobin Club of Besançon, Antoine had been elected mayor on November 16, 1790, by a very slim margin. However, he had to give up this office when he was elected presiding judge of the revolutionary criminal tribunal of the Doubs department, August 28, 1791. His period of tenure on the bench was marked by severity and weakness: he sold no favors, but at times he sadistically pursued the enemies of the Revolution with the full punishment provided by law. Yet there is a great deal of evidence to support the story that young Charles prevailed upon his father to acquit Madame d'Olivet, the grandniece of the celebrated grammarian and critic, the Abbé d'Olivet. This lady had been accused of sending money to her émigré husband, an act of treason then punishable by death. As Weiss, Charles' boyhood friend and lifelong admirer, tells it,[1] the only proof against her was a written denunciation, which mysteriously disappeared from her file before her case came to trial. Weiss intimates that the judge was only too glad to look away as Charles destroyed the incriminating document in this feeble case.

The simple truth is that Antoine Nodier did not have the stuff to make an equitable judge. He did not possess an adjusted personality and the solid integrity of character that would have enabled him to render calm and impartial decisions. He had never been a judge, yet he was raised in a flash to the highest magistracy in the region, a promotion which certainly went to his head. To make matters worse, through a blunder of the revolutionary authorities in Paris the civil court that Nodier inherited was hastily transformed into a criminal one as well in a legally questionable move to simplify regional jurisdiction. Antoine certainly was not equipped to sit as presiding judge in a criminal court. This may be deduced from his conduct on the bench. After a considerable period of inactivity, which he filled with denunciations of priests who had refused to take the civic oath of allegiance, pursuing aristocrats who had not removed their coats-of-arms from their carriages and the façades of their homes, and squabbling over questions of proctocol (should he wear his official ribbon when he went to the play?, etc.), Nodier moved the tribunal, equipped with guillotine, to try the insurgents of *la petite Vendée*, to Ornans, September 7, 1793. Of the forty or fifty insurgents that faced him in each session, he managed to send three to the guillotine on September 14, four on September 18, and five on September 21. To all these executions his young son Charles, aged thirteen, was an unwilling witness, having been taken along because the Nodiers had some relatives in the area. Antoine opened the first session with a fiery speech to the effect that he had come to *punish* the enemies of the Revolution; hardly the language of a judge. Then, taking a fancy for this barnstorming tour of justice, he moved the court to the adjacent town of Bourg to continue the trials there. Upon learning from an informant that one of the rebels he had pardoned at Ornans was a detractor of the quondam government and should have been punished, Judge Nodier summoned that gentleman to appear in Bourg to be tried again for the same crime!

In view of the foregoing, it is difficult to avoid George Lenôtre's stricture regarding Nodier *père*. "Out of consideration for the son, . . . history has been indulgent toward the father."[2] It is even more difficult to accept Charles Nodier's image of his father as a tower of strength and a symbol of probity whose only fault was a naive zeal in support of a Revolution whose increasing madness ended by filling him with horror.

When his mother died, Antoine took full possession of the house situated at number 11 in the Rue Neuve (now Rue Charles Nodier) in Besançon. Begun by Joseph in 1766 on lands appropriated from the expelled Jesuits, it was finished two years later. Antoine added the court and a little pavilion behind it early in 1798 at a cost of 4,900 francs. There the little family could live together for the first time with a sense of permanence, occupying the second floor and renting out the first for economy's sake. This was the only property the mayor and judge owned. Charles was to become familiar with the wrought-iron railing enclosing the second floor balcony with its proud *N* worked into the center circle and beyond which he could see by twisting his head slightly to the right the dolphin's fountain built by Luc Breton in 1785 and *la sirène* which his grandfather had brought from the gardens of the Palais Granvelle, where it had been since the sixteenth century, and encased in the corner of the building across the street.

Little is known of Charles' childhood prior to the family's coming together in the Rue Neuve, except that he sadly missed his father and resented having to stay with a mother he hated. Suzanne had the reputation of being brusque, cold and stingy, hardly characteristics that would endear her to a gifted son. In 1789 she was known as one of the most boisterous fire-eating members of the female revolutionary club, Les Amies de la Constitution. The children were allowed to shift for themselves while the mother, an illiterate, decided the fate of the nation. Charles inherited his physical characteristics from her, including a predisposition to Addison's disease, which accounted for Suzanne's excessively dark skin pigmentation. Although not properly identified at the time, there is no doubt, according to Dr. Benassis' diagnosis of the symptoms, that both Charles and his mother suffered from this ailment.[3] Perhaps it is well to state here that the weakness, the quick fatigue, the constant irritability, the nervousness and the episodes of hypoglycemia (convulsions due to sugar shortage, which Charles thought were epileptic fits) that he complained of throughout his life are all classic symptoms of an insufficiency of the adrenal gland. That Charles developed this disease is proved by the fact that as a boy he was extremely fairskinned; it was not until he reached maturity that the onset of this disease, producing the increased pigmentation so typical of it, prompted one ignorant observer to publish a stupid newspaper article entitled, "Charles Nodier, négrier."

Charles' predilection for intellectual pursuits he got from his father. The clandestine existence forced upon the family obliged Antoine to take upon himself his son's education, and Charles knew no other tutor until he was ten, when he was sent to the *Pension Mathieu*. However successful the ex-professor may have been with the boys at the *collèges* at Salins and Lyons, he set up a bizarre program of study for his son which seems to have had as its aim the making of a prodigy. At eight he was already reading Montaigne, at nine philosophy, and it seems that by the age of ten he could write themes with equal facility in Latin or French. For relaxation the child could browse in Amyot's translation of Plutarch's *Lives*. Singularly lacking in this program of study was physical exercise, and Charles for the most part had to forego the fun of playing with other children because his playfellows, aware of his parents' irregular connection, called him bastard. For years he was known to the adult world simply as "Suzanne Pâris' son." How deeply these epithets seared into the child's mind can be seen from his earliest adolescent attempt at self-portraiture entitled *Moi-Même*, wherein he refers to himself as "Charles Anonyme Trois Etoiles" (the "trois étoiles" being the three asterisks used by French writers after an initial when a person shall be nameless). That Charles blamed his mother for his unloved childhood, his erratic upbringing, and his wayward youth is evident in his later correspondence: his letters to his father are always long, confiding, affectionate chats; his infrequent letters to his mother are cold, formal notes, announcing births, baptisms, and illnesses. Moreover, when in 1825, as head of the Arsenal Library, he was announcing to his correspondents that he was mourning the "loss of our mother" it was to his mother-in-law, Madame Charve, that he was referring. When his own mother died the following year he made no mention of it, though both he and Elise went to Besançon to settle the estate.

An anecdote drawn from an eyewitness account of Nodier's early youth amply illustrates Charles' unfilial attitude toward his mother:

As for Madame Nodier, she entertained a respect for her son based upon the instinctive premonitions she had of his talents. In spite of this admiration, she had to admit to herself that he got up too late or did not return home until early morning; that he had slept with all his clothes on and that his room was in a hopeless disarray. From time to time she allowed herself to make some observations on these subjects, but our poet listened to her with such solemn gravity, or answered her in such high-sounding phrases ending so unexpectedly for her that, not knowing what to think and not finding a ready answer she would go away after a moment's silence taking with her the better half of what she had intended to say to him. One example taken from these domestic scenes will suffice to give the reader an idea of all the rest.

About the time he was writing *Le Dernier Chapitre de mon roman,* Nodier told one of his friends one evening to come to his room next morning to hear what he had already written and make such comment as he thought fit. When the friend arrived Nodier was still in bed. Our critic takes a seat near the bed and prepares to listen. The reading begins. Soon it is interrupted by Madame Nodier, who asks through the half-opened doorway, "Charles, aren't you getting up?" "You can see that I am not, mother," answers Nodier. Then he returns to his reading. Madame Nodier withdraws. About ten minutes later she returns: "Charles," she calls, "don't you want to get up yet?" "No, mother," he answers in the same phlegmatic tone. Madame Nodier retires again and patiently waits a little longer than the first time. Then, she comes back again and, still not advancing any farther than the door: "Charles, it is almost nine o'clock, the maid wants to go to church and has barely enough time to make up your room. After mass, she will have to prepare dinner and tend to other duties. This is the only time she has to put your room in order and for her to do that, you will have to get up." This time Nodier answers more fully: "Mother," he says after a moment's hesitation, assuming a grave and solemn tone of voice, "I see in all that only one extremity which I will have to face without trepidation, that is, that my room will not be made up today and I . . . I'm resigned to it." Madame Nodier, taken aback, went away and did not return.[4]

The scene speaks for itself: Madame Nodier seems not a little afraid of her talented son, while young Charles' attitude is one of condescension toward a menial.

In January, 1790, Antoine Melchior had already taken his seat as one of the fourteen municipal councilmen elected to insure a local government favorable to the triumphant Third Estate. The obscure provincial lawyer had been catapulted into prominence by the sudden turn of political events in Paris. Charles found this change in the family's fortune's entirely to his liking, and though he was not as yet the legally avowed son of Antoine, he set about emulating his idol and begged to play a part. It is clear that Antoine was not adverse to thrusting his charge into the public arena, but the opportunity did not present itself until midsummer.

It was the Festival of the Federation, set to commemorate the first anniversary of the taking of the Bastille. On the Champs de Mars, Talleyrand, Bishop of Autun, said a solemn high mass and La Fayette, at the head of the National Guard, took the oath of allegiance—along with the King—to the Constitution. Delegates from the citizens' militia and the regular army had been sent from Besançon to Paris to mark the event. To celebrate their return two weeks later, the patriots of Besançon organized a welcoming committee which went out to meet them on the Dijon road. Enthusiasm was at its highest. The Enfants de la Patrie, the most recent proliferation of the Revolution which favored youth, led the procession, dressed in their little blue uniforms, complete with shining miniature sabres which still managed to seem grotesquely long. In the midst of a group representing the *Pension Mathieu* rose a Roman standard, an eagle with wings spread wide, holding in its beak a tricolor banner bearing the inscription CONSTITUTION, the word of the hour. The proud bearer of this flag was Charles Nodier, who had earned the honor by memorizing a speech of welcome for the jubilant delegation which was bringing back from Paris the banner of liberty.

After two days of feasting—the children were also taken to the theater to see a comedy—the celebration closed with the ceremony of the deposition of the flags into the hands of the departmental directorate. Charles came forward in the name of his comrades and delivered the following speech:

"We offer to the fatherland the flag under which we came together to celebrate the happy return of our confederates. We place this in your hands and beg you to lay it at the feet of the august ensign which attests the union of the great family of the French. The rods, emblem of the strength of the Roman eagle, symbol of grandeur, must naturally take their place alongside that of union, which will make France the first empire in the world. Too young to serve and protect our country, we are eager to walk in the footsteps of our brothers; instructed by your teaching and prepared by your example, fired with the zeal and the courage which inspire you, we will in our turn uphold the Constitution, and we will make our nation, our law and our king respected."

No doubt other children made or read speeches that day in Besançon as elsewhere in France. It is also rather certain that Charles' allocution was written by his father, or by Mathieu. But the events of these three days remained vividly etched in Charles' memory as days of glory and notoriety, days he was eager to renew and multiply by further participation in the invigorating Revolution. Accordingly, after his father's November victory over the legally constituted authorities, thanks to the local Jacobins, the Friends of the Constitution, now affiliated with the powerful parent club in Paris, he pestered the incumbent mayor with pleas to let him speak in public again.

Knowing the boy to be mature beyond his years, the following autumn Antoine set Charles the task of writing a speech in praise of liberty, the watchword of the Revolution. Whether the results far exceeded the indulgent parent's expectations, or whether the judge had decided to exploit his son's literary and forensic gifts to cement his own position with the bigwigs in Paris, the youthful orator was thrust upon the rostrum of the Society of the Friends of the Constitution, December 22, 1791. For fifteen minutes the Jacobins' Club listened in hushed attention to the shrill rhetorical piping of an eleven-year-old boy. There is nothing worthy of retaining our attention in this childish elocutionary exercise, but in the topsy-turvy social situation of the time this speech was considered a success. It was accorded the eternity of print by the Society of the Friends of the Constitution. With mounting pride Charles could read on the title page, "by master Nodier, aged 11 years."

The members of the Jacobins' Club were sufficiently impressed with this juvenile offering to invite the young author and orator to join their ranks the next year. After his reception speech, which was also printed, Charles took the oath of allegiance. Thus Nodier was a full-fledged member of the provincial Jacobins' Club with two published works to his credit at the tender age of twelve. His speeches show that in his brief political life he had already changed from a fiery Constitutionalist to a moderate Girondist.

The following September, 1793, the young revolutionist was initiated to the not-so-pretty side of the Revolution. A peasant uprising in the uplands of the Doubs department having failed, those that had not been able to escape to Switzerland were brought to the village of Ornans for trial. From September 14 to 21, they appeared before Judge Nodier at the rate of forty or fifty per day. Charles heard a dozen of the ringleaders condemned to death on the guillotine after a rather perfunctory examination. The curious child was allowed to follow them to the place of execution on the afternoon of the day of sentence and witness the decapitation of these poor wretches. Out of this unfortunate experience were to come unforgettable scenes in his later novels depicting with raw realism the beheading of Lucius in *Smarra*, the butchering of the unlucky Helen by the executioner in *L'Histoire d'Hélène Gillet*, and many similar scenes in his *Souvenirs de la Révolution et de l'Empire*.

This was followed by a trip to Strasbourg where Charles already had more than a nodding acquaintance with the revolutionary leaders. In March of 1793, the mayor of Strasbourg was sent to Besançon to be tried by the revolutionary tribunal. The demagogue Euloge Schneider accompanied him there and stayed at the Nodiers' during the weeks of the trial. A familiarity grew between the boy Charles and the renegade priest

Schneider which led to an exchange of letters between the two after the accuser's return to Strasbourg. Unfortunately, when Charles arrived in the Alsatian capital in December Schneider himself was in trouble with the Popular Society, having been denounced for kidnapping a young girl and similar flagrant acts which led to his downfall and eventual execution in Paris. After a brief visit with his father's friend, General Pichegru, in his headquarters on the Rhine, Charles returned to Besançon. His stay in the camp among the grizzled veterans, where sanitary conditions were practically unheard of, left Charles with a bad case of scabies, which Weiss tells us plagued him for many months thereafter.

The next political utterance of the precocious interloper was to end in near disaster for both father and son. The story of Joseph Barra, the young Vendean hero, is soon told. Challenged by Royalists, he was summoned to cry "Long live the king!" He shouted "Long live the Republic!" and was shot dead. He was fourteen years old. In the Convention, Robespierre proposed that Barra be granted the honors of the Pantheon, December 28, 1793. The Convention meantime was considering—also under Robespierre's urging, May 7, 1794—according similar rites to the remains of a youthful Marseillais hero, Agricola Viala, who was slain while attempting to destroy a bridge to prevent counterrevolutionaries from crossing the river Durance. On May 16, 1794, the Convention decreed the fête of Barra and Viala. Struck by the similarity in age of these heroes to that of his son, Antoine Nodier nudged officials of the Comité d'Instruction de la Société Populaire de Besançon, and they invited the fourteen-year-old Charles to commemorate the event locally in a speech. It is likely, though not certain, that Papa Nodier had a hand in preparing the speeches Charles delivered earlier to the Friends of the Constitution. In the more ambitious apotheosis of Barra and Viala, the elder Nodier not only guided the young orator as to background material but may have even taken the pen from his hand to sketch a telling period or two. The imitation of Robespierre's oratorical style, the bloodthirsty raving, the extolling of the uniqueness of the virtues of the French Revolution, the fulminations against Pitt, are all too unashamed a reflection of the master in Paris to plead coincidence. All are excoriated here but the purest of the pure: the enemies at the gates, foreign and émigrés; the counterrevolutionary enemies within France, the corrupt Federalists and the traitorous Girondins.

"These monsters have been punished for their crimes . . . insofar, at least, as it is possible to punish crimes of such heinous nature. . . . The criminal heads of Vergniaud and Brissot have rolled under the terrible sword of the law. Gaudet, who made a laughing-matter of the most sacred dogmas, has brought to an end his immoral existence. Buzot and Pétion have met death in the plains of La Gironde and the bloody carcasses of the conspirators bear witness to the justice of the eternal and the vengeance of the people."

Even the lower-case usage of *l'éternel* for God, a peculiar manifestation of Robespierre's late "religious" ejaculations, is here repeated. The opportunistic judge was obviously trying to bend with the wind from the capital, eager to proclaim through his son's voice his adherence to the "incorruptible." But the 242 miles that separate Besançon from Paris made it difficult to catch the tunes from the fitful fiddlers in Paris. Little did he know that even as his son was pronouncing his bombastic eulogy of Barra and Viala the trap was being sprung that hurtled Robespierre into oblivion. The cheers of the Friends of Liberty and Equality had hardly died down when the news of Robespierre's fall reached Besançon. So the speech the boy-orator delivered on that afternoon late in July, 1794, was never published, and the angry looks, the uncomplimentary remarks, and the hostile press that hounded the Nodiers, father and son, convinced Antoine that the air of Besançon was no longer good for Charles.

He sent him to spend the rest of the summer with a friend of the family, Girod de Chantrans, engineer and ex-aristocrat, whom the Revolution had exiled from the fortified walls of Besançon. As presiding judge of the revolutionary tribunal of the Doubs department, Nodier senior had permitted Girod to withdraw quietly to his country house at Novillars, only five miles away. There, under the kindly guidance of Girod, young Nodier had the only days of carefree youth he was to know. But Girod provided more than companionship, more than fatherly love; he gave Charles enlightened, systematic instruction in mathematics, history, botany, and literature. In the morning, there were butterfly-chasing expeditions along the banks of the Longeaux, a naturalist's paradise. In the afternoon, there was the laboratory with its miscellany of instruments, fascinating for a fourteen-year-old boy. Thirty-seven years later, the ailing writer could still recall nostalgically, but with arresting vividness, the inventory of this makeshift workshop. The evenings were devoted to reading, scientific and literary. The cultured Girod knew his Shakespeare in English and treated the boy to extemporaneous translations that must have retained some of the master's touch, for Nodier became one of the few Frenchmen who thoroughly appreciated the genius of Shakespeare. This memorable, idyllic summer was to furnish Nodier two lifelong friends: entomology and books. Thanks to the gentle tutelage of a grateful ex-noble, the precocious zeal of the budding revolutionist was diverted to humanistic channels.

Unfortunately, the pastoral education did not last long enough. The Thermidorian reaction having calmed the ferocious temper of the Revolution, Girod de Chantrans on October 12, 1794, was permitted to return to Besançon two days out of ten. Gradually supervision relaxed, and by the end of the year both mentor and pupil were permanently returned to the city. Charles wasted no time in bringing to fruition the excellent lessons of the aristocrat naturalist. The study habits learned at Novillars turned him into a serious student of the literary masters of his country, whose works we find him absorbing, pen in hand, throughout the year 1795. His manuscript comments on Montaigne, La Fontaine, Racine, Rousseau, Bernardin de St. Pierre, though patently those of a student, show a maturity of judgment uncommon in a fifteen-year-old. Occasional imitation and translation of the ancient classics, especially Martial, mark this period. Most interesting perhaps of the literary activity resulting from Charles' association with Girod are the original poems, both verse and prose, especially the Ossianesque prose poem, *De-*

scription d'une nuit orageuse, so filled with the romantic overtones we usually associate with *Atala*.

Toward the end of the summer Charles came under the
influence of the proscribed revolutionary Louis Maribon
Montaut, newly released from prison. Did the fiery Jacobin
come to compare notes with his anxious colleague, Antoine
Melchior? In any event, to this brief acquaintance we owe the
boy Nodier's unpublished *Essai historique sur la Montagne*,
confirming his faith with the revolutionary cause of 1789,
and eulogizing Montaut's part in its proceedings. Two letters
from this *Montagnard* show how seriously mature men of
the time considered this precocious boy. The correspondence
of young Nodier up to 1795 demonstrates ease in a mutual
exchange of ideas with such men as Gaume, secretary to
General Sparre, the commander of Strasbourg; the naturalist
Lacroix, for a time professor in Besançon; and with the arch-
rebel, Euloge Schneider, on a variety of topics spanning
literature, politics, and science.

Early in 1796, Charles registered for the courses that
Badot (Latin), Joseph Droz (rhetoric), and Glo de Besses
(natural history) were offering at the Besançon Central
School, a brilliant new venture in secondary-school education
initiated by the Revolution. Enthusiasm for student esprit
de corps and learning inspired a group, led by Charles, to
form a society of Philadelphoi. There was considerable background in the Nodier family for this sort of free association:
Nodier's father was a Freemason, and in 1790 a gastronomic-
literary club was formed in Besançon which boasted cousin
Pajol as one of its members. Nodier's by-laws in the constitution of Philadelphia indicate he had in mind a fraternity
in the American college sense of the word: a bond that would
help the brothers on their way through life.

"I wanted to give society a moral and political code and
strengthen the ties between its members," Charles wrote.
(Besançon Library MS 1417, folios 121-122.) It was in
reference to his failure to accomplish this that he included a
wryly reminiscent passage in the course of an article on the
"Coutumes des Morlaques" for the *Télégraphe Officiel* July
15, 1813: "Not more than twenty years ago a young en-

thusiast who had received from nature an unbounded imagination and who had contracted in the schools a ridiculous
love for the institutions of the ancients got the idea of pro-
posing to France a society of friends." At first this harmless
adolescent literary club, complete with mystic signs and ritual
copied from Freemasonry, numbered only five or six members besides Nodier: Charles Weiss, the brothers Pierre and
Joseph Deis, Jean-Joseph Goy, Charles Pertuisier and Luczot
de la Thébaudais. The society degenerated into a noisy gang
in the course of a year. To make matters worse, at the
instigation of Charles, the society extended membership to
a twenty-five-year-old army captain, Jacques Joseph Oudet,
whose two nephews, Gabriel and Jean François Arbey, had
just become Philadelphoi.

In the course of human relations it is often difficult to
chart with any degree of accuracy the reasons for the as-
cendancy of one person over another. In the case of Oudet
and Nodier, the age differential of nine years is not enough
to account for the lifelong adoration of the army officer by
the writer. In other accounts Oudet is pictured as a soft-
spoken, likable chap with a flair for the ladies. He was a
good officer, brave in battle and a capable administrator.
He bore his wounds stoically and accepted his assignments
without criticism. In 1796 he was already a captain and
General Malet's adjutant in Besançon. He was killed at the
battle of Wagram in 1809 at the age of 38. Out of this exemplary career-officer Nodier made a god, the greatest orator
of the revolutionary era, and the most feared conspirator
since Brutus. As a boy Nodier worshipped Oudet; as a man
he spent a considerable part of his literary activity in spinning a legend to his memory.

There are signs that Nodier's political thinking was under-
going a change before the eulogy of Barra and Viala, his
last Jacobin pronouncement, which was really a concession
to his father's career. At Novillars the rereading of Amyot's
translation of Plutarch's *Lives* opened his eyes to the true
stature of the Girondins, whose ideals and heroic death were
not far removed from those of the Greek and Roman leaders.
Also the brief but important contact with Montaut could

not fail to have a sobering effect on the youth. Charmed by the silvertongued persuasiveness of Oudet, Charles easily shifted to the ranks of the moderate republicans who rightly preached that the Directorate could not last. This new political conviction was revealed in a shocking illegal act of violence, all the more disturbing since it indicated not only an infringement of the law, but an open revolt against his father's political commitments. The authorities of the city of Besançon having decreed the permanence of the guillotine on St. Peter's Square, Nodier and five or six Philadelphoi, egged on by Oudet, one night went with this officer to overturn and destroy the dread instrument of death. Thus Oudet, upon being elected archon of the society of Philadelphoi, transformed this group from a literary drinking club into an adolescent league for political action. The perpetrators of the mischief on St. Peter's Square were never apprehended, though it is unlikely that the city officials were ignorant of their identity.

Oudet also instituted reforms of the by-laws of Philadelphia. One, stipulating that new members must be elected by unanimous vote, very nearly brought the society's activities to an end. By this measure Oudet no doubt intended to restrict knowledge of the club's past acts of violence to a select few. It had the double effect of bringing to a halt the admission of new members and of frightening off some of the more peace-loving ones, who were overawed by Oudet's dominating personality and tyrannical assumption of power. At this point Oudet was transferred to another station. A few stalwarts, of which Nodier was the most sanguine, tried to keep the society alive; but never again did Philadelphia flourish except as a boy's memory. Oudet's ability to knit together a group and drive it to action with his dynamic personality fascinated Nodier. Not being a leader himself, he did what any hero-worshipping youth would have done: he drew as close to imitation of him as possible by means of unswerving loyalty in executing unquestioningly acts which the leader had decided were important to the movement. This capacity for getting things done haunted Nodier after Oudet's disappearance and he stubbornly insisted that he never met it again. Significantly, it was not until long after Napoleon's death that Nodier grudgingly conceded that the ex-emperor may have possessed the quality he so admired in Oudet. But Nodier did not know nor long serve Napoleon.

After Oudet's departure, Nodier's political thinking took another sharp conservative turn. The heritage of Oudet's ideal republicanism had vaguely sketched in Charles' maturing political consciousness the possibility of a compromise between the interests born of the Revolution and those which it had set out to destroy. This alliance of revolutionary tendencies with aristocratic beliefs, drafted by émigrés sobered and chastened by nearly ten years of exile, was encouraged by Charles' new royalist friend, Edouard de Charnage. But this youngster was no Oudet, and Nodier was not yet ready to discard the legacy of his hero, to whose doctrine and example of republican idealism he was to remain faithful for a long time to come.

There is more to being seventeen than endless discussions about politics, even if one is living in the time of a great revolution. Nor do literature and dreams of creative writing, however lofty, furnish daily bread. There was the matter of a career to be settled upon to give direction to carefree, aimless speculation. Charles had distinguished himself in natural history as de Besses' favorite student. Droz, who was one of the examining professors, has reported the embarrassment caused the judges by Nodier's learned and audacious answers at the orals terminating the course: it seems the jury accepted the seventeen-year-old youth's insights into the field of entomology with reservations.

The Nodiers toyed with the idea of having Charles become a lawyer like his father, but there is reason to believe Charles did not entertain this prospect for very long, if at all. The urgency of gainful employment became more acute as Charles approached his eighteenth birthday. More tolerated than supported by the Directorate, Antoine Nodier had been permitted to reenter politics in 1795, when he was elected first member of the *Directoire de département*. Later, 11 frimaire, an IV (December 2, 1795), he was named *commissaire du pouvoir exécutif près les tribunaux civil et criminel du Doubs,*

Besançon City Hall

Antoine Melchior Nodier, Charles' father, as Mayor of Besancon

Portrait of Nodier usually attributed to Franque,
but believed by some to be the work of Guérin

or, in contemporary French legal parlance, *procureur de la république,* a sort of district attorney. He was still bailiff of the archbishop of Besançon in his principality of Madeure, orator of the Masonic Lodge, administrator of the Public Assistance Bureau established in the old abbey of Bellevaux, and member of the Board of Education of the Doubs department. Successive attempts to secure Charles the post of secretary to his uncle, the captain of gendarmerie at Lons-le-Saulnier and of special lecturer in natural history in the Besançon Central School failed. The ex-mayor then used his influence, as one of the three members of the Board of Education, to have Charles appointed assistant librarian of the Central School, October 31, 1798.

Charles had been preparing in some measure for the eventuality of this appointment by making a classified bibliography of the holdings of the local bibliophile and esthete, the Abbé Claude Antoine Pellier. He furthered his interests in entomology in the company of Luczot de la Thébaudais, a brilliant young engineer then residing and studying in Besançon. Together they published a *Dissertation sur l'usage des antennes dans les insectes, et sur l'organe de l'ouïe dans les mêmes animaux.* In the winter of 1798, Charles was also busy learning the art of playwriting under the guidance of the minor poet and songwriter, Francis d'Allarde.

Nodier's interest in the theater of a lighter sort can be traced back to the period of his inflammatory speeches. In the summer of 1793, he successfully appeared in a play in a minor role. In the summer of 1794, after the Viala episode, when Charles attempted to make his second appearance as an actor, he was hooted and whistled off the boards by the politically-minded audience. This reversal may have discouraged the budding actor and playwright. In any event, there is no further evidence of dramatic activity until Charles' encounter with Francis.

And there were girls. Thin, somewhat above the average in height, Charles' wispy figure was almost too girlish to appeal to the opposite sex. His long, narrow, brooding countenance, his long tapering fingers, and his long spindly legs gave him too ethereal an aspect to attract the solid *bour-*

geoises of Besançon. Add to this an excessive timidity in the presence of women, frequent blushing, averted, downcast looks indicative of mental and physical discomfort, and one can understand that the girls responded to the boy's plight with titters and giggles rather than with sympathy. This did not prevent Charles from fancying himself a highly romantic lover, and he gave his schoolmates to understand that he was a veteran of many an encounter with the opposite sex.

In a city the size of Besançon, it is inconceivable, even in the fumbling confidences of adolescents, that a youth could air his romantic attachments without being obliged by his fellows to descend to personalities. Drawing upon a fertile imagination, Charles supplied the expected details with such assurance that his friends' skepticism turned to wonderment and ultimately, one supposes, to belief. How deeply Charles regretted having put his talent as a narrator to such nasty use—to revenge himself upon the Besançon girls for having slighted his essentially virile nature—can be judged from his abortive attempt to take his own life while in the company of the very boys he had duped. Fortunately the penknife was not very sharp, Charles fainted at the sight of his blood, and his friends immediately disarmed him and took him home. After Goy and Joseph Deis had left, Charles, still suffering the aftermath of the crisis, tearfully confided to Weiss that he was conscience-stricken because his wild tales had embarrassed many of his neighbors and had done irreparable harm to the good name of half a dozen Besançon girls. He made Weiss promise that he would undertake to deny the slanderous boasts and give assurance that Nodier would do whatever was necessary to make amends to the persons involved.

The matter seems to have ended there, but Charles' friends, fearful that he might again attempt suicide, set a round-the-clock surveillance over him for several days. Goy, who had gone home to Domblans, bombarded him with long letters to keep up his courage, but daily expected the news of Nodier's death. Instead, he received equally long letters from the would-be suicide setting forth reasons why he should destroy himself. These weighty protestations, apparently intended to convince the reader more than the writer, had the desired effect upon Goy, who came posthaste to Besançon. Breathlessly questioning the first mutual acquaintance he chanced to meet, Goy was surprised to learn Nodier had not only conquered his melancholy fit but was carrying on as before with even more doubtful companions. Disgusted, Goy returned to Domblans and bitterly complained to Weiss of Nodier's behavior toward him; he felt Charles had toyed with him merely to elicit expressions of concern and alarm.[5] The pity of this demonstration was that Charles could have moved in the most brilliant social circles. However, he felt that the family finances—the judge was an idealist, and like his model Robespierre did not make money out of the Revolution—did not permit him to appear in all the splendor befitting his father's political standing. He preferred therefore to spend his evenings in cafés, engaged in idle conversations and drinking bouts with congenial companions of his own sex.

Young Nodier attempted to overcome the momentary check offered his ego through creative writing. Besides the autobiographical novel *Moi-Même* already mentioned, a fragment of penetrating insight published by Jean Larat in 1921, Nodier tried verse and prose in the *galante* manner of the eighteenth century, literary essays, translations of Sallust and Virgil, and bibliographical studies. To stimulate his imagination, he resorted to strong doses of opium, which on occasion made him deathly ill. This unfortunate habit, coupled with the heavy drinking, was said to have brought on acute neurasthenia. Since his friends had prevented him from committing suicide, Charles now charged them with the responsibility of having condemned him to a slow death by tuberculosis; he told them he woke up one morning spitting blood.

Nodier's father, meanwhile, when it appeared that the *Directoire* would be superseded by a more fervent Jacobin government, addressed the revived Jacobin Club of Besançon in a stirring allocution "against the tyrants." Only two days later, August 12, 1799, Charles elected to air his reactionary views publicly on Granvelle Square in a little skit satirizing the Jacobins which he, Weiss, and remnants of Philadelphia had mounted. The performance was interrupted by the arrival of the police, who seized Weiss and two or three others. Charles eluded their grasp by taking refuge in the home of Girod de Chantrans nearby, hiding there until the storm blew over. The participants in this anti-Jacobin demonstration were later acquitted by a criminal court, but Charles nonetheless was fired from his post of assistant librarian for harboring Chouanist (royalist) tendencies. Napoleon's *coup d'état* of 18 brumaire three months later restored him to his position, but the father's political fortunes suffered a severe reversal as a result of the law of reorganization of 27 ventôse, an VIII (March 18, 1800). He was named one of three judges to the civil tribunal of the first instance of Besançon, a sort of minor assessorship which carried a stipend of 1,200 gold francs per annum. According to his own expression, this reduced him to the status of the petty judges of the little arrondissement of Besançon.

Late in the year 1800, the first of the Consulate, Charles turned to journalism. Under the patronage of the prefect of the Doubs department, Marsson, Nodier founded a newspaper called *Le Bulletin Politique et Littéraire.* In Paris the Arena-Ceracchi conspiracy against the First Consul had just been uncovered and the young editor seized on this copy to reveal the remnants of Jacobinism still extant in Besançon. These did not allow the accusation to go unchallenged, protesting vehemently in the press that Nodier and his father were both in the forefront of the Jacobins' Club, and suing the *Bulletin* for 12,000 francs damages. Luckily Marsson was in agreement with the accusation and Charles and his colleagues got off with a scolding. But the campaign of mutual denigration continued until late November, when Charles published a scurrilous pamphlet entitled "Charles Nodier to his fellow-citizens" in which he set about castigating the old Jacobin die-hards, whom he termed revolutionary lickspittles (*la valétaille révolutionnaire*). However, wishing to make an exception of his father, he undertook the defense of the ex-mayor and ex-presiding judge by calling attention to his "sixty years of exemplary political life." The burghers of Besançon were not above retaliating in a most vicious manner. Maddened by the attack, a few erstwhile members of the extinct Jacobin Club, the renegade priest Dormoy, the prefect's secretary Briot, the friend and correspondent of Nodier who had formerly been a member of the Council of 500, and the mayor Janson brought out an anonymous pamphlet entitled *Jacquemard Carillonneur*, in which Nodier's father was reminded of his terroristic revolutionary exploits and of his illegal connection with Suzanne Pâris. Charles could see a copy of his birth certificate proving his illegitimate birth. Not content with bringing father and son to heel with this foul blow, they derided Charles' filial piety and his literary pretensions. The circulation of this document scotched Charles' journalistic venture with the thirteenth issue. The ensuing embarrassment caused Nodier *père* to send Charles on his first visit to Paris, in December, 1800. There was also some hope that his connections in Paris would procure for his son a more attractive position than he held in Besançon.

Charles' duties at the library were not very trying, so there had been ample time for the composition of two or three playlets, a novel, *Les Proscrits* (*Exiles*), based on his readings of German romanticists in translation, the unfinished autobiographical essay *Moi-Même*, imitated from *Tristram Shandy*, and a *Bibliographie entomologique*. In the evenings, the Spartan meals and the Falstaffian drinking continued in the local cafés, generously spiced with topical gossip, criticism of La Harpe's literary dicta, and infrequent yet disparaging remarks about the Consul's government, which the youths hated because the return to order meant the closing of careers to all except future soldiers, financiers, and administrators. Out of these ruminations grew *La Napoléone*, a satiric ode, which Charles intended as a battle cry for the vanishing Philadelphoi, when it had been set to music by Francis d'Allarde.

One of their group, Pertuisier, had gone to Paris to attend the Ecole Polytechnique so that he could prepare himself to fit in with the new order. His glowing letters beckoned one and all to come to Paris and see for themselves the wonders wrought by Napoleon in one short year. Pertuisier had been careful to include in his letters references to successful bookhunting expeditions, an appeal that the young librarian found irresistible. Having obtained leave of absence toward the end of December, 1800, Nodier packed his slight literary baggage and climbed into the stagecoach. Four days later he was taking possession of a dingy room in the Hôtel de Hambourg, 69 and 70 Rue de Grenelle Saint-Honoré, run by Madame Pagnest, the wife of the stagecoach driver between Besançon and Paris. She had tacit orders from Nodier *père* to advance Charles odd sums if he needed them, while her husband was an occasional guest for dinner on the Besançon end of the mail run. This signal honor was no doubt intended to keep the Nodiers regularly informed of their son's doings in the capital, but it also served to placate the owner of the pension upon whose generosity Charles made frequent demands.

Nodier's first trip to Paris was a three-month voyage of discovery. His letters to his father glow with enthusiastic reports of literary and social activities. A letter to his sister dated January 18, 1801, describes in ecstatic periods the young author's joy in being permitted to visit the apartments of the First Consul. After some searches in the rich libraries, he completed and published his *Bibliographie entomologique*, at the behest of the great naturalist Lamarck: "M. de Lamarck has approved my entomological bibliography, qualified it as a work welldone, really classical, and encouraged me to hasten its publication."[6]

At this time too he met Lucile Messageot, the stepdaughter of one of his father's colleagues, Judge Charve of Dole near Besançon. Great was his despair when he learned that Lucile had married a painter, Jean Pierre Franque, a pupil of the fashionable David. But the situation was not displeasing to Nodier's Wertherian views on love, so he became a frequent visitor at the Franques'. Many years later, long after Lucile's death, Franque was to paint an idealized portrait of Charles; and Charles was to make Lucile the heroine of his *Werther*-inspired novel, *Le Peintre de Saltzbourg* (1803). Paris was really wonderful to the twenty-one-year-old visitor in that spring of 1801; in fact, he was in such demand that he barely had time for an occasional get-together with his old crony

Pertuisier, busy with his engineering studies. But the brilliant situation Charles had hoped to find had not materialized. In spite of his many economies, Charles' little hoard of money was so depleted that he had to return home in March.

The return to the stillness of the provincial town after the excitement and gaiety of Paris was quite a shock to the young traveler. Except for a short trip to Lons-le-Saulnier the previous summer and a three-week visit to Strasbourg in December, 1793 (whither he had been permitted to accompany a deputation of his father's friends from the Popular Society of Besançon, the Public Prosecutor Rambour and the stocking-manufacturer Détrey, sent to testify in favor of their countryman General Perrin, who lay under a charge of treason), Nodier had never been so long nor so far away from home. Neither Lons nor Strasbourg, both provincial cities like Besançon, provided the striking contrast between the populous, alert, busy center of intellectual activity and the quiet, routine-bound momentum of the Franche-Comté capital. Never before had his fellow-citizens seemed so stolid, so uninteresting, so intellectually dead. For weeks he brooded over his books in the library and at home, cursing every minute that took him away from his favorite studies: entomology, Shakespeare, and Goethe. Then in August he snapped out of it with his publication of *Les Pensées de Shakespeare*. Despite the fact that the edition was limited to only twelve copies and that, as Weiss reported rather smugly in a letter to Pertuisier later in the month, "it pleased no one," this was easily Nodier's most significant publication to date.

It is striking that Nodier's first published literary venture deals with Shakespeare, the giant introduced to France by Voltaire and then renounced by him when he found others turning to the great works with admiration. Notwithstanding the many translations of Shakespeare into French by Ducis, Letourneur, Laplace, etc., the Bard was still considered in France a brutal, formless primitive. It was not until a quarter of a century later, when the romantic school espoused him, that the French began to understand and appreciate Shakespeare. The visit of Kemble's Shakespearean troupe to Paris in the late summer of 1827 was followed immediately by adaptations of the great plays by the elder Dumas, Vigny, and Berlioz. The English actors presented the great tragedies: *Othello, Romeo and Juliet, Hamlet*. In the third edition of *Les Pensées* (1822) Nodier was already pointing out the beauties in the historical plays: The assassination of the nephew princes from *Richard III,* the disgrace of Wolsey from *Henry VIII* (Act III, Scene 2) and *King John* (Act IV, Scene 5), *Henry IV* (Act IV, Scene 5), and many more. He also published for the first time in French the famous will. It is true that the references are not always neatly tied down. However, this may have been no clumsy oversight, since, as Pingaud suggests, Nodier was floating in a few *pensées* of his own to test how they would fare in company with the authentic excerpts from Shakespeare's plays. In any case, if the popularity of a genuine Shakespeare was a facet of romanticism, then Nodier must certainly be given credit for having foreshadowed it at least a quarter of a century before the others.

In August and September, 1801, letters trundled back and forth between the friends in Besançon—often anthologies signed by several hands—and the distant Pertuisier, enthusiastic over Charles' literary activities. Thus Joseph Deis, in a footnote to Weiss' letter of September 9: "On the 23rd they are going to present Nodier's new *vaudeville*; I say new because this is the first one of his plays to receive the honor of performance, but you know that he has already written about a dozen."[7] Nodier had finally consented, with encouragement and some help from Francis d'Allarde, the light-hearted and popular *chansonnier*, to mount one of his comedies, *Lequel des deux? ou l'Amant incognito* (*Which of the Two? or The Disguised Lover*). But Nodier was right, the play was not a success, and it cannot be found in his published works or among the various manuscript sources.

In October, 1801, Charles made his second trip to Paris. This time the anxious parents were careful to take advantage of Francis' return to the capital after a tour of provincial theaters and asked the poet to see that Charles was delivered safely into the hands of another friend of the family, at the Hôtel de Béarn, Rue Coq-Héron. Carping, censorious, undisciplined, Charles' first act of defiance was to take the form of a visit to the notorious gardens of the Palais Royal, where he contracted gonorrhea from one of the many prostitutes who haunted that place. In a letter to Weiss, on the last day of the year, he complained about the discomfort this disease caused him, "the virulence of which all the ministrations of doctors Segond, Nayme, Favre, and de Bailly were powerless to alleviate."[8] He advised Weiss to destroy the letter so that the secret would be kept. But a pharmacist of Besançon, one Joseph Bailly, visiting Paris at this time, called on Nodier and upon learning the cause of Charles' malady revealed it in a letter to Weiss, January 9, 1802, and presumably to others as well.

When Charles was well enough to go out, he accompanied the Franques to meetings of the *méditateurs*, a group of the painter David's students, more frequently referred to as *les primitifs*, who seem to have been dedicated to a reform of religion, society, and costume through a revival of the arts and a resuscitation of the way of life of the philosophers of antiquity. Vegetarians, they believed that abstention from meat would save the world. The devotees let their hair grow long and sat around in flowing white gowns, eating oranges and dates and smoking oriental tobacco, discussing Pythagorean philosophy, reading the Bible and each other's works. Their mysticism took the form of a theosophy which coupled a vague sense of the grandeur of creation with an intuition of immortality.

Nodier's interest in mysticism reached back to his childhood, when, with his father, he had listened enraptured to the tales of a strange guest, the illuminist Jacques Cazotte. Similarly, he gave a childish mystical framework to the Philadelphoi, which he gathered from Masonic rites learned from his father. Adept in botany and entomology, he early came into contact with Rosicrucians, who taught that a life-lengthening panacea would be revealed to students of natural science. He had also written an essay on Lavater's *Physiognomonie*, but it was not until his arrival in Paris that Charles was able to meet the leading representatives of the various illuminist cults that were to flourish under the Empire.

Thanks to Mercier, he met the Bavarian mystic Dr. Freimuth Sayffert, who believed in material reincarnation, and Nicolas Bonneville, Sayffert's interpreter and also a translator of works of German romanticism. Together they initiated Nodier to German illuminist doctrine. Bonneville favored a specialized form of Pythagoreanism, an adoration of nature instead of gods, which Charles was to find again in his new hero, Maurice Quaï, leader of the *méditateurs*. According to August Viatte,[9] besides communicating his enthusiasm for Pythagoras, Quaï sketched for Charles the filiation of Christian love from Pythagoras to Plato, to the Essenians of Syria and the Therapeutics of Lake Moeris, perhaps even indicating the analogy with Hindu philosophy, but he left the working out of these ideas to his disciple, Auguste Gleizes, who stated, in his *Thalysia*, that Nodier was completely won over to his views. But Charles' recorded enthusiasm was reserved for Maurice Quaï, who led the meetings draped in a purple mantle, a white turban, and sandals, and heavily scented with perfume. His "god-like" serenity Charles compared to the prophets of old; his "literary potential effaced the great Chateaubriand," he wrote in a glowing letter about this period to Weiss. "He is Job, he is Isaiah, he is Klopstock; imagine what a man this must be who joins to everything that is most distinguished in geniuses the brush of Poussin, the way of life of Pythagoras and the face of Jupiter Ammon."[10]

An entirely different view of Maurice Quaï was offered by E. J. Delécluze,[11] a contemporary of both the future author and the budding painter-mystic. Himself a pupil of David, Delécluze had ample opportunity to observe the antics of Quaï in the great man's school and later in his own atelier. At first a young painter not without promise, Quaï soon became known to his fellow-students as the Don Quixote of the studio for his strange behavior and extreme opinions on art. Later, when he left David to form a sect of *primitifs* in art, the same group young Nodier knew as the *méditateurs*, he earned the further appelation of Agamemnon. It was at this period, Delécluze tells us, that Quaï would fly into fits of rage when presented with a painting he thought old hat;

screaming such epithets as *vieille Pompadour* and *rococo*—
he hated everything reminiscent of Louis XV—he would rush
about the offender's studio wrecking whatever he could lay
his hands on: bibelots, objets d'art, canvases, easels and, if
not arrested in time, even the furniture. This picture of a
demented painter who had not long to live contrasts strangely
with Charles' estimate of the calm, Olympian philosopher
who could be compared favorably to the prophets of old and
who overshadowed Chateaubriand. It may be that Nodier's
lifelong hatred of Voltaire sprang from the same source, for
Quaï's series of scornful epithets usually ended with, "C'est
comme M. de Voltaire!" We are alerted again as to how far
Charles could go in his admiration of contemporaries who
stirred his imagination.

His excitement over meeting the *méditateurs* did not prevent Charles from frequenting Francis' favorite haunts,
among them the Théâtre des Variétés, where he was introduced to the popular *vaudevillistes* and *chansonniers* of Paris.
Francis contributed heavily to Nodier's support on this trip,
no doubt hoping that one of the young poet's little plays
might be produced with success in the giddy capital. But the
two or three comedies Charles brought with him never left
his portmanteau. The repertory of the Théâtre des Variétés
and the conversations of the actors and playwrights in the
café of the playhouse convinced him, as Weiss tells us, "that
his literary talent did not extend to the theater." He also
visited the Café Putode where he might foregather with such
diverse literary lights as Bonneville, Marie Joseph Chénier,
Sébastien Mercier, and Villetard. It was then he began circulating clandestinely *La Napoléone*, his proud attack against
the tyrant, Charles' second act of defiance within six weeks.
The anonymous ode was passed from hand to hand in manuscript form just after the Peace of Amiens, and a copy even
reached a young man in Besançon, who together with a friend
sat up all night reproducing it. The next day the talk in
Besançon was filled with knowing guesses as to the identity
of the author of the diatribe against Napoleon. In Paris the
authorities took no notice of the little poem, so Charles published his novelette, *Les Proscrits*, in which many of the

invectives used in *La Napoléone* against tyranny reappear, thus making a confrontation of the published work with the manuscript a simple lesson in sleuthing that would have led inevitably to the author of both. But if the consular government, whose agents had matters of greater moment to attend to just then, could afford to treat Nodier's third defiant act with the same contempt as the second, the apprehensive father in Besançon would not, and Charles was called home for the second time in June, 1802.

Another of the bizarre incidents which were to stud Charles' career occurred on the way. Influenced by his association with the *méditateurs*, Charles had let his hair grow till it was almost a foot long and he had not shaved in many months. At Troyes, where the courier stopped to refresh the horses, Charles' emaciated and hirsute appearance caused the local authorities to suspect him of being a deserter. (Charles was of the class of 1801, but his father had paid a substitute to go in his stead.) His papers were not in order, and despite the recriminations and protestations of the courier, Mathieu Paquin, Nodier was held in custody. Paquin arrived in Besançon with the news of Charles' mishap, but added that he felt certain the young writer would be released in time to take the next post. Nodier's father immediately had a complaint sent out from the mayor's office and Charles was set free at once. This is the story, as we learn it in a letter from Joseph Deis to Weiss, dated 12 prairial, an X (June 1, 1802), that was to form another link in the chain of supposed Napoleonic persecutions.

The short novel *Les Proscrits* is only incidentally a political pamphlet against Napoleon: it is primarily, along with *Atala*, one of the first essays in romantic literature in France. Unlike *Atala*, *Les Proscrits* pays its debt to the ubiquitous shadow of *Werther*, which Nodier held to be the first modern novel. Charles wanted to be the French exponent of what he considered the fountainhead of European literature. He originally entitled his first effort in imaginative literature *Stella*, after the name of the heroine—really the female counterpart of Werther, who commits suicide because she has been unfaithful to her exiled husband—but the publisher thought it sounded too much like *Atala*, or perhaps was too reminiscent of Goethe's play of the same title. Stella has been identified as Thérèse Kriss, by Nodier in a letter to Weiss,[12] and as Thérèse Burtscher of Giromagny in the Vosges mountains of Alsace.[13] But there is no reason to believe that Stella was anything more than a figment of Nodier's imagination, a romantic heroine that became a familiar type in the literature of the early nineteenth century.

Nodier was not very satisfied with *Les Proscrits*, although the novel did have a slight vogue in 1802. Even before publication Nodier thought it "ignoble" and "trivial." After publication he termed it "detestable," "but it is the last bad novel I shall write." Weiss, to whom these remarks were addressed, did not let himself be taken in by the author's professed disdain of his brainchild; in a letter to Pertuisier in December, 1802, we find him saying as usual all the right things: "*Les Proscrits* is Nodier's favorite genre for the moment, but it's not the only one he has. In a few years, when age has somewhat ripened his conceptions, I do not doubt that he will take his place, if he works, among our most prized writers."[14] A famous *salonnière* of the day, Mme Hamelin, named her pug dog Lovely, after the original name of the hero of the novel, and Charles was pointed out to the crowd in the Palais Royal gardens as the author of *Les Proscrits*, a fleeting foretaste of literary fame.

Charles' return to Besançon in the late spring of 1802 was not marked by any untoward events. The hubbub over *La Napoléone* had died down and the young author was allowed to work quietly on his new novel, *Le Peintre de Saltzbourg*. More than a year of good behavior convinced the Nodiers that Charles had learned his lesson. Moreover, the ever-present need of finding suitable employment for their capricious son caused them to look favorably on his request to return to Paris in the autumn of 1803. On November 1 he took lodgings at the Hôtel de Berlin, 25 Rue des Frondeurs.

Nodier's third trip to Paris began auspiciously enough with the publication of his second Wertherian novel, *Le Peintre de Saltzbourg*. Charles is easily identified with the hero, Charles Munster, the same vaporous sort of lover we meet in the novels of Ramon de Carbonnières and of Senancour. Charles finds that the girl he loves, Eulalie, is married to another, one Spronck, just as Lucile with Jean Pierre Franque. When Spronck dies a suicide, Eulalie enters a convent and Charles drowns himself. The theme of unrequited or frustrated love, the inability of two young people in love to come together even when all hindrances to their union have disappeared, seems to have fascinated Nodier's imagination. How far this theme wanders from actual autobiographical material we may judge from the fact that another sexual indiscretion earned Charles a second attack of gonorrhea. We may partially excuse the rashness of this second visit to the Palais Royal gardens as an act of despondency: Charles had learned that both Maurice Quaï and Lucile Franque had died of tuberculosis in his absence. Gone forever were the delightful outings to the convent of the Visitation of Sainte-Marie in Chaillot in the company of the *méditateurs*—for Nodier their star had set—and the intimate *parties à trois* at the home of the Franques. So Charles had to make new friends. In his despair, he chose unwisely; they led him from platonic love to debauchery, from Pythagorean metaphysics to the gambling dens. He was impoverished and diseased, and his fortunes were at the lowest possible ebb, when the police came to arrest him, at his own bidding, for writing *La Napoléone.*

The little satire had been completely forgotten when it suddenly appeared, October 10, 1803, in the *émigré* Peltier's *Ambigu*, a French-language newspaper printed in London under Tory auspices. My rather free translation may give some idea of the incendiary nature of the ode.

La Napoléone

Let the vulgar kneel
Before the gilt portals of Sylla's palace,
Julia's chariot, Claudius' or Caligula's sceptre!
They reigned as gods over the truckling crowd,
Their bloody dominion did but smother a declining race.
Posterity hates their memory which survives
But as a forfeit to history.

Let others sow incense and reap shame with mercenary
  hands;
My muse, freer and prouder, rises up unhindered, un-
  bought.
You will not see me buy slavery
Nor for shameful homage vile celebrity.
When people groan under their yoke I shake it off,
And my rebellious soul breathes deep the air of liberty.

Insolently the perfidious foreigner comes to sit above our
  laws,
Cowardly heir of parricides
He fights the executioner for the spoil of kings.
Sycophant spewn from the walls of Alexandria
To the opprobrium of France and the wrath of Europe,
Why did our vessels and our ports receive the renegade?
From betrayed France he earned a haven and she a set
  of chains.

Why do you destroy your work
You who wrote *glory* on the French flag?
The people loved your courage;
Now liberty ceases and the earth mourns your victories.
Your star has pitched its flight too high,
Descend from your insensate pomp,
Return to the bosom of your army.
Think you to be absolved by hiding under laurels?
Does hope allay the thunder?

In your drunken dreams of Empire,
When your mad ambitions branded us with shame,
Was your sleep troubled by the sight of Brutus' dagger?
Did you see the hour of vengeance approaching
To fling the sceptre from your grasp
And dim the bauble of your destiny?
Remember the Tarpeian Rock rubs elbows with the Capitol;
The abyss succeeds the throne
And the cypress the shriveled palm of Arcole.

In vain does back-bowed fear create a cult of adulation
To worship at the altar of your pride;

The spell is broken, the tyrant dies
And truth stops at his bier.
But justice implacable, upright in eternity
Cuts off his guilt-soaked glory,
The widow's rags of his illusions.
Hear the cries of the oppressed rain down upon your ashes;
Your name is anathema, symbol of hate to all.

A few copies trickled back to Paris and suddenly there was a clamor for more. Sorely in need of money—he had even published a licentious tale in the eighteenth-century manner, *Le Dernier Chapitre de mon roman*, which went through two editions in 1803—Nodier gave up his copy of *La Napoléone* to the publisher Dabin, who fully appreciated the risk involved in this venture.

According to Charles, copies of the ode mushroomed all over the capital and the police were making numerous arrests in the hope of discovering the culprit.[15] Dabin was picked up for questioning, and Nodier, fearing that the publisher would be severely punished, nobly admitted authorship of *La Napoléone* in a letter delivered to Napoleon's minister of police, Fouché, December 19, 1803.

To the First Consul—or in his stead, to one of the prefects of the palace.

In the depths of misfortune and despair, abandoned by all I loved, the widower of all my affections, at twenty-three I have outlived all love and friendship.

There remains to me at least the happiness of being guilty and of being able to ask for imprisonment, exile, or execution.

A work entitled *La Napoléone*, directed against the First Consul, appeared two years ago. The police have been seeking the author of this pamphlet. It is I.

Expecting neither quarter nor pity, I bring you my freedom. Who knows what use I may make of it tomorrow? Whoever has loved deeply can hate to excess, and my time has come.

My name is Charles Nodier.

I am living at the Hôtel Berlin, 25 Rue des Frondeurs.

Persuaded that he would be arrested the same day, Charles warned his landlady not to be frightened at the arrival of the police. He waited all day in his room; as night approached and no one had come, he exclaimed, "What is the meaning of this? Am I allowed to go free, when the Temple Prison is full of people who have less reason to be there than I?" The police arrived on the 20th. Taken to Sainte Pélagie Prison, he was briefly interrogated by Inspector Dubois, then sent to La Force to be treated for his venereal disease. A search of his lodgings by the police had revealed a few letters, fragments of a manuscript, and a copy of a truly incriminating work, William Allen's political treatise in a French translation, wherein he proves that "To kill a tyrant is not murder." For some unaccountable reason, nothing was made of this in Dubois' report; but knowing Charles' bibliomania, we may assume that this represented a harmless book find. Indeed, as late as 1829 this work seems to have remained in Nodier's collection, for he mentions it in his *Mélanges tirés d'une petite bibliothèque,* "William Allen, *Traicté politique,* Lugduni, 1658, in-12, 94 p."[16] The police were simply not acquainted with Allen's inflammatory tract and did not bother to read it during Nodier's detention.

Dubois' interrogation began, as do all French police interrogations to this day, with a description of the offender: "height, 1 meter 88 centimeters [6 feet], dark-brown hair, high forehead, brown eye-brows, gray-brown eyes, large nose, small mouth, pointed chin, oval face."[17] Under interrogation Charles was very contrite: he said he was sorry he had written *La Napoléone* because a good citizen should never allow himself to write against the government in power, even if he did not approve of it. He alleged extenuating circumstances, excessive misfortune, heartbreaking disappointment. When pressed on this point, Charles aswered, "I was intimately connected with a Miss [*sic!*] Lucile Franque, painter of historical subjects, and Maurice Quaï. . . . They both died just before my return to Paris."

Dubois concluded his letter to the minister of justice, the *grand juge* Régnier, December 21, 1803, with the remark that he had found nothing suspect in his papers, but that an examination of the "diary of his life for the two months since he has been in Paris proved that he had been frequenting only the most doubtful company. . . . I have reason to believe that a lack of resources of every description has led him to denounce himself as the author of the infamous document in question." A marginal note bears the terse comment that *La Napoléone*, despite Nodier's statements, was "little known," and that "no one has been arrested, the police merely having suspected various men of letters."

Letters went out from the *grand juge* to the prefect of the Doubs department and the mayor of Besançon requesting information about Charles' activities there. At the same time Mathieu Oudet, Fouché's secretary and librarian, wrote to his fellow ex-Oratorian Antoine Nodier to inform him of his son's plight. Antoine immediately addressed letters to all his friends in Paris who could be of help: Oudet, General Lefebvre, and Fouché. He called on the new prefect and mayor in Besançon, whose answers to the minister did Charles no harm. Jean De Bry's report, dated January 5, 1804, from the prefecture of the Doubs department stated that according to Charles' sister, Elise, *La Napoléone* was written at the end of the year 1800. The prefect pleaded Charles' ill-health and his opium-taking habit to draw the minister's indulgence. Daclin's letter, probably written by the mayor's secretary, Charles Weiss, Nodier's best friend, went into more details: young Nodier had never expressed or circulated any anti-Napoleonic sentiments while in Besançon. Charles had always possessed a vivid imagination which at times led him to acts of insanity or near-insanity. He cited the opium habit as Charles' source of literary inspiration; that he continued to increase the dose until he became violently ill, permanently damaging his nervous system. Nodier's personality was reported to be flighty, inconsistent, indiscreet; in short, he was a young man without character whose impetuous acts could not be taken seriously. In support of Charles' favorable view of the First Consul, he attached the letter praising Napoleon that Charles had written to Elise. Here Weiss was no doubt taking advantage of a lucky chance. Nodier had dated his letter to his sister no further than "Paris, le 25 nivôse à dix heures du soir." Weiss had no trouble making it appear that the letter had been written in 1802, whereas other elements in the letter, known only to the Nodier family and intimates, clearly prove that Charles had visited Napoleon's apartments on his first visit to Paris in 1801. The mayor concluded by drawing the minister's attention to the "good company" Charles had kept on his first two visits to the capital.

Fouché, an ex-Oratorian like Antoine Melchior, is generally given credit for obtaining Nodier's release from prison, but the means employed by Fouché, devious as always, have yet to be told. General Lefebvre, who had been visiting Charles in prison at Nodier *père*'s instigation, suggested that he compose an ode in favor of the First Consul. The invasion of England in flat-bottomed boats or rafts was then being widely discussed as Napoleon's next move to knock out "perfidious Albion," so Nodier wrote a *Prophétie contre Albion,* in which the First Consul is compared to Jupiter throwing thunderbolts. At the right moment Lefebvre placed the poem before Napoleon, who pushed the paper away with an impatient gesture. "Your scribblers bore me," he said to the general. "I have better things to do than read their flattery." Then his eagle's eye fell on the manuscript; he read a few verses and asked who the author was. "A poor devil your police have jailed on a charge of literary misdemeanor. I urge his release." The same evening Nodier was set free and placed under surveillance. Napoleon, in signing the order of release, was still unaware that he was dealing with the author of *La Napoléone.* Fouché—who apparently had concocted the whole plan in conjunction with Oudet and Lefebvre—when the order reached him for processing, ran to his master to apprise him of this fact. But Napoleon would not change his decision.

Charles had spent thirty-six days in the prison hospital. The release order emanated from La Force, showing clearly that Nodier had only passed through Sainte-Pélagie. The freedom he returned to on January 26, 1804, was only relative, since he lived under the watchful eye of the police. He was under orders to return to Besançon and place himself in the custody of his parents and to report to the prefect of the Doubs department, Jean De Bry. He took advantage of the ten days granted to put his affairs in order and to publish an Ossianesque rhapsody of prose and poetry, *Les Essais d'un jeune barde*, containing his fulsome *Prophétie*, a "translation" into verse of Goethe's *Das Veilchen*, more *pensées* of Shakespeare, and a tribute to those "two perfect beings," Maurice Quaï and Lucile Franque, and to contribute a dozen articles to the newspaper *La Décade Philosophique*. Nodier was loath to return to Besançon, as may be seen in his letters to his friends. When he expected to be charged with high treason and executed—"They have great things in store for me; I'll see you in this world or the next."—he was merely reprimanded like a bad boy and sent home. The treatment exasperated and humiliated him. But there was no trifling with the order to return home within ten days or forfeit his passport. So on February 13th, Charles re-entered Besançon, the most inglorious of his three returns, the one that bit deepest into his deflated ego.

II

The Exile
(1804-1815)

As for me, I readily admit that I did not appreciate the true greatness of this giant until he was dead. I must be excused for not looking sooner: he had his foot on my head.

NODIER, writing on Napoleon in *Les Prisons de Paris sous le Consulat*

THE CAFÉ MARULLIER (now Café de l'Hôtel de Ville) in the center of Besançon was the rendezvous of royalists and royalist sympathizers in the fall of 1804. In between games of billiards, the newly amnestied *émigrés* looked beyond Napoleon and generously restored the throne of France to the Bourbons. Indeed, the parties, fêtes, and balls given in their honor imparted a foretaste of the Congress of Vienna to the holiday atmosphere of the gaily festooned town. It was as if Napoleon, in creating himself Emperor, had merely announced the return of Louis XVIII. The Empire would be a brief prelude to the Restoration. If the repatriated nobles would only be patient, they would be restored to their former titles and positions by the Corsican adventurer. In the meantime they danced, and, lest the prelude take too long to unfold, they plotted.

To them came the exile from Paris, technically a prisoner in his own home town; he was not allowed to leave without permission. The prefect, Jean De Bry, had gently but firmly explained the conditions of his freedom, and Charles had given his word that he would remain within the city limits. He was remanded to the custody of his father, who was made responsible to the prefect for the activities of his son.

For the space of one year Charles behaved himself. Then, the long period of probation hanging heavily on his hands, he began to pester the authorities to be allowed to return to Paris. He even had a friendly publisher, Demonville, write from Grenoble to his cousin, the State Councillor Miot, pleading his case. "Charles Nodier is quite harmless," wrote this gentleman. "Women, ease, and literature take up all his time. He doesn't bother much with political affairs, his ode against Napoleon was no doubt an impulse he could not resist and no evil was intended by it. Moreover, he has talent, and the government cannot afford to embitter men of talent."[1] Five days later, March 3, 1805, De Bry received a note from his superiors in Paris asking if it was safe to permit Charles to return to the capital. Demonville's letter and Charles' request accompanied this note. After studying the Nodier dossier, De Bry duly took cognizance of the Demonville letter and advised against lifting the restriction on Charles. Ten days later De Bry's decision was justified to a degree; he had to send to Paris a report inculpating Charles in the Pyrault-Léclanché conspiracy, March 27, 1805.

Did Charles disobey the terms of his probation by consorting with the Chouanist, Henri de Monnier, and the ex-*émigrés,* Hôtelane and Pyrault? These, together with the *républicain* Léclanché of Dole and the law-student Buguet, were suspect. Pyrault had been a member of the royal household whom the emigration had elevated to a commission in Mirabeau's legion. After a few missions to Lyons and the Juras on behalf of the princes, he had returned penniless to Besançon under the Consulate. Léclanché was an ex-demagogue who had been in trouble with the authorities in 1795 and again in 1800 when he was jailed as an agitator. Buguet was a deserter from the republican army in which he had served eight years. A police informer was "planted" in the café because Marullier himself was reported to be "an inept but extreme Jacobin."[2] When the prefect learned of Charles' visits to the Café Marullier, the surveillance was tightened. Now Charles had friends in both camps of the opposition, having been finally seduced by the charm of the royalists' superior instruction and breeding. Together they hatched a fantastic conspiracy to rid France of the usurper.

The plot, which Nodier was to call later "The Conspiracy of the Alliance"—assembling as it did the ill-assorted but natural enemies of Napoleon, republicans and royalists—was to waylay Napoleon on his way to be crowned king of Italy in May. At a carefully selected point on the road from Dole to Lons-le-Saulnier, between the village of Tassenières and the forest of Souvans, Buguet was to spring out of ambush with 400 men, overcome the guard, and take the Emperor prisoner. Warned in time by the provincial authorities, Napoleon changed his itinerary at the last moment, passing through Semur, Châlons, Mâcon, and Brou.

The Conspiracy was revealed in an undated anonymous letter to the subprefect in Poligny (Jura). The informant stated that the leader of the movement was the exterrorist Léclanché, whose movements he had been watching closely. Though settled in Dole, the letter went on, Léclanché, made frequent trips to Besançon to stir up the hotheads there. His plan was ostensibly to act in concert with the émigrés in favor of the return of the Bourbons, but in reality he hoped to foment a state of confusion in which the Terror of 1793 would be restored. The rapprochement with the *émigrés* was also designed to raise much-needed funds for the movement, whereupon Léclanché would continue his feint by wooing the royalists in Mittau. This plan did not meet with general approval in Besançon but correspondents in Lyons, Paris, and other large centers were in sympathy with it. The letter ended by saying the conspiracy counted 8,000 men in the Juras.

The above report reached Paris toward the middle of March. The prefect of the Jura Department, General Poncet, requested to furnish more information on Léclanché, dismissed him as lacking the prudence and the influence to be dangerous. De Bry preferred to be more cautious. He admitted that it was certain there were still dangerous men at large, but the vast numbers in favor of the imperial government rendered them helpless. As for those who had been irrevocably compromised by their acts against the Empire, all were known and under surveillance. It was true, however, his report continued, that many recent events pointed to an evident intrigue: the posting of signs in Besançon and Baume, and the reunion of ex-nobles to reestablish with pomp and costume the old Confrérie de la Croix, were cases in point, but these should merely "encourage us to increase our vigilance."

A second report dated March 30 expanded this theme. "The anonymous letter writer is obviously a crack-pot who cannot be taken seriously. Pyrault, a former royalist, has to borrow twelve francs to keep up a wretched existence. He is allied closely with Moris, *entrepreneur de diligence,* and young No-

dier, a highly excitable character. Then there are Major
Talmet, who has been under surveillance since last July, a
fellow named Crétin de St. Hypolite, a fire-eating radical, and
Huot de Neuvieu, an *émigré*. Their common meeting place is
the Café Marullier, where d'Hôtelane has been seen playing
the role of observer, after he had been introduced to the place
by an ex-nobleman, Maranche." De Bry placed the rendezvous
of this motley group under surveillance, planned to have Moris'
coach searched and Talmet sent to Metz as he had requested.
The prefect reported he was worried because there was only
a small force of 1,000 to 1,200 troops in Besançon.

Another anonymous letter from the same source a few days
later gave more alarming details about the subversive organization. It was more widespread than the writer at first thought.
"The conspirators boast a membership of 12,000 to 20,000
men, with recruiting heavy among retired and reserve army
officers, especially malcontents. They intend to proclaim a
Bourbon at Dole, then march on to Lyons. Their present objective is to increase rumors of discontent; when the Emperor
is absent, there will be uprisings in the Vendée and in Franche-
Comté. No movement is on foot in Paris, as the capital is too
closely watched."

Jean De Bry's second report had the bad luck to arrive in
Paris on the heels of this bombshell transmitted through the
office of General Poncet. His Excellency, the Senator-Minister
of Police Fouché, was stirred to action. He demanded a complete repertory of the actions of all the cast of characters involved in this plot. The prefect did not keep him waiting. His
third report, dated March 31, gave a day-by-day account of
the Marullier clique activities. "On the night of March 27
Pyrault, Léclanché, and Nodier met a new recruit from Dole
named Buguet. These last three were enjoying a game of billiards in the café when Pyrault entered, drew Nodier into the
laboratoire du café and spoke with him in a low voice until the
other players called Nodier back to finish the game. Then all
four left together. On the 28th they met again. On the afternoon of the 29th they met with Marullier and a carpenter
called Olivier and talked politics. The upshot of their conversation was that the present order could not last as there was a

good deal of discontent. The soldiers of the Ninth Infantry, passing through Besançon that same afternoon, would have much to say about Bonaparte, for they had seen him in Egypt. Marullier guessed they would show the Emperor to be a man consumed with ambition whose government would fail because the soldiery was disaffected. He was overheard to say that there are only two kinds of government: republican and royalist. In the evening Nodier and Léclanché went to the theater but left after the first play to go to a café run by Thomas, an ex-servant of the *émigré* Sozans. Léclanché does not say much at these meetings."

De Bry concluded this report with the observation that the group did not seem to have any contacts elsewhere in France, nor abroad. He suggested closing the Café Marullier, searching the homes of suspects for incriminating material, and arresting those who were implicated in the plot, or having them placed under special surveillance at a safe distance from Besançon.

In Paris, Fouché's police had uncovered the following information. "Léclanché, Talmet, Crétin, Nodier, and Moris are known anarchists. Léclanché had been noticed earlier in Paris for his loose tongue. Pyrault, (Noel Abraham, *gendarme*) had served in Mirabeau's corps of Condé's army. Talmet had been closely connected with the late General Pichegru. He was expelled from Paris the previous July for spreading false rumors about the condition of the fleet. None of the above, including Nodier, was capable of leading an underground movement." On the 11th—Napoleon having long since bypassed Dole on his way to Italy—Fouché included all this and a few remarks about Nodier in a rescript to the prefect of the Doubs and Jura departments. He urged them to "check any possible connection between the Besançon group and Tinseau, the London agent of the Bourbon princes, Couchery, also originating from Besançon and recently returned from England, and the elder Bayard, an *émigré* who was long the agent of Wickham; this last-mentioned agitator may have returned to his home in St. Claude (Jura) after disappearing from Paris a year ago."

De Bry returned answer four days later. "Léclanché was the *agent provocateur* who was involved in the so-called Dutch conspiracy of the year VIII (1800). Pyrault, known for his pro-Bourbon sentiments, may be the real leader. Moris, an ex-Oratorian, was running the mail for the group. The disgruntled Talmet, a retired army officer, is under surveillance. His passport for Metz was delivered to him ten days ago, but he has not yet left Besançon. However, it is hard to see a connection between him and the others. As for Nodier, though capable of a good deal of fervor in political matters, he has shown himself to be entirely without character. Beginning as a rabble-rouser in the Jacobin Club, he soon passed over to the opposition. He could write glowing letters about Napoleon at the same time he was publishing against the First Consul the work which occasioned his arrest. It is hard to assess precisely under which guise he has enlisted in Pyrault's intrigues; but this trip to Dole to alert Léclanché that, judging from the movements of the *gendarmerie* in Besançon, an order of arrest had been issued against him [Léclanché], and his departure from Besançon when Léclanché was taken there under arrest from Dole, indicate that Nodier's was not the least active part in the movement. The law-student Buguet, who has been studying in Besançon for the past two years, was interrogated yesterday." De Bry found him very impudent and ordered him placed under special surveillance and to report to him every day at a certain hour. He would like authority to send his twenty-three-year-old student back home to Louhans (Saône et Loire) under the surveillance of his parents.

"However, all the above are very unimportant. I believe that the Tinseaus, the Coucherys, the Devezets, and others who played a part in the Pichegru and Georges affair have not been discouraged by the failure of their detestable projects." De Bry tried to keep the attention of Fouché focused on Besançon as a danger spot by pointing out the activity of the *émigrés* as still representing a threat. As if to say, "the Léclanché movement may not be significant, but we have other groups here that need watching; to do this, I must have agents and a complete reorganization of the police system so that I can work properly on a case like this."

General Poncet's response of the 19th was more direct. As

per authority of the State Councillor dated April 3 he had moved to the arrest of Léclanché in Dole. Pyrault was to be apprehended on the same day in Besançon. On the 8th, De Bry had informed him that Léclanché had been arrested in Dole and taken to Besançon. He had been interrogated on the 11th and again on the 15th. Then he was to be sent to Poncet with a copy of the interrogation.

A summary of the Doubs and Jura case delivered to Fouché on the 24th of April showed that Léclanché had been taken into custody, Pyrault and Nodier had disappeared, Huot, Buguet, Marullier, and Moris had been interrogated without result. "All the suspects unanimously denied any participation in the plot. In the absence of any proof to give substance to projects rumored by the anonymous informer, whose identity still remains a mystery, we suggest continued observation and search." In the margin Fouché gave his view of this report: "Bring the affair to an end; these are fairy tales."

Poncet's final report of May 1 admitted that Léclanché continued to deny everything. Pyrault, who fled to Switzerland, was probably the real culprit. Here are the prefect's observations on Nodier, who was also missing: "He knows something about books, he has composed a few bad novels to earn money. He tries to attract attention by the exaggeration of his ideas and the singularity of his habits, such, for instance, as that of taking a heavy dose of opium every day."

As soon as Charles learned the authorities were looking for Léclanché, he set off in the direction of Dole to warn him but arrived too late; Léclanché had been arrested the previous day. We learn this from De Bry's letter of April 13 to Miot, warning him that Nodier had absconded in spite of the order requiring him to keep within the Besançon city limits unless otherwise authorized. In view of Nodier *père*'s public character, the letter ran on, De Bry had represented to that gentleman the rashness of his son's act; whereupon Charles' father stated that he had sent his son to Dole to prevent him from associating with bad companions, such as Léclanché, whom he had always condemned. Thus Papa Nodier took upon himself the responsibility for Charles' breaking his word and promised to bring him back within 24 hours.

Charles, when he learned of Léclanché's arrest, returned immediately to Besançon; however, as De Bry stated in his letter to the minister of police dated April 16, as the conspirator was being taken to Besançon for trial, Charles, fearing interrogation, again left Besançon without permission, this time taking refuge in the Jura mountains. The prefect summoned the judge to bring Charles back and keep him in Besançon. By April 19 Nodier *père* had still not succeeded in carrying out his promise; so De Bry asked Daclin, the mayor of Besançon, to grant a delay in issuing the order of arrest against Charles, since he did not think it ethical that the judge should seem to participate in the arrest of his own son. But Franche-Comté officialdom was most insistent: on April 20 General Poncet wrote to De Bry requesting information as to the whereabouts of Charles Nodier. De Bry asked for and obtained further delays; finally, on May 1, Nodier *père* decided to go after his wayward son himself. Ten days later, weary and quite ill over the unsavory business, he wrote to De Bry to acquaint him with his failure and to beg his forgiveness for having caused him so much embarrassment. On May 17 Miot issued the order of arrest against Charles as a participant in the Léclanché-Pyrault plot. The order was acknowledged by De Bry, who informed Miot that both Pyrault and Nodier had been placed on the *gendarmerie's* wanted list, May 23, 1805.

The following description of Charles was circulated among the local constabulary: "age 25, height six feet, hair and eyebrows chestnut-colored, hair cut short *à la Titus* [with curls tight to the scalp], large, prominent nose, protruding chin, brown eyes, large mouth, oval face, carries his head a little to one side, has an indolent manner of walking, speaks distinctly and expresses himself very well." This is a somewhat more complete catalogue of Charles' characteristics than we were offered earlier in the hasty description by Inspector Dubois of the Paris police.

On August 1 Charles and Pyrault were still at large. When, toward the end of the summer, Léclanché was moved from Besançon to Strasbourg to carry out his sentence, De Bry thought the two fugitives might turn up in the Alsatian capital, so he sent their descriptions to the prefect of the Bas-Rhin department. This letter was acknowledged September 26, 1805, but no further news of the outlaws came from that quarter.

In October Charles returned to Besançon voluntarily, having learned from his father that the order of arrest had been lifted. Nonetheless, he was immediately brought in for questioning. The *procès-verbal* of the interrogation of October 28, 1805, conducted by De Bry and the chief of police, Lagrénée, shows Charles as brazen as ever. Asked why he had broken parole to go to Dole in order to warn Léclanché of his impending arrest, he answered, "I would have done as much for an enemy; you can imagine how much more willing I was to warn a person with whom I had a certain intimacy." De Bry, who seems to have taken upon himself the task of converting the exile to Napoleonic views, preferred to overlook the impudent remarks, having in mind perhaps Charles' impending departure for the army. He had been called up with the class of 1801 and remanded to the custody of his parents until the unit of reserve conscripts left Besançon.

The details in this case demonstrated, if indeed it need be demonstrated again, the thoroughness and despatch with which Napoleon's police system worked. An anonymous informant had given rise to an imaginary uprising in a distant province of France; yet within hours Fouché had enough information on his desk to be able to classify the affair as nonsense. And we must note in passing that his agents had files on all the really significant and dangerous enemies to Napoleon in that area. Thus if it had not been for Charles' participation in and later fictional magnification of the conspiracy to give weight to his demands on the restored monarchy by urging his active opposition to Napoleon, no one would ever have heard of the Conspiration de l'Alliance, police files notwithstanding; these must necessarily be full of notations, many of which amount to nothing.

In November the prefect reclassified Charles in the inactive reserve and suggested that he would give him permission to visit with some of his relatives in the environs of Besançon provided he promised to stay away from the Café Marullier and its *habitués* and keep the police informed as to his whereabouts. It was then that Charles went to live with a friend of his childhood, his cousin Dr. Dumont of Arbois, in whose house he remained quietly for the next three months. Early in 1806 he appeared in Besançon just long enough to lampoon the city authorities for removing the stone benches of the Promenade Granvelle. The satiric verse met with such popular approval that the benches were restored.

In the spring and summer Charles had ample opportunity to renew acquaintance with relatives and friends of the family in the neighboring villages of Aumont, Grozon, Vadans, and Valdois. When he tired of visiting the Barochins, the Coulons, and the Pârises, he would call on the learned *curés* there and in Arbois, Colonne, La Ferté, Pupilien, Saint-Cyr, and Villers-les-Bois. These priests always had a warm welcome for the inquisitive exile, who was busy with a dictionary of onomatopoeias of the French language. The itinerant lexicographer explored in this manner many vestry libraries to check word origins, definitions, and usage in the miscellaneous French dictionaries held there. In between scholarly disquisitions on onomatopoeia, Charles recaptured the thrill of naturalist expeditions along the valley of the Doubs, or he dreamed hours together perched on a promontory in the Jura Mountains.

In the autumn, word came from Mathieu Oudet that the order restricting Charles to Besançon had been lifted, but he was still not permitted to visit Paris. The lure of the city and the need of work brought Charles eventually to Dole. He paid his respects to his father's old friend and colleague, Judge Charve, who presented him to the subprefect of the Jura department, P. G. de Roujoux, an enthusiastic *littérateur* and historian. De Bry granted Charles permission to remain in Dole where Roujoux assigned him to the minor post of *expéditionnaire* in the subprefecture, which meant that the great lover of the outdoors, the poet of freedom, had to sit in a stuffy office from morning until night copying such prosaic matters as accounts, administrative rolls, correspondence, and reports. The subprefect hinted that if all went well, Nodier might be appointed later to the staff of the Dole Public Library, but this post never materialized. The one bright spot in all this drudgery was the hospitality of the Charve family.

Nodier at about twenty-five, author of La Napoléone and fugitive from insouciant police

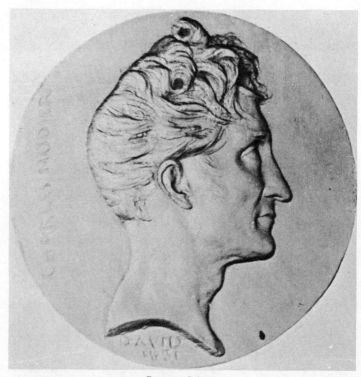

Besançon Library

Idealized relief profile of Nodier cast by David d'Angers in 1831

Charles had not forgotten his attachment to Lucile Franque, *née* Messageot, daughter of the judge's wife by a former marriage. Madame Charve's striking resemblance to her first daughter attracted the young clerk, who also found the Charves' two grown daughters, Françoise, or Fanny, and Désirée, like enough to their dead half-sister to stir his memories. At first Charles seemed to be courting the older sister, Fanny, but when he began to show interest in Désirée, who was just sixteen, the judge objected that she was too young to be thinking of marriage.

In 1806 Charles published *Les Tristes, ou Mélanges tirés des tablettes d'un suicide,* a collection of short pieces in the melancholic vein of *Werther.* In fact, the first story in this edition, known later as *La Filleule du Seigneur,* is entitled *La Nouvelle Wertherie (A Wertherlike girl).* The majority of the prose excerpts are a tribute to the defunct *méditateurs,* to Lucile, or are *souvenirs romantiques* of Ossian and Schiller. More important in the history of the development of Nodier's literary formation is the tale entitled *Une Heure, ou la vision (The One O'Clock Vision)* in which we are introduced to his preoccupation with the occult and the supernatural. The extrasensory perception of its epileptic hero, presented in a compact, tense, eerie masterpiece, was the first thread of an endless spool of a truly original theme in Nodier's best vein: that the idiot, the fool, the mentally unbalanced possess supersensitive faculties that permit them to communicate directly with the unknown.

The systematic and intelligent indoctrination of the exile by Jean De Bry began to bear fruit as Charles entered a contest sponsored by the *Académie de Besançon* in 1807 for the best eulogy of Napoleon. The prize was to be a gold medal worth 200 francs. None of the essays submitted by the seven contestants was judged good enough to win. Nodier's effort was a fulsome document of fawning hyperbole, which so little impressed the judges that they did not even open the letter identifying the author of the essay. So Charles' first attempt to bend the knee to the Emperor went unrewarded and unnoticed.

Tragedy struck the Nodiers in the decision of the *sénatus-*

consulte authorizing the government to purge the magistracy. By the imperial decree of March 24, 1808, seven magistrates of the Franche-Comté were dismissed from the bench; the list opened with the name of Nodier and closed with that of Charve. In a letter of March 28 to Mathieu Oudet complaining of the forced retirement, Nodier *père* bitterly observed that it was clear he was being punished for the faults of his son. This is the sole written expression that has come down to us of the chagrin and disappointment Charles' conduct brought upon his father. The humiliation of summary dismissal after almost twenty years service was more than the old man could bear. For six months after the news of his destitution reached him, he continued to exist in misery and ill health, never leaving the house and rarely his old armchair by the fire. On October 9, 1808, Antoine Melchior Nodier died of lung congestion.

In April, 1808, unaware of the interpretation his father had placed upon the abovementioned decree, Charles went ahead with his plans for marrying Désirée, although both ex-judges secretely opposed the match. At the last minute, *grand enfant* that he was, he learned that the ceremony could not take place without copies of his birth and baptismal certificates. The afternoon before the wedding, he set out on foot for Besançon and returned the next noon, having accomplished the 55-mile roundtrip in less than twenty hours. He was so tired that he went to bed and slept beyond the hour appointed for the wedding. Years later he would relate with a chuckle how he would have missed his own wedding if his worried friend Weiss had not thought to look for him in his room at the Grand Hôtel Chandioux in the Place Grévy. (Room 18 is still preserved by a reverent management, furniture intact, as a memorial to Nodier's stay there in 1807-08.) Thus Charles married Liberté Constitution Désirée Charve, as she had been christened by an exultant parent in the throes of enthusiastic support of the Revolution when she was born on June 25, 1790.

In the meantime, letters from various officials had been pouring into the office of the Senator Minister of Police in Paris beseeching him to lift the surveillance of Charles Nodier. Charles had begun the assault in a letter to Fouché of October

28, 1807, in which he deplored his implication in the Léclanché affair and denied any participation in the plot. He urged as a recommendation to relieve him of the confining surveillance his authorship of the *Dictionnaire des onomatopées*. Daclin, De Bry, Roujoux, even Mathieu Oudet in Paris, seconded his request in April and May of the following year; but all they could obtain for the poor exile was partial exoneration. On July 14, 1808, Nodier was informed through channels that the surveillance was at an end, but he could not go to Paris.

The marriage was good for Charles; it had a sobering effect upon him. He spent no more idle hours in cafés with questionable companions; the conspirator and plotter died in him as he faced up to the reality of Napoleon's power. As a responsible married man, Charles frequented only the best people in the judge's circle at Dole, such as Roujoux, Benjamin Constant, also under surveillance at Brevans, the future mayor Auguste Dusillet, Cournot, Jobard, and Persan, who by their influence or their talent could help him make his way in the intellectual and literary world. Dusillet has left us an eye-witness account of Nodier's life at Dole in 1808 in the remarks prefacing his speech on Nodier's lecture course delivered at the Academy of Besançon in 1846. Nodier and Constant, surrounded by the attentive youth of Dole, would read passages from their current writings. Charles, whose erudition was the fable of the Dolois, would read two or three articles from his *Dictionnaire des onomatopées*. "It was there that the naturally timid Nodier, feeling relaxed and admired, would become gay and vivacious. His conversation, which had substance and grace, was spiced with a good-humored raillery. . . . The life he led at Dole suited him to perfection, for if his mind was alert his body was indolent, and never was a man suspected of having definite ambitions less troubled than he about what the morrow might bring."[3]

The admiration of the studious youths inspired Charles to offer them a course in literature, if they could obtain the permission of the prefect. The patient and paternal De Bry now openly became Charles' protector, satisfied at last that the young exile had turned over a new leaf. Together with Roujoux, he arranged for Charles to give a course in "ancient and

modern literature" without going through the examinations
and formalities prescribed by a recent law for all professors.
The course, which began on July 4, was given at the ex-
Cordeliers' monastery, formerly the seat of the University of
Dole, before Louis XIV shifted that faculty to Besançon,
now the courthouse of the Jura department.

According to Dusillet's notes on the lectures preserved in
the Public Library at Dole, Nodier divided his material on
literary art into two sections: oratorical and poetic. The
latter included a literate appreciation of Shakespeare which the
citizens of Dole found so appealing that they petitioned the
authorities for a prolongation of the course through the summer vacation. Charles was in ecstasy over the success of his
lectures, which may well have been an indication that he had
at last found himself. It is unfortunate that a plea to repeat
the course at Dijon the following year was denied, for Nodier
was a good speaker who knew how to communicate his ideas
to an audience in a stimulating manner. Although there was
talk some years later of offering him the first Chair of Natural
Science to be established at the University of Besançon,
Charles was never to teach again. The decision against offering another course in 1809 and the press of financial need
forced him to turn his attention to other fields.

The death of Antoine Nodier not only left a vacuum in the
family but gave rise to a quarrel between his children. Considering Charles' way of life up to this point, Antoine wisely
deeded his house to Elise, a bequest which caused Charles
much chagrin. It is true Antoine had expressed the hope that
Charles and Désirée would come to live with her, but Elise,
justifiably enough, did not like this arrangement; so Charles
went to live with relatives of his wife in Quintigny, the Gesse
family. And what about their mother, Antoine's widow? Having been left a mere pittance of 395 francs per annum as a
pension and no rights to the family house, she had to sell her
furniture to make ends meet. After four years of living in
penury, it became clear that Madame Nodier desperately
needed additional help, so Elise, who on March 28, 1812, had
married Jean François Tourtelle, a master in pharmacy, sold
the house to a Mademoiselle Rose, October 21, 1812, who con-

tracted to supply an adequate pension for the rest of Madame
Veuve Nodier's natural life "in the place of her two children,
as part of the purchase price."[4]

But Suzanne had to quit the house in the Rue Neuve. For a
time she lived in the Rue du Clos; after 1824 she inhabited
number 3 Place Saint-Quentin, not fifty meters distant from
the scene of her first love affair with Antoine. She died on
July 21, 1826, having survived her husband by nearly eighteen
years. Her inheritance, which amounted to 836 francs *less
debts*, was immediately refused by both her children. Meanwhile, in the heat of argument over the succession to Antoine
Nodier's goods, neither Charles nor his sister thought to
settle the little item of the beloved father's burial expenses;
the receipt acknowledging payment of the amount, 69 francs
and 4 centimes, signed by the clerk of Notre Dame, October
12, 1808, bears the name of Charles Weiss.

Nodier marked the passing of Antoine Melchior with a
dedicatory volume of translations from Pythagorean philosophers. Privately printed by Joseph Deis, who had set up a
bookselling and publishing business at Besançon, and limited
to 17 copies, the *Apothéose de Pythagore* was really Charles'
way of expressing his indebtedness to his friends, teachers,
mentors and benefactors: Regnault de Saint-Jean d'Angély,
Girod de Chantrans, Jean De Bry, Roujoux, Bernardin de
Saint-Pierre, Chateaubriand, Gleizes, Ballanche, Senancour,
Weiss, Dusillet, Considérant, Tercy, Benjamin Constant,
Bonneville, and finally, the inscription to the greatest and best
of fathers, Antoine Nodier. The death of his father gave
Charles the opportunity to pay appropriate respects to his
many foster fathers: Girod, Regnault, Roujoux, De Bry; only
the name of General Pichegru is missing from this list. Pichegru, whose reputation Nodier was bound to redeem, had
perished in the Cadoudal bomb-plot against Napoleon; his
name would have clashed with those of the Napoleonic administrators, De Bry and Roujoux. Significant too is the
absence from this table of honor of the high priest of asceti-
cism, Maurice Quaï, for Nodier's adherence to the mystic
brotherhood had lapsed with the death of its greatest exponent.
We may assume then that the tribute here offered is symbolic

of Charles' new orientation toward the realities of literary and social engagement.

When it had seemed inevitable that Charles would embrace the teaching profession, he brought to an end his musings on French onomatopoeias and published them in a monograph, *Dictionnaire raisonné des onomatopées françaises*. The importance of Nodier's contribution to lexicography and linguistics has been discussed in specialized studies elsewhere;[5] but the influence of his lifelong preoccupations (with neologisms, onomatopoeias, semantics, and love for the beautiful archaic language of Rabelais) on the literature of the romantic movement in France has not yet been properly assessed. At any rate, as a letter from Fourcroy, the minister of education, informed him, the *Dictionnaire* was adopted by the Committee of Public Instruction to be placed among the classic dictionaries that composed the *Lycée* libraries. It is certainly marvelous that a manual of such painstaking accuracy could have been written by a vagabond who did not have access to libraries and other sources of information available in a large center.

Charles had not been gainfully employed since the summer and though he and Désirée were still living with her relatives, the young couple was in debt. Charles Etienne was trying to secure for Nodier the post of *inspecteur d'instruction publique* at Dole. Among other possibilities of future employment for the recently married exile were a clerkship to Egypt, a planter's life in Louisiana, and a postman's route in Lons-le-Saulnier. Charles decided on this last occupation and wrote a letter of application to Baron Destouches, the new prefect of the Jura department. Madame Charve's first husband, Messageot, had been postmaster at Lons-le-Saulnier, and perhaps his mother-in-law's reminiscences on the postman's life painted for Charles a picture of security and ease not incompatible with scholarly research. While awaiting results of his application, Charles wrote in the summer of 1809 to M. Coste, curator of the Besançon Municipal Library, requesting the loan of books to aid him in his works in progress: a theory of the natural alphabet, a commentary on the *Fables* of La Fontaine, and a philosophical essay on the insects' ability to adapt themselves to their natural surroundings. This last, in his own words "the closest to completion," was the only one of the three projects never realized. The *Commentaires sur les Fables de La Fontaine* appeared in 1818—considerably altered, as he had left the 1808 manuscript in Quintigny—and the theory on the natural alphabet received expression in many later linguistic essays.

Encouraged by the adoption of his *Dictionnaire,* Charles sought to have his *Commentaires* endorsed in a similar manner. He had learned from the dramatist Antoine Vincent Arnault, secretary-general of the imperial universities, that the Committee on Public Instruction was in search of commentaries on French classic writers. Thanks to the friendliness of Etienne, while still living in Dole Nodier had contributed occasional articles on entomology and literary criticism to the *Journal de l'Empire.* He therefore wrote to Boissonnade, a professor of Greek literature and a critic of that newspaper, to urge adoption of the *Commentaires,* and to propose a new edition of *Télémaque.* Boissonnade, who had been popularizing English literature in France, was in correspondence with Sir Herbert Croft, eccentric English scholar, a former collaborator on Johnson's *Dictionary,* author of the biography of Young in *The Lives of the Most Eminent English Poets,* and of *Love and Madness,* a life of the wonder boy poet Chatterton. Residing in Amiens and currently at work on an edition of *Télémaque,* Sir Herbert was looking for a bright young scholar to act as his secretary and assistant in preparing a new edition of *Les Fables de La Fontaine.* Boissonnade, struck by the community of interests of these two men, arranged to bring them together. Impatient to meet his future employer, who had sent him 600 *livres* and had deposited a similar amount for him in Paris to defray the expense of the journey, Charles wrote a letter to Fouché asking permission to cross Paris on his way to Amiens, August 18, 1809. Without waiting for an answer, he and Désirée departed for the capital. Upon arriving in Paris, August 28, Charles collected the remainder of his travel money, visited with a few friends, and pushed on to Amiens, September 2. (It was not until September 7 that his request to spend 24 hours in Paris was granted.) In Amiens, Sir Herbert, taken with Charles' enthusiasm and encyclopedic grasp, made him a stunning offer: in return for his services Nodier was to receive a monthly stipend of 400 francs, board and lodging in a separate apartment manned by two servants, and a horse and carriage at his disposal for trips to Paris.

The baronet's household consisted of the aging novelist, Lady Mary Hamilton, several servants, pets, and a magnificent library. Lady Mary's daughter, Lady Bell Hamilton and her husband, General Etienne Jouy, dramatist and librettist of Spontini's *La Vestale,* were frequent visitors to the Croft estate in the Rue Gloriette. Charles had no sooner entered the expatriates' house than he realized that the kindly old souls were being plundered by English and French bankers, by their managers, caretakers, and servants. Lady Mary's extensive holdings in Jamaica had produced not a shilling in the past ten years, and Sir Herbert, with 200,000 *livres de rentes,* was constantly out of pocket. Sublimely oblivious to the depredations foreign and domestic on their income, the "millionaire" writers, as Charles lovingly called them, pursued their self-appointed literary tasks with the regularity of clockwork. Here are the first impressions of the new secretary.

This is our household. The sixty-year-old knight, sprightly and in excellent health, simple, frank, and as true as M. Friport, possessed of a lively and penetrating wit, always busy, always full of discoveries and new projects, blessed apparently with limitless knowledge, a frighteningly accurate memory, endowed with endless energy upon which he makes continual and exaggerated demands incredible in one of his years, equipped with a mind which seizes the most minute, the most fugitive details, a unique tact in sensing the most delicate shades in linguistic meaning, an instinct which does not allow anything to escape him, which sees faults everywhere and proves them to be such, all in all, a rare and an excellent man distinguished in every respect, whom no one could refuse as a teacher and everyone wants as a friend.

Lady Mary Hamilton, granddaughter of the author of the same name, niece of Lord Hope, related to the Duke of Cumberland and to the royal family, author of a dozen

volumes on education published in England and pillaged
in France, more than seventy years old, but still prim, fresh
and almost pretty, an angel in woman's clothing, which is
really extraordinary; the most noble, the most generous,
and at the same time the simplest, the most modest, the
most natural person, possessed of a rich, cultivated, and
fertile—perhaps too fertile—mind, but one which frets, so
to speak, because it distrusts itself so. What more can I
say? One can give a more or less satisfactory account of
the knight's qualities, but for Lady Mary the pen falters.[6]

Charles was soon to descend from this pinnacle of rhapsodic
praise to the humdrum routine of the Herculean task he had
to perform. Besides the edition of *Télémaque,* Croft was busy
with a pedantic crotchet of his, correcting the classics by
altering their time-honored punctuation. The current victim
of this punctilious exercise in minutiae was Horace. Charles
found this work most unrewarding and boring. When his
daily chores for the baronet had been completed, he was required to assist Lady Mary in translating her wordy novels
into French. Since the old lady knew little French, Charles had
the backbreaking job of rewriting these senile mediocrities in
his own language. The success of these "translations" inspired
Sir Herbert to set Nodier translating Johnson's *Lives of the
Poets* in his spare time. Of his own works, the commentaries of
La Fontaine, the entomological compendium and the theories
on the origins of the alphabet, there was naturally no question
after 14 to 18 hours of drudgery. Even during meals the tire-
less pair hounded him with dictation. Since Croft had generously paid Charles the first quarter honorarium in advance
so that he could satisfy his most demanding creditors, the in-
centive to carry on flagged after the first rosy weeks. Nonetheless, Charles entertained with enthusiasm Sir Herbert's
plan to set up a printing press which would involve hiring
additional men of letters. He immediately thought of his old
friend Weiss and of his future brother-in-law—through his
eventual marriage with Fanny, Désirée's sister—François de
Tercy. Cognizant of Nodier's tendency to espouse grandiose
schemes which came to nothing, neither of these gentlemen
rose to his ecstatic proposals.

As Christmas approached and the Englishman gave no sign of paying the second quarter, Charles increased his visits to Paris, where he furthered his acquaintance with Arnault, Barbier, Boissonnade, Jouy, A. A. Renouard, and the *Journal de l'Empire* staff. He also began to spend more time on his own projects, neglecting those of Lady Mary and Sir Herbert. He contributed articles—notably one on Alfieri—to Prud'homme's *Dictionnaire,* sold collections of insects to fond amateurs in Paris, and contemplated competing for the prize of fifty Danish ducats set by the Academy of Copenhagen to resolve the question raised more than a century earlier by Leibnitz on a universal language.[7] Summoned to give an account of this new schedule, Charles ruefully explained that he had expected to be paid for the second quarter in November, that he had a wife to support and many old debts to pay. After some consultation with Lady Mary, the baronet confessed that he was temporarily short of funds, due to the failure of the House of Virnet in Lille, which had carried off a full year's subsistence of the "two millionaires'" living. Charles sensed in the excuse a trap to keep him indefinitely on a servant status without pay. He reasoned that his position would be rendered even more footling if children came; then he would never be able to break away from the wearisome toil. However, seeing no other solution in the immediate future, Charles consented to remain.

Visiting the Nodiers in June, 1810, Fanny, Désirée's sister, found the couple immured in the house on the Rue Gloriette as in a prison. Lady Mary, unable to communicate with the young Frenchwomen, had taken kindly to Désirée but looked down her nose at the intrusion of the sister. Bilingual discord rose to a strident pitch in the early summer, and by July Nodier's need to extricate himself from the Amiens impasse really became acute. He implored his patrons to release him because of his own ill-health, Désirée's pregnancy, and—since there was no further talk of payment—his many debts. Lady Mary would not hear of it, retorting that Désirée could have her child in Amiens as well as in Quintigny. Sir Herbert, she said, was expecting funds to arrive from England and Nodier could have a few days to himself in Paris.

Charles turned to Croft, who was brokenhearted at the prospect of losing his faithful amanuensis. He admitted his currently depleted treasury did not permit him to offer a financial solution, nor did he hold out any hope for the foreseeable future. In a grand gesture born in despair, he confided to Charles that he had come to regard him as a son and that he planned to make him his universal heir. The baronet had been twice married and as often widowed; his two children were dead and he longed to pass on his title and goods to a worthy adopted son. They would all remove to an old manse near Quintigny which could easily be transformed into a printing house; think of it, "Croft and Nodier, publishers." Together they would edit fine copies of the classics on fine paper with wide margins. A touching scene involving mutual avowals of trust and admiration ensued, but Nodier's determination to leave remained unshaken. With Sir Herbert's blessing and a parting gift of the manuscripts of the philologist David de Saint-Georges, Charles said goodbye to the quaint old couple in the Rue Gloriette and made haste to retire to the quiet of Quintigny.

The measure of Charles' growth while under the tutelage of the English scholar was considerable. The awareness of almost microscopic detail, the respect for meticulous accuracy, and the love of authenticity in the establishment of an ancient text, were all earmarks of Nodier's future literary production. While it is true that his only publication during his stay in Amiens, the *Archéologue, ou système raisonné des langues*, February 1, 1810, was but a prospectus of a vast treatise on language, unfortunately never completed, one sees in his writings on linguistics and in his critical articles of other philologists on the subject a storehouse of erudition gathered from Sir Herbert's method. Painful and trying as the experience in Amiens no doubt was, especially the "translations" of Lady Hamilton's novels, from which he learned nothing, Charles needed the discipline that the patient, unglamorous Croft was able to give him. He was to remain eternally grateful to the scholar from across the channel, with whom he kept up a friendly correspondence, and about whom he wrote one of his most delicate and sensitive tales of young love unfolded during a scholar's quest for a breathtaking commentary of Pindar, *Amélie,* in which the happy love of books, the depiction of bookish characters and their adventures in a library, are seen by the mature writer as being much more vital and engrossing than the account of the coming together of the two sexes. Furthermore, Charles was honored by the citizens of Amiens, who elected him to their Academy on May 2. He had also formed many new friendships in Paris: Bouvier, Bayard de Plinville, Portalis, and Suard.

It may seem strange that Nodier decided to go all the way back to Quintigny instead of stopping at nearby Paris, now that the interdict had been virtually lifted. In Paris were many friends, opportunities for literary journalism, and well-stocked libraries and museums. Add to these the theaters and galleries, the exciting exchanges of views in the cafés and on the promenades, the *cirques,* the *chansonniers,* the restaurants and gaming tables, and the lure of the big city would seem irresistible. However, Charles had no money and Désirée was pregnant. Moreover, as has been mentioned, a change had come over Charles since his marriage. At thirty he was perhaps most dedicated to making a career as a savant in two fields; entomology and linguistics. To further his projects he needed the quiet routine of the little hamlet tucked away in the Jura department.

In a letter to Weiss dated from Amiens, June 23, 1810, Charles explained that he did not want a job for three reasons, and two of these reasons arose from his compelling need to get back to Quintigny. "I miss my village very much; I would no sooner be set up in work in Paris than I would regret not having a watch to sell so that I could return to Lons on foot." So Charles turned his back on Paris for financial and psychological reasons. In the latter category must be classed his increasing moroseness, due in part to the prospect of adding another member to the family when there was no money, but more important perhaps to Charles' depression at not receiving the recognition he felt he deserved. He had started out as a child prodigy in literature and was esteemed a master of style and content from his earliest essays. Almost twenty years had passed since then and Charles had not given the world a single work marked by his maturity. The artificial exhilaration of conspiring against Napoleon for the common good had worn off and, though he had paid dearly for his foolishness, his dedication had gone as unrewarded in political circles as had his writings in the literary world. A great man in potential, yes; but he was rapidly coming to the realization that as the years slipped away the promise of his youth was taking on a fixed patina that did not become an unknown writer and an unemployed prospective father approaching his thirty-first year.

Another reason for Charles' eagerness to return to Quintigny was the warmth and hospitality he and Désirée had enjoyed in the heart of the Gesse family; for the next two years no incident disturbed these wonderful relations. He continued to work on the proofs of Lady Hamilton's novels, and although he was loath to have his name connected with her works, he managed to see at least two of them through the press in 1811: *Le Village de Munster* and *La Famille du duc de Popoli*. The whining theme of a desire to break loose that typified his correspondence in earlier episodes of forced dependency is singularly lacking in this period; on the whole, his letters from Quintigny reveal a glow of well-being, satisfaction, and security. Charles never forgot the happiness of those years in Quintigny, to which he was to return in imagination again and again during moments of defeat and depression.

He was within easy walking distance, for him, of Lons-le-Saulnier, whence much of his correspondence emanated. The quiet walk to town provided a capital form of exercise and relaxation as he easily fell into the regular stride of the outdoorsman. The chance of a chat there with such an invigorating local character as Rouget de Lisle of *Marseillaise* fame delighted him. He took stock of the many fine acquaintances he had in the literary world; of Duméril, the savant; of the poet Millevoye; of Francis, the light-hearted *chansonnier* of Besançon and Paris; of Desaugiers, the renowned *vaudevilliste;* of wonderful Etienne, the journalist and playwright, director of *Le Journal de l'Empire;* of the scholars Boissonnade and Croft; and many others. He counted his protectors and patrons: Regnault de Saint-Jean d'Angély, the statesman; his

brother-in-law Arnault; their nephew, the publisher Demonville; Senator Volney; the legislator Bouvier; Prince Cam-
bacérès; and even the informer Veyrat who arrested him for
the *Napoléone* in 1803 and invited him to dinner in 1810.

On these walks, new literary projects suggested themselves
to Charles. To defend Etienne against the odious charge of
plagiarism that had been leveled against his recent comedy
success, *Les Deux Gendres,* he initiated a bibliographical undertaking dealing with the legal aspects of writing and publishing;
the edition of the *Fables* of La Fontaine, almost ready for the
press, was sent to Taulin for consideration; a new edition of
Grainville's *Le Dernier Homme* was a publisher's success in
1811. Drawing upon his notes for the Dole course on literature,
he published four articles on epic poetry in the *Journal du
Jura.* He wrote to Gabriel Peignot, bibliographer and scholar
in Vésoul, asking him to find an outlet for his philological
essays. Amid all this literary productivity and plans for future
research, Charles announced to Weiss—upon whose store of
erudition he had been leaning heavily since his return to
Quintigny—the birth of a daughter, Marie Antoinette Elisabeth, April 26, 1811. The coming into the world in Quintigny
of the beloved Marie, the future darling of the Arsenal and the
only offspring of the Nodiers to survive, made that place
doubly precious to the young couple.

In the interim Elise and Weiss in Besançon were busy seeking to obtain for Charles the chair of Latin in the *Lycée d'Etat,*
established by Napoleon in all municipalities large enough to
boast a Court of Appeals. An earlier attempt to secure for him
the post of teacher of rhetoric and belles-lettres at Poligny
was frowned upon by Charles because he could not face the
humdrum routine of an obscure provincial classroom. He now
was reluctant to take up the teaching of Latin, for which he
claimed he was unprepared; any student could translate
Tacitus and Horace better than he, he was utterly incapable
of instructing a third-form scholar who could read his Livy,
etc. What Nodier really meant, in these letters to Weiss, was
that he hated to leave his wife and daughter, his works in
progress, and his idyllic existence at Quintigny to take up
the grueling schedule of teaching Latin grammar. Visiting the

Nodiers in September to see the baby, Elise found Charles in bed with a fever, delirious. He had been complaining of an "oppressive phlegm" on his chest, which he thought meant a worsening of his "tuberculosis." There was no further talk then of going to work, and Charles retreated deeper within himself because he thought he did not have long to live. In this condition he readied and published, in 1812, his *Questions de littérature légale*.

The *Questions on the Legal Aspects of Literary Production,* a bibliographic miscellany on plagiarism, imitation, quotation, allusion, similarity of ideas due to reminiscence or analogy, literary theft, false attributions, forgeries, hoaxes, and other literary misdemeanors, was intended by Nodier as a supplement to A. A. Barbier's *Dictionnaire des anonymes* and "to all bibliographies." The subject matter is presented in a series of scholarly essays which reveal a brilliant method of dating and attribution based on the internal evidence of linguistic usage, style, historical data, and an intimate knowledge of an author's mannerisms. A discussion of authors' rights, contracts with publishers, pirated editions, and the creation of spurious rarities in the bookselling business rounds out the volume. This work, Nodier's first bibliographical study since the *Bibliographie entomologique* eleven years earlier, attracted considerable attention as a pioneer in a little-known field. Where others were content to state the arid facts of bibliography, Nodier, combining boldness with imagination, revealed the romance and adventure of the detective work involved in establishing the authenticity of a manuscript, the genuineness of a text, and the originality of an author. Sixteen years later, the *Questions* being still in demand, Nodier brought out a second edition, augmented to twice the size of the first. Both editions were fittingly inscribed to Charles Weiss. In gratitude for the generous *apologia* of *Les Deux Gendres* the *Questions* contained, Etienne opened wide the columns of *Le Journal de l'Empire* to Charles' articles. The *Académie de Besançon* admitted Charles to membership on March 12, 1812.

Such books and honors, though interesting and important, did not increase the family exchequer. Since the previous Christmas Charles had been pestering influential literary personalities—Arnault, de Bonald, Chateaubriand, Victor Considérant—to have his La Fontaine commentaries adopted in the imperial *Lycées* for four or five thousand francs. He could have sold them to Taulin for 1,500 francs. The appearance of an obscure *Etude sur La Fontaine* caused a sudden drop in the market value of Nodier's edition, and the *Commentaries* were shelved until 1818.

Charles circulated a new batch of letters advertising his interest in securing a position as librarian or newspaper editor. He even wrote to Sir Herbert Croft in the hope of obtaining the salary for three quarters still due him. It was the future brother-in-law, François de Tercy, then general secretary for the management of Illyrian affairs, later alternate delegate for Kranj (subprefect of Krainburg) and ultimately mayor of the city of Fiume, who secured for Charles late in September the ideal combination Nodier dreamed of: the post of librarian and newspaper editor in the city of Laybach, now Ljubljana. It was true he would have to leave France, but his salary was to be 9,000 francs per annum—more than seven times the amount he had received as Croft's secretary—with an additional 9,000 for expenses. In the letter to Weiss on October 19, Nodier announced, "The Emperor has appointed me librarian of the city of Laybach," which offers a glimpse of Nodier's reconciled attitude to Napoleon.

Ironically, the Paris police were at the very moment seeking to learn Nodier's whereabouts. They suspected he was on a mission to England and wrote, in November, 1812, to Sir Herbert Croft for information. Sir Herbert replied that he had not seen Charles in eighteen months, but that he was in correspondence with him and had just learned that Charles had recently accepted a government post in Illyria. Paradoxically, this honest Englishman, whom the imperial police must have suspected of employing Nodier in some nefarious dealings with the enemy, was the one who informed French officials of the government's endorsement of Charles' loyalty.[8]

Before entering upon his new duties, Charles, out of pocket as usual, had to borrow money to finance his trip. He obtained 600 francs from De Bry and Weiss and an equal amount from Roujoux, whom he had slighted by ignoring his correspondence once he had landed the lucrative Amiens post. However, when it became apparent that security and permanency did not lie in that direction, Charles had suddenly remembered his former protector and patron. Now he appealed to Roujoux for the balance of the 1,200 francs he needed; then, typically, he forgot to acknowledge receipt of the money Roujoux sent him.[9]

He took his little family on a tour of Geneva, Savoy, the Mont Cenis, Turin, Milan, Lake Garda, Verona, Padua, Venice, and the Adriatic coast in November and December. On January 2, 1813, they had their first view of Ljubljana, which was to be their home for almost a year. They were met by de Tercy, who introduced them to his superior, Count Chabrol, *intendant général des provinces*. After the usual official visits, Charles was installed in his new post on January 6.

The Dalmation coast had fallen to Napoleon's lot with the Peace of Schönbrunn, October 14, 1809. Detaching Trieste and a part of Venezia Giulia to form an addition to the kingdom of Italy, he reserved the remainder as a province, administered from Paris, later to be turned into a friendly Slovene buffer state between France and Austria. Thus the southern Slavs were brought into a national consciousness which was to result eventually in the creation of Yugoslavia. Before this desideratum could be achieved, a program of intensive propaganda in favor of the mother country had to be effected. As early as 1810 the imperial government envisaged this friendly orientation of the Slovenes in a rescript on general policy in the new province. Article III of that document decreed, "General Censorship will have a newspaper or official Gazette published, setting forth government acts, political news, and other items of interest. This newspaper will appear twice a week in two separate editions, one in French and German and the other in Italian and Slavic." Successive administrations by the Marshal Marmont, the Duc de Ragusa, General Bertrand, and General Junot had done little to advance this design in the first two years of French occupation, as Benincasa, Beaumes, and Paris, Nodier's journalist predecessors, had made a mess of the newspaper.

When Nodier was made editor of the *Télégraphe Officiel*

he found it had been reprinting *in extenso* stale articles drawn from French periodicals to fill out the columns surrounding the announcement of the few government acts. On the same day as he took over editorship of the *Télégraphe,* Nodier was installed as librarian. Immediately there was trouble, as the Slovene mayor of Ljubljana had previously awarded the post to Matija Kalister, a friend and supporter. After some wrangling, it was decided for the sake of Franco-Slovene relations, to confirm Kalister in his post, Nodier ceding 2,600 francs of his salary to that gentleman as his assistant. Charles preserved the title of chief librarian, which office he had indeed come to Illyria to fulfill; however, he did not set foot in the library from that date except for purposes of research. Thus Charles' willingness to compromise insured amicable relations with the native government, which already felt a freer hand in managing its own affairs than it had enjoyed under Austrian domination.

As luck would have it, in the summer of 1813 Nodier's superior became Fouché, Duke of Otranto. The feared ex-minister of police had been suffering a protracted eclipse of his fortunes, thanks to Napoleon's discovery of his scheme for world peace concocted with Ouvrard, Wellesley, Fagan and company in 1810. The master was loath to leave the conniving politician in France while he took the field against an aroused Europe, so he called Fouché out of his forced exile in the south of France and sent him to succeed the demented General Junot as governor of the province of Illyria, thus putting a thousand miles between the inveterate schemer and the center of intrigue in Paris. He found there a handfull of sleepy functionaries, no army, and a disgruntled mixed population of Serbo-Croats, Italians, and Austrians.

The two exiles were not unknown to each other. Fouché and Nodier *père* had been Oratorians together, and Fouché, while he was minister of police, had always maintained in his service two or more of the former pupils of the elder Nodier. We have already seen the part played by Fouché in the liberation of young Nodier after the *Napoléone* incident some ten years earlier. Charles has left a searching portrait of Fouché in his essay on him in the *Souvenirs de la Révolution et de l'Empire.*

He noted his angular, muscular frame, somewhat above the average but bent by cares, his vitreous blue eyes which no emotion excited, and his complete mastery of the art of dissembling, learned after long years of practice as a courtier during an administration crisscrossed with intrigue.

The governor of Illyria did not leave his impression of Nodier at this time; the wily ex-minister of police was not addicted to writing memoirs. (Most authorities attribute Fouché's *Mémoires* to Nodier.) If he had been, his remembrance of Charles probably would have been limited to a mental note of one he had befriended, and upon whom he could depend for an eventual favor. However, Charles has left a portrait of himself in the spurious *Mémoires d'une contemporaine,* supposedly by the adventuress and spy Ida St. Elme, but mostly, as so many other *mémoires* of the 1820's and 1830's, ghost-written by Nodier. "She" is describing a visit to Fouché's headquarters in Ljubljana:

> In the third office there was a somewhat taller young man —the clerks got up as his excellency approached—who was distinguished only by a gentle, tired, and lazy aspect. "Well done, *mon Moniteur,*" the duke said to him. "I was delighted with your last issue. There are some good things in it, based on solid research, though a little too scientific, too literary, too specialized for the times. Let them appreciate the advantages of French influence on public education, speak of the abolition of fiefs, speak to them of liberty; there's a word that sounds well in any language. Point up anything that may do us honor, deny whatever tends to stigmatize us."[10]

This cynical little scene of window-dressing, ideally suited to impress the supposed Gallophile and Napoleon-idolizing French visitor, was not at all typical of Fouché's policy in Illyria, which blew hot and cold depending on whether the Austrians or the French had the upper hand on the international chessboard of unsettled power. Fouché kept the avenue to France open in case Napoleon were to fashion another miracle after the Russian débâcle; at the same time he courted Metternich in Vienna, hoping to be awarded an influential post in the new European scheme, if Napoleon was unseated. Of this double game Nodier showed not the slightest awareness either in his *Souvenirs* or his letters. According to these last, Nodier was nonplussed by Fouché's habit of waking him up in the middle of the night to air his views on the day's happenings in a peripatetic excursion around the room. Seemingly unaware of the journalist's presence, Fouché would set his policy with regard to the occupied area in a protracted monologue. Charles was apparently free to make copy for the next issue of the *Télégraphe* out of these mumbled lucubrations, subject to immediate denial by the governor if it was greeted by disapproval from any quarter. In this manner the faults of policy were laid completely at Nodier's door as an inept interpreter of the governor's wishes, while the foxy Fouché kept his own record clear.

This jumbled state of affairs regarding the governor's decisions concerning the province of Illyria did not prevent Nodier from taking his job seriously, with the result that the *Télégraphe* improved in all departments during his editorship. Charles saw at once the advantage of talking to the local people about their own country, about their history, geography, art, and language. He set them collecting poems, songs, legendary tales, and other manifestations of an autochthonous folklore. He encouraged them to keep distinct their own superstitions, beliefs, and customs. He urged the Slovene scientists to study Illyrian botany, entomology, and geology, studies which would be published, if nowhere else, in the *Télégraphe*. In short, Nodier fostered a growth of national consciousness in the occupied territory through a revival of and an enthusiasm for their own native culture.

It was the inclusive aspect of the compilation of the *Statistique illyrienne*—*statistique* is a borrowed German word meaning in this context the full description of a country including geography, population (racial composition), agricultural and industrial resources, art, literature, and science, a word largely replaced by modern anthropologists with the expression "culture pattern"—it was this thoroughness that caused Fouché to categorize Nodier's work as "too specialized, too scientific, too literary," but which may be regarded as a perfect fulfillment of the propaganda-conscious imperial rescript of 1810. Unfortunately, before either Fouché or Nodier arrived in Illyria, by the agreement of March 14, 1812, Napoleon had decided to cede the province to Austria in exchange for Galicia in southern Poland for Austrian aid in the war against Russia. Modern Slovenian scholars, France Dobrovoljc and Janko Tavzes, have made thorough studies of the essays in this collection, esteeming them to be of the utmost importance in the development of the history and literature of Yugoslavia.

"The *Statistique* would have systematically revealed the history of the country, its beauties and peculiarities, its customs and mores, and would have resuscitated interest in poetry, the national literature, and the mother tongue. . . . Before Nodier, our country represented for the Empire merely a section of an immense tract of land on the road to the Orient. By means of his work on the spot as well as in his recollections later, Nodier stirred an undeniable interest in the suppressed nation, whose aims he served even by his exaggerations."[11] In improving the political role of the newspaper, Nodier was not content to act simply as the genial editor of an encyclopedia on Illyrian affairs. In the columns of the *Télégraphe* he defended Slovene peasants accused of rebellion, and offered to act as mediator between lord and serf.

Nodier's active interest in Slovenian politics and society opened the doors of the cultured élite of Ljubljana, notably of the *salon* of Baron Sigismund de Zoïs. Louis Madelin's telling phrase describing the atmosphere of the city of Ljubljana at this time may well serve as a setting for the circle of Baron Zoïs, where Nodier found "an indistinct Oriental flavor mingled with all the elegance of the Faubourg Saint-Honoré."[12] There Nodier heard discussions of European movements in art and letters on a continental level divorced from French bias. The experience was refreshing to his soul, already dedicated to German models of the end of the eighteenth century. Gradually his articles in the *Télégraphe* took on a more literary and a less administrative tone, and revealed his true position on the main currents of European literary thought.

In an article, "De l'influence de Goethe et de Schiller sur les nouvelles écoles dans la littérature française," Nodier stated that, though the French hated to admit this influence, *Werther* was certainly lurking behind the important French novels of the day, and for the past twenty years, 1793 to 1813, the French owed Schiller "all the tragedies played as *mélodrames* and all the *mélodrames* played as tragedies," or, in other words, all the serious theater. In dedicating a whole number of the *Télégraphe* to a review of a new edition of Bartolommeo Gamba's *Serie dell 'edizioni de 'testi di lingua italiana,* Nodier takes occasion to speak of the state of French bibliography. "The science of bibliography is not very highly held in France, and I am inclined to think—considering how they treat it there —that it can hardly be classed as a literary genre." He does make exception of two or three works whose merits he recognizes, and of one bibliographer by name, his friend Charles Weiss.

What is the upshot of this sniping at French letters from foreign soil? Judging from Nodier's literary allegiances to this time, and from his later preoccupation with the really golden ages of French literature of the past, the pronouncements recorded above would certainly seem to add substance to Nodier's contention that the great literature of the early nineteenth century was not being produced in France—*Atala, René, Corinne,* and *Obermann* notwithstanding—but in Germany. The international orientation of Nodier's literary preferences, remarkable since he knew no German and learned surprisingly little Slavic during his stay in Illyria, was thus intensified by his sojourn in Ljubljana, not as a result of firsthand contact with foreign literature, but through his physical remove from France and Frenchmen. He gleaned his knowledge of Serbo-Croatian literature from Alberto Fortis' *Viaggio in Dalmazia,* Venice, 1744, which had been in the library of Ljubljana since 1778.

It may be that Charles' uneasy suspicion that he was a "foreigner" in his own country, because he came from Franche-Comté, exempted him from the characteristic French xenophobia, thus allowing him a more dispassionate view of foreign literary achievements. In the eyes of Frenchmen, united behind Napoleon in a life-or-death struggle, this kind of disaffection, though superficially expressing only a difference of literary taste, was perhaps not to be tolerated. We are confronted here with Nodier's ability to accept a fact he thought necessary to his existence, but not everything that that fact represented. Nodier was to become quite adept at making these subtle distinctions. Prior to his election to the Academy in 1833, he had been viciously attacking that institution, its members, and the *Dictionnaire de l'Académie Française*. After his election, Nodier accepted the Acadamy and its dictionary, but not the academicians, whom he continued to castigate. In the present case, Nodier had accepted Napoleon—whom he termed a "demigod" in the first number of the *Télégraphe*—and his administration, but not Napoleonic French culture.

In August, Nodier was made inspector of the national lottery,[13] an appointment which carried an annual remuneration of 5,000 francs. This sinecure was granted to help him meet expenses and to offset the disbursement to Kalister of part of his salary as librarian. When Charles accepted the appointment as librarian and editor of the newspaper, he exulted that his annual income would be seven times what he had received from Sir Herbert. He did not reckon, however, with the exigencies of court dress. As a government functionary Nodier was required to be dressed to the teeth at all times, even when Fouché called on him in the middle of the night. One of the items of apparel that was *de rigueur* for officials of the Napoleonic court, where external magnificence was accounted more than half the battle, was a florid doublet dotted with frightfully expensive buttons. Fouché, who had been obliged to wear the showy and uncomfortable costume when he was minister of police, affected a simpler habit as governor of Illyria, but he required his staff to display the uniform of Napoleonic officialdom. And as editor of the government newspaper, Nodier had social obligations which were much more demanding of his time and money than those on the country gentleman's estate in Amiens. Désirée's wardrobe too had to be more pretentious, as she was called upon to entertain other French officials, Slovene dignitaries, literary and scientific guests. In a letter of August 16 to the lawyer Tamisier of Lons-le-Saulnier, Nodier complained that because of the heavy expenses, he was poorer on his impressive base salary in Ljubljana than he had been on his modest income in Amiens.

When it became clear that the tide of war had turned in favor of the Allies and that in the resulting dismemberment of the Napoleonic empire Austria would soon be reclaiming her outlet to the Adriatic, Fouché moved his headquarters to Trieste. The last issue of the *Télégraphe* to appear in Ljubljana is dated August 31. Nodier was able to publish only four editions of the newspaper in Trieste between September 16 and 26. Then in October, as the Austrians were invading the Dalmatian coast, the remainder of the slender occupation staff made its way back to France, Fouché having preceded them by several days.

In retreating across the frontier the ex-governor had taken precautions to protect his staff in the event they fell into the hands of the enemy. He used in the case of Nodier the simple device of sending him a written order to cease publication of the newspaper. The order went on to inform Nodier that he was fired from his post for conniving with the enemy, conspiring against the emperor, and corresponding with the internal and external agents of the deposed monarchy. Nodier had been guilty of all these charges, but not since 1805. Fouché had cleverly summed up the Napoleonic government's extinct griefs against Nodier as a natural expedient to "cover" Charles in case of capture. Fouché's ingenious order was all the more amazing since he had never alluded to Nodier's past activities while working with him in Ljubljana, as if he had ignored or forgotten them. Charles was flabbergasted by the shock, for, as we have seen, he had been basically guilty of the accusations contained in the order, and his essential naiveté in political matters did not permit him to recognize the canny subterfuge of the seasoned diplomat. He hurried to Fouché to protest, only to find that the thoughtful ex-governer of the province of Illyria had thus secured for his ex-editor safe conduct across the invaded territory. Through the ever-benevolent Etienne, in November Charles was attached to the *Journal de l'Empire* as *rédacteur* at 3,600 francs per annum.

The experience in Illyria was a fruitful one, not only because of the nine-month sojourn in a foreign city—Nodier's first contact with another culture—but also because it returned Charles to circulation in his natural habitat, the world of letters. He obtained amazing mileage out of his literary articles for the *Télégraphe;* one, on "Poésie illyrienne," he reprinted no less than four times.[14] On the whole, considering his erratic schedule, his health had been good; we find him complaining only once, in a letter of May 13 to his friend Béchet, secretary of the prefecture of the Jura department, of an attack of jaundice accompanied by migraine headaches, from which he seems to have recovered rapidly. While crossing the Alps in that October of 1813, the Nodiers' conveyance overturned, and Désirée broke her leg. The mishap considerably lengthened the return journey, as Désirée was carried on a homemade litter to Sierres, Switzerland, where she lay five weeks convalescing.

When the family finally arrived in Quintigny, travelsore and in rags, Nodier found he had lost 16,000 francs which he had just received as his last salary before leaving Illyria, all his manuscripts, books, collections (relating to the entomology and geology of the Dalmatian coast), furniture, and clothing. So the little family had returned poorer than they had set out, Marie ill, Désirée hobbling about on crutches, and Charles downhearted and disgusted. Had it not been for the letter from the Minister of Police, the Duc de Rovigo, confirming his appointment in the censorship division of the Paris newspapers and ordering him to appear without delay, Nodier would have collapsed into the blackest fit of depression. Even so he was loath to leave Désirée and Marie and the loving ministrations of the Gesse family. After putting his affairs in order, Nodier set out for Paris on November 12, 1813. Except for short trips and another six-month stay in Quintigny in 1818, Paris was to be from that date Charles' permanent home.

Charles took up residence at 17 Rue des Trois Frères at the point where that street formed an angle with the Rue Saint-Lazare. He had his old friend Jouy for a neighbor, and began to receive visits from Ballanche, Millevoye, Etienne, Desaugiers, Colonel Foy, and Duc de Caylus. Occasionally, Alexandre Duval and Aimé Martin dropped in for a chat. Soon Désirée and Marie were able to join him. Toward the end of

the month he learned of his new duties with the *Journal de
l'Empire;* he was to be literary critic and reporter of the new
liberal courses that were being offered to the public, such as
Aimé Martin's lectures on literature at the Athenaeum. When
these tasks were accomplished, he could supply articles on subjects of general literary interest. Occasionally, he was asked to
replace the aging dean of French literary criticism, Goeffroy,
who, for a short time before his death, consented to sign his
name to reviews of the drama written for him by Nodier. This
arrangement must have been satisfactory to all concerned, as
Nodier was moved to the drama criticism desk when Geoffroy
died in April, 1814. Shortly after the Restoration, Nodier received a considerable increase in salary. He was to provide the
newspaper, which had again become the *Journal des Débats,*
seven articles a month, an eighth every third month, at 100
francs each; if he realized his full quota of work, his annual
income would be 8,800 francs. However, at this time Nodier
preferred to review publications that permitted political discussion, since he was eager to prove his adhesion to the restored
monarchy.

Sensing that Napoleon was doomed, Nodier had written a
little poem on December 13, 1813, entitled *La France aux abois
à Bonaparte (France Yapping at Bonaparte's Heels),* which
he had the prudence to keep to himself until the Restoration
had actually taken place. When he published it, along with a
new edition of *La Napoléone,* May 7, 1814, he did so under
the assumed name of Flamen. Suddenly remembering his opposition to Napoleon, his years of exile and his ultraroyalist sentiments, Nodier prepared a highly fictional work, the *Histoire
des Sociétés Secrètes de l'Armée,* which he published anonymously in the beginning of 1815. Purporting to be a history
of the "military conspiracies which had as their aim the destruction of Bonaparte's government," this hoax so baffled and
delighted the reading public that a second edition was recorded
by the *Journal de la Librairie,* March 4, 1815. Charles let his
thwarted conspirator's imagination run riot in this fantasy of
cloak-and-dagger activities, probably the first full-length "historical" novel to appear in French.

It is certainly a *mystique de l'histoire,* as the reader has the

eerie presentiment that Colonel Oudet has been the archcon-
spirator since the beginning of time and that he still is in touch
with all the underground movements in history. Nodier as-
sembled under one roof the known conspiracies against Napoleon: the Cadoudal-Pichegru bomb plot of 1804, the pro-roy-
alist machinations of General Moreau, General Malet's conspiracy of 1812, even the peasants' uprising in the Tyrol under An-
dreas Hofer in 1809 and laid them all at the door of Colonel
Oudet! Using the organization of the adolescent Philadelphes
as a framework, Nodier inflated the Society to several thousand
members with ramifications throughout the Grand Army. Of
all this vast underground movement, according to Charles,
Napoleon had not the slightest knowledge, but fearing Oudet
as a rival, he exiled him to the Island of Ré, then had him
assassinated at the battle of Wagram. The wonderful blending
of fact and fancy is so artfully conceived in this "history" that
serious observers have been startled by the revelations contained in it. Moreover, Charles introduced elements of this
"secret" Society's doings in many spurious memoirs which he
ghost-wrote—a lucrative publishers' venture in the 1820's—so
that the multiplication of the same evidence in various works
purportedly by different hands would lend credence to the
"reality" of Oudet's conspiracy. So successful was he that a
serious historical scholar in the definitive study of Napoleon's
era for the *Histoire générale* series known as *Peuples et civili-
sations* feels bound to mention that "we are not informed about
the Philadelphes which Colonel Oudet, killed at Wagram, was
supposed to have directed,"[15] and an earlier historian, G.
Caudrillier, in an article on the Conspiracy of the year XII,
stated that the *Histoire Secrète* was "not entirely a novel."[16]
On his deathbed Nodier could still laugh at this hoax.

The entire fabric of this novel had been germinating in his
mind as a tribute to Oudet from the moment he learned of his
idol's death in 1809. He now produced it as a testimonial of
his continued opposition to Napoleon, since only a trusted
henchman of Oudet could be informed of the Empire-wide conspiracy. Charles veiled his own identity but thinly, reproducing
the whole of *La Napoléone* as the *Marseillaise* of the underground movement. Moreover, the fiction of Oudet's assassina-

tion in an ambush immediately following the battle of Wagram and the ensuing suicide of his men at the sight of his dead body is a Nodier creation, reported for the first time as early as 1811. In this version we read that "he received thirty-two wounds, and forty-one of his officers let themselves be cut to pieces over his corpse."[17] When this incident was published for the first time in the *Histoire* we are discussing, the number of those massacred was reduced to twenty-two; then three days later, at the sight of Oudet's corpse being carried from the hospital, "a young sergeant-major who had been following the burial party fell upon his sword a few paces from the grave. A lieutenant who had served under him in the 68th half-brigade blew his brains out."

In the "Portrait" of Colonel Oudet, which Charles published in the *Revue de Paris* in 1830, the incident on Oudet's grave is again recalled: "Two of them [i.e., Oudet's despairing friends] committed suicide on his grave, a lieutenant with a pistol shot, a noncommissioned officer with a sabre thrust." In all the other so-called *mémoires* and histories, the details of the suicide—the trademark of Nodier's participation in those works—were reported verbatim, as in a prayer. Charles added another stroke in his "Portrait" of 1830, intended to identify him more closely with his idol: at the point of dying, Oudet mumbled five names, "Lahorie, Malet, Charles Nodier, Gindre, Piquerel." Notice that Nodier's is the only name given in full. Were the others sufficiently known, or was Nodier busy linking once and for all his fate with that of his elusive hero, the only opponent among Napoleon's contemporaries who had the status and the power to unseat the tyrant, *if he had lived?*

Of all the voices that were raised to stem this crescendo of falsification, at least one, that of General Vasserot, belonged to a man who was in a position to give the actual facts surrounding Oudet's death. He had succeeded Colonel Oudet in command of the seventeenth regiment at Wagram and had witnessed his predecessor's last moments. Here is his deposition: "Jacques-Joseph Oudet, wounded in the Battle of Wagram, was taken to the home of Baron Arnstein in a Vienna suburb. He died as a result of his wounds a few days later and was buried in the cemetery of that suburb. The officers of his regiment caused a tablet to be erected on his resting-place. *No one committed suicide on his grave.*"[18] That would seem to be final enough, but Nodier had done his work too well; other memorialists, wishing to seem well-informed of the organized opposition to Napoleon, seized upon Nodier's fictions regarding Oudet and the Philadelphes and reproduced them as a sign of their own participation in the anti-Napoleonic movement. Indeed, how could a nation of intelligent people be expected to submit unquestioningly to fifteen years of tyranny?

Just as *Les Proscrits* had been the fictional counterpart of *La Napoléone, l'Histoire des Sociétés Secrètes de l'Armée* was an amplification in novel form of Charles' imagined grievances against the Empire. He had earlier penned a letter to the Comte d'Artois setting forth the persecutions his fidelity to the monarchy had caused him under Napoleon's regime, but he never mailed it because he would have had difficulty in explaining his present position on the *Débats* and his editorship of the *Télégraphe*. So he saved all its elements for the *Histoire*, leaving the letter as a document to posterity, the kernel of one of the most fantastic tours de force in the annals of literary history.[19]

When Napoleon returned from Elba, Charles was summoned by the hastily regrouped Empire censorship staff and the reinstated Minister of Police to justify his continuance on the *Journal des Débats*. Nodier consulted his ex-patron Fouché, who had also been bombarding the restored monarchy with protestations of devotion to the legitimate incumbent. Fouché advised him to transfer his allegiance to the Empire, but Charles, enervated and exhausted by the continual change of governments, decided to risk all on the side of legitimacy and published anonymously a violent attack against the Emperor in the last issue of the *Journal des Débats,* Wednesday, March 20, urging that the French could expect nothing but grief from Napoleon's return to power. The next day the newspaper became *Le Journal de l'Empire* again and Nodier's friends, alerted by Désirée's apprehensions, tried to persuade him to leave Paris.

The bookloving Duc de Caylus offered Charles and his family refuge in his Chateau de Buis at the Ville-d'Avray near Versailles. Instead, the unheeding journalist published another blast against Napoleon Friday, May 10, 1815, entitled "Bonaparte au 4 mai" in *Le Nain Jaune*. Reproduced separately in the provinces shortly thereafter, the energetic pamphlet caused him considerable uneasiness. To make matters worse, little Terence, the Nodiers' son born in 1814, a feeble child at best throughout his short life, sickened visibly and required constant nursing and care. Taking advantage finally of the hospitality offered by the Duc de Caylus since April, the Nodiers retired to that gentleman's estate, where Charles kept silent for the remainder of the Hundred Days. At the second Restoration of the monarchy, Louis XVIII rewarded Nodier for his loyalty by granting him letters of nobility—Charles' application was sponsored by four noblemen of Franche-Comté—and an author's pension. His position on the *Débats* was assured.

Perhaps Nodier's political maneuvering at the end of the Empire should not be judged too harshly. He had really been moving toward a royalist point of view, but the responsibilities of parenthood forced him to take a realistic view and bend the knee to the tyrant. At the downfall of Napoleon, Nodier was one of the first to rally to the side of the king, a position he did not leave during the Hundred Days because it represented his true political convictions. Other writers were far less consistent in their political thinking. His friend Benjamin Constant, for instance, published a violent attack against the returning Emperor in the columns of the *Débats* on March 19, 1815; yet a few days later we find him closeted with Napoleon helping him draw up the Additional Act to the Constitutions of the Empire. In the crazy-quilt shifting of governments of the years 1814 and 1815 in France, it was difficult for anyone— with the exception perhaps of the master calculator Fouché —to keep a cool head on political matters. Charles at least showed the courage of his convictions, preferring absence to recantation when Napoleon returned from Elba. Nodier's retirement to the Paris suburb of Ville-d'Avray in the spring of 1815 was his last flight and episode of hiding from the police. It was with a light heart that he took leave of his host at the Château de Buis at the end of June. The long exile was over.

III

The Critical Campaign
(1815-1820)

André Chénier once said, "Let us make ancient verses on new subjects." *That idea singularly haunted me in my youth, and I must say, in order to explain and excuse my reasoning, that I was the only one at the time who foresaw the inevitable coming of a new literature. For a genius, that might have been a revelation; for me, it was only a torment.*

NODIER, in *Smarra,*
Préface nouvelle

REGARDLESS of how changeable Nodier may have been in his political allegiance, determined mostly by the exigencies of the moment, he showed a dogged consistency in his stand on the coming of romanticism. His earliest writings exhibited an acceptance of all the features which were to constitute the basic doctrines of the new school: the cult of Shakespeare,[1] the adoption of foreign literary models, and the reverence for the national past, including the veneration of monuments and shrines.

At the age of fourteen, Charles was afforded an excellent introduction to the works of Shakespeare by the engineer and amateur naturalist Girod de Chantrans at Novillars. In the evening and on rainy days, Girod would translate for the admiring youth select passages from the great plays. These readings bore their first fruit in the *Pensées de Shakespeare* seven years later. In the *Observation préliminaire* to that work, Nodier began his campaign in favor of romanticism by an attack on the so-called unities, fully twenty-six years before the famous *Préface de Cromwell*.

> I do not know to what extent the unities established by the ancients must be considered as an essential and constituent part of the dramatic poem; I respect these hindrances, because they seem to be imposed by taste and consecrated by usage; but are they appropriate to the author of *Macbeth* and *Othello*?

This question was the core of the romantic view of Shakespeare that French writers were to share a quarter of a century later: Shakespeare is as vast as nature itself and must be accepted on his own terms or not at all. The strictures on the confining unities were the focal points of both romantic manifestoes of the 1820's, Stendhal's *Racine et Shakespeare* and

85

Hugo's *Préface de Cromwell*. Nodier's appeal to sentiment rather than reason in these same observations was also an important romantic gambit because it permitted the poets of the new school to escape the witty *pièces de salon*—which had plagued the verse of the preceding century—and ultimately gave rise to lyrical poetry, the most significant aspect of romanticism.

Seven years later, beginning in July, 1808, Nodier offered a course on literature in Dole. In the second semester, under the general heading of *Art Poétique*, the young professor had perforce to take up the art of drama. His opening remarks concerned the unities and were more detailed and more mature than those set forth in the *Pensées*. The tenor of the remarks was that some nations succeeded in ignoring them altogether, yet wrote first class plays, and that the French, who had used them to advantage, were wrong to judge the worth of a play on the strength of whether it adhered to or violated these same unities, each work having to be considered in terms of theater and dramatic merit. Nodier then approached his idol. In an eloquent speech, the most brilliant tribute tendered Shakespeare by a Frenchman since the great dramatist was first introduced by the critic De La Roche in 1717, he reviewed all the elements of Shakespeare appreciation that were to render the romanticists famous: the universal grasp of Shakespeare's genius; the superb delineation of character, especially of women, considered at that time negligible even in England; his use of the macabre, the eerie, even the horrible to balance the noble and sublime; the creation of sprites and goblins to enliven the canvas with gossamer, airy, intermediate creatures. His image of Shakespeare, as a giant who had his head in the clouds but had feet of clay, shows that Nodier at twenty-eight was a more perceptive critic than the later eulogists, Lamartine, Hugo, and Vigny. He saw that not everything was to be admired in Shakespeare's plays. But this recognition of weaknesses, which did not dampen his enthusiasm, bespeaks a sureness of judgment which makes his comments all the more noteworthy and his tribute all the more sound. In truth, of the four or five world poets usually ranked with Shakespeare, whose work is more uneven? Yet, as Nodier said so beautifully, who can notice the spots in the sun?

Proceeding, he discussed the various reasons why Shakespeare can never be translated successfully into French. Topical circumstances which are peculiar to a period or to a locality, to the genius of a people or of an age, render translations flabby and pointless. Despite the fine efforts of Letourneur, the French do not have an adequate Shakespeare. As for Ducis' imitations, they are no longer Shakespeare.

Addressing a much larger audience in his review of Ducis' *Hamlet* for the *Journal des Débats*, May 14, 1814, and thoroughly aware of the reticence expected of a responsible critic, Nodier softened his earlier judgment of Ducis and was somewhat less sanguine in his praise of Shakespeare, but not less real. He allowed again that Shakespeare's plays, *qua* Shakespeare, can never be transferred to the French language, and that *Hamlet*, the most complicated of all Shakespeare's tragedies, is the least susceptible of French adaptation. Yet there are many beauties in it which call for universal admiration, he went on; the character delineation of Ophelia and Gertrude, Hamlet's predicament, his sadness, which logically puts him in contact with the supernatural apparition of his father's ghost, the great soliloquies which reveal the heart of man in all its madness, so typical of modern society and developed later with so much power, but never with so much genius, by Goethe, Schiller, and Chateaubriand. Of all this, Nodier continued, Ducis made what he could, and it took all of his talent to transmit as much of it as he did to a literary atmosphere that differs so radically from the English; but Voltaire, in a monument of bad faith, chose the very scenes which he knew would appear ridiculous to the French, thanks to his exaggerations and travesties of them, in order to cast derision on the great playwright. Voltaire may not have known English very well, he concludes, but he was well enough acquainted with the plays in their original at home to know that the English did not find those scenes laughable. In fine, Voltaire "treated Shakespeare as if he should have been writing for the French, as if French literature was the essential type of all possible literatures." It is evident from this article that

Nodier was aware that the beauty of Shakespeare's original English could never be translated into French; yet he was certain the impact of the great tragedies on French drama would be tremendous.

Nodier's first and only dramatic success came as the result of his study of Shakespeare. *Le Vampire,* 1820, was the natural outgrowth of Nodier's cogitations on the rise of romanticism; what it meant, what it tried to do in England and Germany, and where it was going in France. The play was a conscious attempt to realize the adaptation of a foreign literary model, Shakespeare, to the French stage in terms of the ideals of the successful German romantic drama modified to suit popular French taste and at the same time to indicate, if possible, the path the rising new school was to follow. That he did this *à contre coeur* is evident in the excerpt given below: he would have preferred Shakespeare in the original, to achieve the impact Goethe and Schiller had on German audiences; but these were out of the question on a national basis in France for the time being, so he settled for the sugar and spice of the *mélodrame.*

In reviewing *La Rançon de Du Guesclin* by his friend Antoine Vincent Arnault for the *Débats,* March 20, 1814, Nodier concludes his remarks by stating: "If a Shakespeare were to be born in France, this great man would doubtless have the wit to become the people's poet and, unfortunately, write *mélodrames."* At the outset of his review of Marchangy's *La Gaule poétique* (*Débats,* November 27, 1817) Nodier reaffirms his position that new political needs lead to new morality and a new literature, typified by the *mélodrame.* He pursues the thesis of the emergence of the *mélodrame* as a result of the Revolution in the first of his three essays on Madame de Stael's *De l'Allemagne* (*Débats,* November 8, 1818).

I shall not have to look far to find an example of the inevitable influence of revolutions on literature. What would the *mélodrame* in France have been before the invasion of new political doctrines, before the great events which fired public imagination, before the terrible scenes which exercised its passions, courage and sensibilities and created a painful need of continuous emotion and alarm, of pity and terror? Under Louis XIV, such a spectacle, placed entirely outside the pattern of usual behavior, would have excited only painful astonishment promptly followed by disgust. That was to be expected then; today, the *mélodrame* is indispensable. I cannot conceive of anything that could be put in its place, and whatever efforts are made to destroy it, or to render it ridiculous, . . . will never succeed, because this kind of composition has become popular, and public taste, normally preceding by a century that of the academies, ends by becoming the national will. Moreover, political leaders should not fly in the face of public taste when it is based on moral need and can be employed to serve the moral education of a people. Well, the *mélodrame,* leaving aside for the moment considerations of technique, is German romantic tragedy. If among the people of wit who make a habit of poking fun at it, there had been found a genius who had the courage to face adverse criticism, to desire to earn the first palm in a new career, to evoke that masculine and terrifying muse of Schiller and Goethe whose secrets Madame de Stael reveals so eloquently, do you know where the second Théâtre Français would be? Most likely on the Boulevards.

Plays like *Le Vampire* would be staged, no doubt, as he suggests in his review of Faber's translation of that work from the English of Byron-Polidori (*Débats*, July 1, 1819).

There are no errors in the beliefs of men which are not the offspring of some truth; and therein lies their charm, for positive truths do not flatter the imagination, which so loves untruth that it prefers frightening illusions to the depiction of an agreeable, but natural, emotion. This latest shift in human idiosyncrasy, tired of ordinary emotions, is what is called the romantic genre. A strange type of poetry that is well suited, however, to the present moral state of a blasé society, which demands sensations at any cost, even to the point of sacrificing the welfare of generations to come. The ideals of early and classic poets, and of their elegant imitators, were premised on the perfection of human nature; those of the romantic poets derive from our woes. This is not a defect of art, it is a necessary result of our social progress. We know where we are in politics; in poetry we have reached the age of the nightmare and of the vampires.

In thus reducing Shakespeare to the stature of a Guilbert de Pixerécourt, we must not be misled into thinking that Nodier had lost his lifelong admiration of the great English dramatist; he is only concerned in this conjuncture with the practical application of the new breath in German drama, aided by some aspects of Shakespeare's plays which were never present in French playwriting: the eerie, the macabre, the grotesque, the weird, and the supernatural, to a rejuvenation of the sagging French theater.

Subsequent events show that Nodier was not far off the mark, for what are Hugo's plays but glorified *mélodrames?* When Bellini turned Nodier's adaptation of Maturin's *Bertram ou Le Château d'Aldobrand* into the opera *Il pirata*, he began a trend that reached its apogee in Verdi's setting of many of Hugo's plays, including *Hernani* (*Ernani*). It is significant too that Shakespeare, of whom some French romanticists spoke as though he were a contemporary, whose tragedies and histories were in great part the well-spring of the romantic drama in France, met the same fate at the hands of the Italian master. Verdi, who was said to have destroyed a *King Lear* after many frustrating years because of an inadequate libretto, finally succeeded in producing an operatic masterpiece out of *Othello*, a play "written by Shakespeare in the style of Italian opera," as Shaw shrewdly observed. According to the *Témoin*, Hugo was moving more and more toward the inclusion of music in his dramas. Was not this an acknowledgment that his dramatic efforts, *mélodrames* after all, were more libretto than play and went thirsting for the musical fulfillment they finally received?[2]

It was not for nothing that Charles continued to style himself *ancien bibliothécaire de la Carniole* after his return to Paris. Since he was busy courting the restored Louis XVIII at this time, it would be folly to assume that he wished to recall his service to Napoleon by this appellation. It was rather the romantic aura of having served abroad, a popular pose in the post-Napoleonic era, that prompted him to use this signature, as if to say, "I am proud to represent a foreign culture," an attitude ideally suited to impress the rising generation of young writers who turned eagerly to Nodier for guidance on foreign literature. As the oracle of life and letters abroad, it was natural that Charles should undertake to defend and propagate foreign models among the French.

"It seems to be in our interest to at least know that we are judging, and not to condemn without a hearing those numberless generations of poets who have delighted the rest of Europe," Nodier states in a review of Madame de Stael's *De l'Allemagne* for the *Journal des Débats*, November 8, 9, 10, 1818.

> It is not by overwhelming them with profound scorn and rating them below the savage bards of the most barbarous nations nor by exhibiting them to public derision in unworthy travesties that we will succeed in destroying the favorable impression they have made upon other nations. Voltaire showed more partiality than wisdom in his violent attacks against Shakespeare. . . .
>
> I repeat: it cannot be useless for us to know in detail the literature of our neighbors, even if these literatures are in marked opposition to the eternal principles of the beautiful, which cannot be the case, for people do not differ so radically that they cannot agree on certain fundamental ideas which are common to all. Even for the most austere tests there is unquestionably a precious mine to be exploited in the romantic writers, and our language has arrived at that point of advanced maturity where it is no longer permissible to ignore new sources.

That the above statement represented Nodier's conviction from the beginning may be seen not only in his correspondence and novels at the turn of the century, but also in his reading notes and studies left in manuscript. His mania for *Werther* in his teens led him to adopt the dress of that sorrowing hero: blue doublet and yellow breeches. To this volume, which he took with him like a Bible wherever he went, he soon added the works of Sterne, especially *Tristram Shandy,* a healthy antidote. Just before the turn of the century, Charles began the translation of an Italian work by Martin Sherlock, entitled *Consiglio ad un giovane poeta* (1779).

The fragment of the Nodier manuscript, now in the Library of Besançon, MS 1417, folios 97-105, shows that Nodier was treated to a view of Italian literature from Dante to Goldoni, with generous quotations from Petrarch, *l'Orlando furioso,* and *La Gerusalemme liberata.* In citing the fifth law of Bettinelli's *Codice* of good taste, Sherlock's patriotism rises in anger against this precept: "You will not read French or English poets until you are forty, when you can no longer be influenced by them." Ironically, Sherlock's whole thesis was meant to guide the young poet away from Dante, Ariosto, and Tasso, whom he deemed unsuitable. In the fury of his attack on Ariosto, Sherlock lets himself say: "Ariosto corrupted Italian taste in poetry. The genre that he chose suffices to condemn him: a romanesque poem. The title alone announces the height of ridicule and absurdity. What is a novel in prose? An insignificant and frivolous work." Here the young translator and romantic novelist-to-be raps the master's knuckles in a footnote: "Mr. Sherlock does not remember on this occasion the sublime novels of Richardson, or perhaps, like Diderot, he does not wish to call them novels." Curiously, Charles did not translate the bulk of the second part of Sherlock's essay, pages 50 to 85, a brilliant study of Shakespeare's plays.

On his second trip to Paris, in 1802, Nodier had met Nicolas Bonneville, the translator, with Friedel, of the *Théâtre allemand,* published in Paris between 1782 and 1785 in twelve volumes, and of the later *Choix de petits romans imités de l'allemand,* 1786. In these volumes Charles became acquainted with a brief history of the German theater and twenty-seven plays by Arenhof, Babo, Brandès, Bertuch, Dahlberg, J. Engel, Gebler, Gemmingen, Goethe, Grossmann, Klopstock, Leisewitz, Lessing, Richter, Schiller, Unzer,

Weisse, and Wegel. Some of the plays that attracted him most were Brandès' *Graf von Olsbach*, Leisewitz' *Julius von Tarent*, Lessing's *Emilia Galotti*, Goethe's *Clavigo* and *Stella*, and Klopstock's *Adamstod*. In the second Bonneville anthology he found *novellen by* Meissner, Wall, Sturz, and Wieland. Again and again in his correspondence with Weiss, and later with Van Praet, the curator of the Bibliothèque Royale, Nodier requested the loan of these volumes. In the preface to the novels of 1803, *Le Dernier Chapitre de mon roman* and *Le Peintre de Saltzbourg,* Charles admitted his indebtedness to English and German models. The *Essais d'un jeune barde*, 1804, contain pieces imitated or translated from the German: *Le Suicide et le Pélerin, imitation de l'allemand, La Violette de Goethe, traduction littérale de la romance.* The 1806 miscellany, *Les Tristes,* includes *Ophelia, traduction d'une complainte anglaise,* a dialogue between Ophelia and her attendants, a free interpretation of Ophelia's last moments, and *Le Jugement Dernier de Schiller,* a translation of the parricide's dream.

In the Dole course on literature (1808) Nodier showed a wide range of familiarity with western European writers and evinced particular enthusiasm for English and German authors. In discussing the epic, for instance, Charles dismisses Dante with a few sentences and Camoens with a few words; but Milton and Ossian are awarded four pages each and Klopstock's *Messiah* calls forth several pages of praise. The following excerpt is typical of his open-mindedness.

Klopstock is little known in France through two translations, the one weak, languishing and paraphrased, the other exalted, emphatic, and incorrect, giving only a faint idea of the original. We would therefore be unjust to reproach the poet with raving exaggeration, obscure mysticism and the gloomy indistinctness in which his imagination so often seems to wander, since these defects may result from basic differences in the two languages, and especially to the impotence of ours. But even if these weaknesses did exist in the *Messiah,* they are more than compensated by so many beauties that the critic can find in them but scant nourishment. The admirable canticles of Eloah would still be among the most delightful productions of the lyre and the aspect of that sad and unfortunate Abbandona, consumed by the eternal regret of his rebellion, will always remain what it seemed to us at first, the most touching, the most sublime episode in human destiny.

This paragraph (Folios 28-31) shows more than a passing acquaintance with the German religious poet, and a deeper insight into his masterpiece than was exhibited by Madame de Stael.

In the section devoted to the drama Nodier underlines the contempt of foreign nations for the unities and breaks a lance in favor of tragedies in prose: "Two or three works of genius would have settled that question."(Folio 49) After passing in rapid review foreign attempts at tragedy by Calderón, Metastasio, and Alfieri, at comedy by Wycherley, Sheridan, and Goldoni, Nodier expatiates on the German dramas of the *Sturm und Drang* school (Folio 84):

Germany, whose hardy authors were from the beginning liberated from cloying rules, had no other guide than a free and ardent imagination, no other system than the inspiration of the moment, no other model than nature itself, Germany so rich in the vast tableaux of Goethe, the touching compositions of Lessing, and the raving though often sublime rhapsodies of Schiller, did not frequently smile on the gambols of Thalia. Yet it was from her breast that sprang that equivocal muse unknown to the ancients and which she does not owe to us, that muse which wears the buskin on one foot and the cothurnus on the other, carrying the masque and the bauble in one hand and the poignard in the other, and thus singularly accoutred in ill-assorted raiment deploys a mantle composed of a mixture of purple and coarse woolen. It was from this source that we received the mixed genre called *le drame*, still flourishing in the hands of the ingenious, fertile, and romanesque Kotzbue, naturalized here in the cold but often interesting declamations of La Chaussée, and in the impetuous and engaging sallies of Diderot, finally found its

true home on the Boulevards where everything indicates
it will remain.

Nodier's later dramatic efforts were to help keep it there.
Charles had met the flower of Slovene literati, among them
Valentin Vodnik, in the home of the cultured Baron Zoïs. At
his leisure and in the quiet of his own study he was to make
a systematic discovery of the great Slovene and Serbo-Croatian writers of the past, whom he examined and translated,
with the aid of local scholars, in four articles for the *Télégraphe Officiel* on "La poésie illyrienne." We can be fairly
certain, thanks to the excellent scholia France Dobrovoljc has
drawn up in his French edition of the *Statistique illyrienne*,[3]
that Nodier made a partial translation of the Serbo-Croatian
popular ballad *Asanaginica* and of the *Firefly*, which he compared to Goethe's *Das Veilchen*, by Ignjat Djordjić, the first
based on an anonymous French translation of Alberto Fortis'
Viaggio in Dalmazia (Berne, 1778) and the second on an
Italian translation by Giacchino Stulli (Stulić), which he
found in F. M. Appendini's *Notizie storico-critiche sulle anti-
chità, storia e letteratura de Ragusei* (1802-03). To these
must be added the great Ragusan dramatic poet, John Gon-
dola or Gundulić of the early seventeenth century, of whose
Osman Charles promised but did not give an appreciation.
In this brilliant voyage of discovery of the authors of the
eastern shore of the Adriatic, where he had been preceded by
Alberto Fortis in Italy and Goethe in Germany and was to
be followed by Mérimée, Gérard de Nerval, and Claude Fau-
riel among others in France, Nodier opened up for the French
the vein of Slavic literature.

In a review of Dr. Tantini's *Rapido sguardo* or *Quick
Glance at the State of Science and Literature in Germany*
(Plon, 1812), which Nodier published in the *Télégraphe* May
6, 1813, he took the opportunity to assess the influence of
German authors, especially Goethe and Schiller, "on the
spirit and the taste of the century." Nodier begins in his
typically discursive manner by stating that perhaps in literature all has been said by the ancients and their works are
so imposing that many young artists have turned their efforts

to other fields; thus Buffon, Bernardin de Saint-Pierre, and Chateaubriand were often poetic, whereas one could search in vain for real poetry in volumes of versification pompously masquerading under that title. (Folio 3)

Yet if some audacious souls had not overcome their fear of competing with the great classics we would never have had Corneille and Racine, he continues in his review of 1813, but many have shown more courage than talent in their desire to be different just for the sake of being different. And are they really different? Is Karl Moor, whom Schiller flattered himself he invented, any one else but Orestes turned robber? And Werther, is he not Orestes in love? The inventions of Schiller and Goethe would then be "limited to some none too happy modifications of village intrigues and highway conspiracies, to a form of mania instead of passion, wherein a road in Franconia is substituted for the palace of Atreus and the blue doublet of a petty bourgeois for the Pelopid tunic."

In the second article of May 27, entitled more candidly "De l'influence de Goethe et de Schiller sur les nouvelles écoles dans la littérature française," Nodier pursues his evaluation of the impact of *Werther*. When this novel first came out, he begins, we were still wallowing in the backstairs literature of the type of *Faublas*. So it was no wonder that *Werther* made its mark on Paris, as it did on Geneva and London. He admits that the character of Werther has some sympathetic traits, but what is the judicious reader to think of this sick man who loves nothing, who does not know what he wants, nor what he regrets, who is disgusted with life before having suffered from it, with passions without having experienced them, with himself without knowing himself, whose cold, melancholy egoism is an insult to the real ills society suffers from, deploring the while imaginary evils which are vain and puerile? This train of thought leads Nodier to a tentative definition of romanticism:

A sadness without object, a vaporous affection resulting from the satiety of experienced sensations or a curiosity of new and powerful emotions, a need for activity which exerts itself perpetually on chimeras and whose very nature is to avoid useful aims, an exaltation which is not in the emotions but in actions and more often in words, a life always busy and always sterile, which consumes itself in false regrets and nourishes itself on false hopes, and which forgets the present in the contemplation of a past which it has lost and of a future which it will lose. . . .

We have here, Nodier concludes, the exact description of the *vague des passions* which was to give birth among us to *René* and *Corinne,* even more exaggerated specimens than their German model.

The most extraordinary feature of the influence which Goethe and Schiller have exerted on us is that our literature refuses to acknowledge it. Our newspapers which are usually staffed by discerning people who should be dedicated to the preservation of good taste and who have, I know not how or why, sacrificed taste to the mode of pathos, show no less scorn for the true founders of the modern school than foolish enthusiasm for their imitators. . . .

It is not Goethe's and Schiller's fault their plagiarists have stolen from them everything but their sensitivity and their genius.

One cannot blame a great innovator if his voice was badly heard and his message misinterpreted.

But it was in lyric poetry that the romantic revolution, inspired by foreign models, was to reap the greatest reward. In the introductory remarks to the poetry section of his lectures in Dole, Nodier had stated that "lyric poetry incontestably brings man closest to divinity." (Folio 95) In a review of his brother-in-law's poem, Tercy's *La Mort et l'apothéose de Marie-Antoinette d'Autriche* for the *Journal des Débats,* February 14, 1817, he added, "In the last analysis, it can hardly be doubted that a new language, and especially a new poetic language, has been forming in France as a result of the great political and moral revolutions." In the three articles he dedicated to Madame de Stael's *De l'Allemagne* for the same newspaper, November 8-10, 1818, Nodier, after paying tribute to that lady for being the first to bring to French notice the beauties of German literature, singles out for especial comment not the epic nor the dramatic poetry, which the classic muse has all but exhausted, "but a branch of poetry where the poetics have never been determined and which is consequently susceptible of modification, even in our own language," the ingenious *poésies fugitives*:

With us, this type of poetry is more often than not dedicated to the palest and most monotonous of sentiments, to that stylized and coquettish *galanterie,* which has taken the place of love in our poetry as well as in our manners. In Germany, all the effects of a more elevated poetic experience have been bestowed on these short pieces whose limited dimensions are perfectly suited to the sudden impulse of inspiration. Terror is very often the aim of this energetic poetry, which does not believe it has moved the reader unless it shocks him. However, at other times the poet evokes a tender and gentle emotion; whose impression persists for a long time in the mind of the reader, charming him with a sadness that has no real object to contemplate.

There follow examples with analyses drawn from Goethe, *Das Veilchen, Der Fischer, Der Erlkönig,* and from Bürger, *Lenore,* and *Der wilde Jäger.* "I persist in believing that my efforts to call attention to these singular works will not have been in vain if they encourage some of our young poets to leave the circle of banal *poésie de salon* and seek in sentiments and passions a more noble and a more abundant source of inspiration." In Chapter Five we shall see how the young Victor Hugo rose to this call.

The new voice raised in German poetry and worthy of being spread to France encouraged Nodier to attempt another definition of romanticism:

In these three consecutive articles on romanticism I will be pleased if I have succeeded in limning the particular characteristics of this type of writing and in transmitting the charm which is peculiar to it, a charm whose effect is admitted by everyone and even the severest critics cannot deny. But how set down what escapes expression, eludes our faculties or impinges on them only by an invisible force whose magic works on the reader as a result of a vague quality which can be explained only through means which are themselves unexplainable? Facets of things hitherto unseen, an order of perception new enough to be bizarre. I don't know what secrets of human emotions which individuals have experienced but never attempted to convey to others, yet when the reader comes across them he knows he is meeting an old friend. I know not what mysteries of nature—which have not escaped us but which we have never analyzed all at once—strike us because the writer, thanks to a happy coincidence, has suddenly placed them in harmony with memories and feelings; above all, the art of speaking to the imagination by inviting it to dwell on the first emotions of childhood, by evoking those fearful, early superstitions which advanced societies have relegated to the domain of foolishness and which succeed in being poetic only in the poetry of the new school; those are some of the traits of romanticism."

In these searching remarks, which include even a perfect example of the pathetic fallacy so dear to the hearts of romanticists foreign and domestic, we see Charles approaching a clearer and more universal definition of the art of the new school. It is perhaps needless to add that his acquaintance and sympathy with foreign literatures considerably aided him in formulating a slogan to which local writers could rally. By thinking out his position on romanticism long before classicists and romanticists came to blows in a life and death struggle for supremacy, Nodier facilitated and in a measure secured in advance the triumph of the new school.

As a budding bibliophile rooting among the books in Abbé Pellier's collection, which he classified and annotated in 1798, or among the holdings of the Ecole Centrale Library in Besançon, where he was engaged as assistant librarian later in the same year, Charles could not fail to develop a deep love of old books and ancient authors. We have seen him reading

Montaigne at eight; at twelve he already had a bibliographical note to his credit on a copy of the works of Amadis Jamyn. In 1800 he was writing in the autobiographical *Moi-Même:* "Have you read Montaigne, Charron, Rabelais, and *Tristram Shandy?* If you haven't, read them; if you have, read them again!"

In 1804 Nodier published the *Essais d'un jeune barde,* whose title alone acknowledges the author's debt to the pseudo-Ossian and whose second selection, "Chant funèbre au tombeau d'un chef scandinave," is replete with the breath of the ancient skalds. Two years later Nodier issued another anthology, *Les Tristes.* The seventh entry in this collection is an essay entitled "De la romance," a form which Charles traces from the Bible to the *trouvères,* and which he defines as "le monument de tous les souvenirs romantiques." (p. 108) He then gives a romance of his own composition, "La Blonde Isaure," imitated from those famous medieval poets. In the 1808 lecture course the young professor exhibited enthusiasm for Cervantes, Dante, and Tasso; but more important for our present concern were his remarks about "La farce de Maître Pathelin" (Folios 84-85):

> Fortunately, comedy has been cultivated among us by authors of more solid taste [than those of the *drame*] and of more agreeable imagination. The old farce of Pathelin that Brueys has thought fit to revive in our day and which offers in effect really comic characteristics, is the most ancient monument of French gaiety. After that work our comedies lost for many years their national character, as we borrowed from the Spanish and the Italians bizarre imbroglios and ridiculous characters.

If Cyrano is mistreated on this same page as one of those who borrowed as proscribed here, Nodier was later to be the first critic to rehabilitate Cyrano as playwright and author of the fantastic *Etats de la lune et du soleil* in a beautiful essay published in the *Revue de Paris,* August, 1831.

Nodier's dictionaries and linguistic studies of the next five years, encouraged in part by his association with Sir Herbert Croft, brought him a richer knowledge of Old French. His proximity to the cathedral of Amiens during his stay in that city made that magnificent example of Gothic architecture the inspiration of his drive to preserve ancient monuments from destruction by vandals. Later, in the first volume of his and Taylor's *Voyages pittoresques et romantiques dans l'ancienne France*, 1820, devoted to Picardy, he was to give a superb description of the Amiens cathedral.

But it was the experience in Illyria in 1813 that taught Charles the value of preserving old monuments and old texts. The plan of the articles for the *Télégraphe Officiel* was to encourage a systematic presentation of the history, economics, geography, laws, customs, literature, art, and archeology of the region. Nodier opened the columns of the *Official Telegraph* to all who might assist in this endeavor to erect a national monument, and urged the Slovenes and Serbo-Croats to set down in anthologies the old songs and traditional ballads before this rich heritage was completely lost. "From all these confused and disparate elements," Nodier concluded his first article, "Statistique illyrienne," January 17, "there will result in the long run a useful and durable monument at no other cost than that of gathering and classifying the material." In the course of pioneering this national drive on the part of the southern Slavs, Charles discovered a few gems that were to serve him later in a similar campaign in France. "It is strange," he says in his second article, "De la manière d'étudier l'histoire d'Illyrie," January 28, "that the most curious part of histories, I mean that which concerns the origins and first institutions of peoples, has undergone in all countries the least contradiction and has been subjected least to the light of solid criticism."

In thus helping to bring to fruition a Yugoslav national consciousness fully one hundred years before it was realized as a geographical fact, Nodier learned that a similar task awaited an enterprising and patriotic Frenchman. So, upon his return to France, he began an active campaign in favor of mediaeval literature, architecture, and history. The titles alone of the plays, books, and lectures he was asked to review in the next few years for the *Journal des Débats* are significant in this respect: 1813, *Cours d'Aimé Martin,*

Séance de l'Athenée (on medieval literature) November 29, and December 13; 1814, *Cours d'Aimé Martin,* January 8, February 15, April 19, and June 1, *La Rançon de Du Guesclin,* March 20, *Ossian ou les bardes,* June 19; 1815, *Essai sur la poésie et les poètes français au XIIe, XIIIe,* et *XIVe siècles,* July 10; 1816, *Jeanne de France,* February 12, *Essai sur la poésie, etc.,* second article, July 23, *Vie privée des français,* November 23; 1817, *Choix des poésies des troubadours,* June 9, *Jeanne d'Arc,* October 8, and 10, *La Gaule poétique,* November 27, *Les Celtes antérieurement aux temps historiques,* December 4.

In the two articles devoted to the *Essai sur la poésie et les poètes français du XIIe, XIIIe, et XIVe siècles* by Benoiston de Chateauneuf, Nodier gives a quick review of the scholarship to date, including a linguistic study of the *langue romane,* on the Middle Ages. He then ridicules the idea that poetry came to France through the Arabs, follows its development in France from the ninth to the fourteenth century, citing examples of religious verse, the *musars* and the *cantadours* of the troubadours, the poems of William IX, duke of Aquitania, of the courts of Foix and Poitiers and the princes of Auvergne and Orange. He then touches upon the *canzon* and *sirvente* of the south, the songs of the northern *trouvères,* the didactic verse, the *Bestiaires,* the *Lapidaires,* the *matière de Bretagne,* the *fabliaux,* the *tensons,* the *lais,* fables, satires, pastorals, the miracle and morality plays, *Amadis, Renard,* and the *Roman de la Rose.* In short, aside from a few omissions, and one blind spot with respect to the value of the *Roman de la Rose,* this review presents essentially the literature of the French Middle Ages as we know it today.

Nodier lauds Raynouard's *Choix des poésies originales des troubadours* as a successful monograph on literary archeology in which the history, dictionary, grammar, and authors of the *langue romane* are observed from the sixth century in an attempt to fix the roots of the *gaie science* and the *langue d'oc,* and eventually of modern French language and literature. A compendium of this nature was eminently suited to Nodier's campaign in favor of the national past for it filled a significant gap and helped dispel the fog of ignorance which hung over the whole subject of the Middle Ages. Similarly, Nodier applauds the recurrent theme of Marchangy's *La Gaule poétique, ou l'histoire de France considérée dans ses rapports avec la poésie, l'éloquence et les beaux-arts*, that the French possessed in their own past history ample subjects of fable, mythology, manners, poetry, and tragedy that made it needless to recur to the threadbare stories of Troy, Argos, Thebes, and Mycenae. So the romantic school, he says, should be grateful to Marchangy for opening up this rich source of literary exploitation and for providing the historical background as well.

In the review of Arnault's play, *La Rançon de Du Guesclin*, Charles deplored the fact that the author had not taken advantage of the extant knowledge of the period in question to give his play a backdrop that was historically accurate, thus missing the opportunity of rendering the dramatic action more vivid. The classicists, he continues in his essay on *La Gaule poétique*, cannot take advantage of this local color because they are interested mainly in universals. And here Charles gives utterance for the first time to his admiration for Gothic architecture:

> It is the same with those ancient monuments which the love of art has salvaged from the fury of revolutionary vandals; we like to see in certain lines, contours, and arrangements of parts something of that inspired grace which lends so much charm to the masterpieces of Greece. But we would enjoy their view less, we would feel less vividly the sense of religious admiration they inspire if we did not find there something rough, incorrect, coarse, which reveals their mysterious antiquity and the imprint of a naive generation which was half savage, which had not yet put off its primitive austerity.

So Nodier was ready to join the great work of preserving through illustrating by sketch and legend the noble ruins of medieval architecture which he undertook with Baron Taylor and Alphonse de Cailleux in the mammoth albums of the *Voyages pittoresques et romantiques dans l'ancienne France* (1820). In the *Introduction* to the second volume of that work, Charles tied together the love of the monuments of the Middle Ages as symbols of christianity on the one hand and the reverence and pride of the national heritage on the other.

> Being the first investigators of the ruins of our country at a time when those ruins were crumbling, never to rise again, we had the good fortune to remind our century that the centuries past had their arts and their genius. We say this without undue pride because the thought was so natural and so generally shared that it only asked to be born, if I may be permitted the expression; but we say it with assurance because no one can dispute our luck in being the first to do what everyone else was thinking of doing. . . . The monuments upon which we impose with such scorn the name of gothic and which we relegate to the construction of barbarians were neither so savage nor so barbarous. . . . They are better than the Greek monuments in religious solemnity and in mysterious harmonies to the same degree that the noble beliefs of christianity surpass the poetic theology of paganism.

That Nodier's ideas on this subject were widely known before the appearance of the *Introduction* from which we have just quoted is attested in the Paris press, whose editors greeted enthusiastically the addition of Charles' services to the *Voyages pittoresques* staff.[4] Three years later Victor Hugo used a quotation from Nodier's prose for that work as an epigraph to his ode, dedicated to Nodier in the first three editions of the *Odes et ballades, La bande noire,* the great poet's contribution to the war against the vandals, the wanton destroyers of medieval grandeur.

Professor Jean Larat has stated that Nodier attempted to substitute national antiquity for classical antiquity and that he made the revival of the Middle Ages in France almost a definition of romanticism.[5] The same could be said of his cult of Shakespeare and of his espousal of foreign writers, for these were the three essential ingredients that Nodier had selected and prepared for the romantic palette. No doubt other writers in France were sympathetic to romanticism and made remarkable contribution to it (Chateaubriand in the gloomy introspection of his morbid prose, brooding over his gothic youth in a medieval castle with a mad, spectral father, a cowed mother, and a frightened sister, his *Essai sur la littérature anglaise,* his *Génie du christianisme,* and *Les Martyrs*) or entertained similar ideas. Madame de Stael, for instance, could state in a resounding paragraph from *De l'Allemagne*:

> The new school maintains the same system in the fine arts, as in literature, and affirms that Christianity is the source of all modern genius; the writers of this school also characterize, in a new manner, all that in gothic architecture agrees with the religious sentiments of Christians. It does not follow, however, that the moderns can and ought to construct gothic churches; neither art nor nature admits of repetition: it is only of consequence to us, in the present silence of genius, to lay aside the contempt which has been thrown on all the conceptions of the Middle Ages; it certainly does not suit us to adopt them, but nothing is more injurious to the development of genius than to consider as barbarous everything that is original.[6]

No other writer in France so consistently represented the cause of romanticism in all its aspects between 1814 and 1820; no one was so vociferous in behalf of the new school where it counted most, i.e., in the great Paris daily newspapers, where his program was in distinct opposition to that of the editors. This must remain Nodier's finest hour, when he stood alone on the threshold of the future and pointed the way to the new writers. He was not a major poet, yet he did not hesitate to admit the evidence of his critical senses, which told him that the new literature would operate most successfully in a branch of the art in which he did not excel and in which he could not even compete. This admission, though it was a fine tribute to Nodier's disinterestedness as a critic, was perhaps the source of the torment he refers to in the quotation used as the epigraph to this chapter.

IV

Literary Experiments

"Sir," insisted Dumas, "if the play is so bad, how does it happen that you have seen it so often? Do you know the author?"

"Intimately," rejoined Nodier. "It is I."

NAPOLEON GONE, Nodier came out openly as the champion of legitimacy. His letters of nobility and literary pension gave him the feeling of solidarity with the restored monarchy he needed to conduct his campaign against the Revolution and Empire in the pages of the *Journal des Débats*. Regarding the value of conservatism in government, his experience of twenty years with republican and tyrannical improvisations had matured him. And, as he wrote to Kératry many years later, he felt that he was carrying out his father's dying wishes in fighting the Revolution with every weapon at his disposal. His father, he said, had told him, "Go, redeem the mistakes of a misled soul. . . . Do against the Revolution as much as I have done for it. . . . Never lend it your voice, or your pen, or your sword. I die in this hope, for the Revolution comes from Hell."[1]

Old Nodier had been understandably embittered by his summary dismissal from the bench. While his son waited almost eight years to fulfill his father's dying wish, at any rate father and son were one again, and Charles could lay about him with a will. Beginning with January 1, 1816, no less than four articles were dedicated to his new mission of flaying the "hated enemies" of France and Europe: "La Convention," January 1, "Le vingt-et-un janvier," January 20, and "La Tyrannie de Buonaparte," two articles, July 30 and August 6.

Nodier's feeling of having finally "arrived" was confirmed by the news that Weiss in Besançon had been asked to do an article on him for the *Biographie universelle ancienne et moderne*. Charles, who had been contributing biographical sketches to that publication, was naturally flattered by the honor of being included in the early nineteenth-century version of *Who's Who* and especially by the selection of Weiss as biographer. Yet he thought it necessary to write to his oldest friend to beg him to be impartial and sparing of praise: "I think you can grant me at best *a remarkable erudition for my age* and nothing more, unless it be a pleasing literary style."[2] Weiss was sufficiently formal in his article on Nodier, having passed the appreciation of his friend through the crucible of many writings.

The spate of good fortune in that year was tempered by domestic tragedy. Désirée, who had not been well since the birth of her son in 1814, had continued in poor health throughout 1815. Visited with a severe illness in the winter, she had to remain in bed until early spring of 1816. As soon as it was considered safe for her to go out, her first thought was of the baptism of her son, delayed because he had been sickly from the start and never completely out of danger. The baptismal ceremony was duly recorded by five-year-old Marie in a note to her grandmother in Besançon. However, little Térence was no sooner christened than he worsened and died. The grieving parents moved to 33 Rue Saint Lazare soon after the burial.

At thirty-seven, Nodier seems to have added some weight to his thin frame, giving him a stocky appearance. In the portrait made of him at that age by C. L. P., we are shown Charles in profile, with closely cropped hair, sideburns, clean-shaven chin and upper lip. His jaw presents a determined, businesslike cast, but the ethereal luminosity has not left his eye. Despite these pictured indications of well-being, he complained of being plagued by continual fever and insomnia, to which the new task of reader of opera librettos for *l'Académie Royale de Musique* offered no relief. Nodier, always a fetichist where his health was concerned, was surrounding himself with medical attendants: the doctors Emonot and Marc were consulted as frequently as the mulatto quack, Fournier-Pescaye, who on one occasion had Nodier drink two ounces of turpentine for tapeworm. If this is true, we can no longer marvel with Weiss that Charles survived giant doses of opium in his youth. He tinkered with his body as if in a laboratory, absorbing untold quantities of the most outlandish nostrums he thought were good for him. He even gave out that he knew as much medicine as any doctor, and their visits to his house usually ended in heated debates on nosology and therapeutics.

But Dr. Baudin has shown that the author missed the chance to show off his medical learning in his novels, where the handling of symptoms and progress of the many diseases his heroines suffer from—tuberculosis, smallpox, meningitis, and neurasthenia—is utterly fantastic.[3] However, his attributions, in the descriptive work *La Seine et ses bords* (1836) of the high incidence of typhoid fever to contaminated water in the Troyes area is hailed as a brilliant guess, fully fifty years before research proved such to be the case. On the credit side too must be mentioned Nodier's reporting that the malaria prevalent along the Dalmatian coast was spread by a fly or a mosquito. This was the extent of his contribution to medical science; in all other respects his convictions in this field led to highly nebulous if not actually harmful results.

In the spring of 1817, a note Charles had co-signed for a Franche-Comté count he had met briefly in Illyria fell due. Unable to pay the 5,000 francs on demand, Nodier solicited loans from the royalist banker, Lapanouze, without success. In despair, Nodier retreated to Saint-Germain-en-Laye, where he met the banker of the liberal party, Laffitte, who, more generous than Charles' political friends, assumed the ruinous debt and granted Nodier a long-term loan.

Early in 1818, Charles, still needing money, seized the opportunity to leave France and repair his finances by accepting the post of professor of political economy at the newly established Lycée Richelieu in Odessa. Charles was to receive 3,000 rubles per annum as professor; in addition, he was to manage a printing press at a salary of 3,000 francs and edit a *Journal Littéraire, Politique et Commercial* of which he was to receive half the proceeds. He sold his furniture, entrusted his library to his new friend Pixerécourt, a bibliophile and author of numerous *mélodrames*, charged Aimé Martin to look after his entomological collections, and transported his family to Quintigny to await the letter of appointment. He waited from March to October, idled the spring and summer away in the Café Rodet at Lons flirting with the *dame du comptoir,* but the letter never came. Inquiring from counsel when he returned to Paris whether he should sue for damages, Nodier learned that the Abbé Nicolle, director of the Lycée and representative of the Duc de Richelieu in Odessa, had done little toward founding the school and nothing in setting up the press and the newspaper. So Nodier was at the expense of the removal from Paris, breaking up one and establishing another household, and sojourning more than six months in Quintigny without pay. At least the warm welcome he had been accorded in Lons and Besançon—Weiss characterized his visit as a "series of fêtes"—showed him his past sins had been forgiven; he was finally a prophet in his own city. In April the Société d'Emulation du Jura accepted him as a member.

Doubtless because it was more romantic, Nodier would have us believe that the reason the Odessa appointment fell through was to be found in the appearance of *Jean Sbogar,* which he was careful to publish anonymously before he left Paris in the spring of 1818. In the fascinating introduction he wrote for the third edition of this novel in 1832, Nodier said, "I was about to enter upon a very serious career . . . and this consideration prevented me from attaching my name to the title page. The politics of Jean Sbogar would have been a poor recommendation indeed for a man who was going to profess political economy in Lesser Tartary (Bessarabia); no one will be surprised, then, that the author, recognized in spite of his precautions, was placed on the Czar's *Index* along with his book."

How can we fail to notice in these words a momentary flare-up of the old conspirator in Charles? The hunted and persecuted enemy of Napoleon favored this typical pose of one victimized in high places and, born under an unlucky star, kept from attaining the eminence he deserved in art and life. Nodier's inability to reconcile his dream of himself as a dominant social and artistic figure with his very real talent formed the basis of his deep-rooted unhappiness. His need to shine at any cost overshadowed his real but latent power to contribute something worthwhile. It made him restless and capricious, and deprived him of the perseverance to see a work of the first magnitude through from conception to realization.

If the career was as serious and important to him as he would have us believe, then why jeopardize it from the very outset with a literary publication which ostensibly would have had no beneficial influence on a diplomatic career? Moreover, in order to escape the charge of imitation, Nodier swears he had written the book in 1812 in Illyria, but chose the very moment when it would do him the least good to publish the novel; apparently, between the two charges of immorality and insanity Nodier preferred the latter; such was his vanity. Unfortunately, the facts do not bear out Nodier's ingenious view of the villainous role *Jean Sbogar* played in cutting short a brilliant diplomatic career hardly begun. They do point to him as a master of the preface, a literary form he regarded as the web into which he lured the reader, coaxing him with artful autobiographical tidbits before spinning him, baffled, into the maze of fiction.

In this 30-page preface, even more fantastic than the ensuing novel, Nodier has a chance to feel sorry for himself, to justify himself, to display his knowledge of world literature, to beckon the reader closer by mentioning the magic name of Napoleon. The Eagle was reported to have spent a night reading and a day annotating *Jean Sbogar* at Saint Helena, or so it was rumored by the publisher Gide, who claimed he read this "fact" in the *journaux anglais* in 1819. When the newspaper *La Renommée* reproduced Gide's remarks on October 17, 1827, it was the first time the "fact" had appeared in print anywhere, though not the last, as another publisher, Delangle, reproduced it again in a footnote to the 1827 edition of Nodier's *Poésies*, adding to the stature of the anecdote by gesturing grandly in the direction of the *Mémoires de Sainte Hélène*, where there is no mention of it. This was all Nodier's doing!

We cannot accept the date 1812 as the period of composition of the novel *Jean Sbogar*, since Nodier, as we have seen, did not arrive in Illyria until January, 1813. Moreover, Charles could not have been present at the trial of the romantic outlaw, since all the bandits that had been plaguing the Austrian administration, including Jean Sbogar, had been captured and executed before the end of the eighteenth century. Naturally, Nodier used his novelist's prerogative of assuming personal contact to lend vividness and credibility to the relation; but the conception of *Jean Sbogar* did not occur to him until he had read Heinrich Zschokke's *Aballino*, which had been fairly popular in France in the translation by La Martelière since 1801. It is hard to believe that Nodier, who was so taken with German literature that he pounced on every translation from that language as the breath of life, did not know Zschokke's play. He would have us believe that he knew of a copy of the translation on fine paper in Renouard's library and that he, the great bibliophile and lover of fine editions, was content to accept Pixerécourt's judgment of *Aballino* as being a worthless play, out of which Pixerécourt had fashioned a *mélodrame* "worth a hundred *Aballinos* and *Jean Sbogars.*" Only then did he read the translation to set his mind at rest, but he saw no connection between the two works.

Despite Nodier's protestations to the contrary, there are more than just superficial similarities between his novel and the German play. Both heroes are of the "noble bandit" type and both Aballino and Sbogar have dual personalities. There the similarity ends, however, as Nodier goes on to exploit his favorite themes; the tenuous love affair between Sbogar and Antonia, who wishes to become a nun because Sbogar will not marry her (since he is loath to soil her good name with his bandit's reputation); the reported suicide of the hero following the heroine's decision to enter a nunnery and the promise of a mystic union after life. Why did Nodier, who was so jealous of the originality of his conception, publish the novel anonymously? Because Sbogar represented the dead conspirator in Nodier, the "noble bandit," the righter of social injustices, the anarchist. He is the ideal outlaw who will usher in a new age by bringing order out of chaos; Nodier is saying that it is always the brigand who saves revolutions and resolves turning points in history.[4]

This anarchist, this Messiah of the downtrodden, this champion of political and social equality was the embodiment of Charles' turbulent revolutionary youth. The identity between the author's past and his literary brainchild was too marked to permit any open acknowledgment of paternity; thence the anonymous publication and the disavowal of the larger implications of Sbogar's political credo as expressed in his *Tablettes* or notebooks. Nodier was rapidly getting beyond the age of running and hiding from the police because of radical doctrines of liberty. He had successfully repressed his desire to be an active revolutionist, but the rebel had gone underground only to appear again in the sublimated transformation of the novel. As a realist, he could support the restored monarchy; as an artist he could hate and yet be fascinated by the romantic potential of the Revolution.

Jean Sbogar was the most successful of the novels in Nodier's early manner, of which it was also the last example. Women especially were captivated by the noble outlaw, and a second, de luxe edition, was brought out in 1820. In the same year, an English translation of the novel was published by Percival Gordon in London. Pushkin, who never left Russian soil, mentioned *Jean Sbogar* among the popular novels of the time, and in *Mistress into Maid* he used Sbogar as the name of a hunting dog. Many years later, when it became clear to Nodier that he would not write a great novel, he fondly hoped that *Jean Sbogar* would be granted that accolade, so he placed it first in the edition of his *Works* which the publisher Renduel began printing in 1832. *Jean Sbogar* was his favorite creation, but in this menu, versatile chef that he was, Nodier made the *hors d'oeuvre* more appetizing than the *pièce de résistance* and we shall have to look elsewhere for his claim to greatness.

Firmly entrenched under the banner of monarchy, Charles gathered the necessary courage to summon the king to remember his promise to amnesty the political exiles of 1815. *Des exilés*, an anonymously published brochure, was a powerful plea for royal clemency, one of the most farsighted and cool-headed political tracts to appear under the Restoration. It urged oblivion of the past, and union and solidarity for the future. Criticizing the decree of exile, which as usual permitted certain flagrant exceptions in high places and penalized such harmless Napoleonic servants as his friends Arnault, Etienne, Bory de Saint-Victor, and other intellectuals who had taken refuge in Brussels, Nodier was bold enough to ask for the return of Jean De Bry, Fouché, and even Louis Bonaparte. But Louis XVIII did not rise to the magnanimity of Nodier's appeal for tolerance; he had the pamphlet seized and forbade discussion of it in the press.

If Charles' grand gesture went unrewarded, we are nonetheless advised that he had obtained a dispassionate perspective on the restored monarchy which allowed him to see some of its shortcomings. This was the gambit of Nodier's political faith, a period of genuine support followed by gradual disillusionment and apathy. In this manner he had rallied to the side of the Revolution, Napoleon, and the Restoration, only to find that in each the hopes of liberty and equality, the promises of social justice, were turned into intolerance and tyranny. As he so beautifully expressed it in *Jean Sbogar*, "Man has belonged to two entirely different states, but he has succeeded in carrying over into the second some memories of the first; every time a political upheaval causes the pendulum of society to swing towards its natural balance, he rushes to its support with incredible ardor, because such is the nature of his make-up, which always leads him from an irresistible authority to the enjoyment of the most complete liberty he can procure for himself."[5] Because of this foible of man's enthusiasm for maximum freedom, he was doomed to see his espousal of three successive governments turn to ashes of disappointment and despair.

In the fall Nodier courted the monarch with a request to dedicate to him his long-awaited *Commentaires sur les Fables de La Fontaine*. Begun as early as 1808, in Quintigny, these commentaries had already earned for Charles a 2,000 franc publisher's advance, thanks to the offices of Renouard. Having temporarily abandoned the work in 1809 to go to Amiens as Croft's secretary, Charles reported he was spending twelve hours daily on it in 1811. His appeal to have the work endorsed for use in the imperial lycées having remained unanswered, Nodier again interrupted the commentaries in favor of other projects and the Laybach appointment in 1813. A study of the manuscript left behind in Quintigny reveals that Charles must have begun this project afresh on his return to Paris in 1814. Despite the many vicissitudes of its preparation, the superb two-volume edition published by Eymery in 1818 will always be consulted by La Fontaine scholars with profit. The appeal to dedicate the work to the king jogged the royal memory on another forgotten account; on November 12 the minister Lainé informed Nodier that he was to be reimbursed 4,000 francs to defray expenses of the aborted trip to Odessa.

When Nodier returned to Paris October 18, 1818, he took up temporary residence in the Rue de Bouloi, until Désirée found larger quarters in the Rue de Choiseul, number 1. There Charles met Isidore, later Baron Taylor, who together with Alphonse de Cailleux and the painter Isabey had dreamed of launching a gigantic illustrated travel series to be known as *Voyages pittoresques et romantiques dans l'ancienne France.* With only 500 francs capital, the aim of the editors was to draw up a pictorial record of beauty spots, shrines, architectural masterpieces, and monuments which were worth preserving for posterity. A printed text was to provide a commentary for the illustrations Isabey drew on the spot. Entering enthusiastically into Taylor's scheme, Charles wrote the general introduction to the work; then the little band set out for Normandy to collect material for the first volume. Strange as it may seem, the vast undertaking, though expensive, was lucrative, for this was an age of keepsake albums. But Charles soon tired of the endless research and wandering. He wrote a good portion of the text on Normandy and practically all of the material for the volumes on Franche-Comté; he then begged Taylor to carry on without him, though he continued to contribute occasional pieces and to suggest artists and writers to the editor, who half a century later was still issuing the cumbersome folios. Both Baron Taylor and Alphonse de Cailleux, who were to lead illustrious lives, the latter as curator of the national museums and the former as a renowned philanthropist, patron of the arts, founder of the Société des Gens de Lettres and director of the Comédie Française, were to remain among Nodier's dearest friends for the rest of his life.

In January, 1819, another financial crisis forced Charles to sell his library. For a moment he toyed with the plan of going to London to seek a buyer, but the scholar Aimé Martin advanced 1,000 francs—really a discreet loan—thus allowing Charles to keep his books.

In order to dispel the haunting memory of Térence's death, Nodier composed the first of his novels of personal reminiscence, *Thérèse Aubert*. The development of this form of autobiographical fiction was an offshoot of Charles' many disappointments. As he grew older and less capable of withstanding the blows of fortune, he took refuge in a sort of waking dream involving his checkered youth. Out of the simple events we have recorded above, Nodier composed a theme with infinite variations that was to lead to harsh criticism and doubts concerning his credibility and sanity. Only Nodier knew the consolation he sucked from these creations, as he had drawn inspiration and exaltation from the opium-eating of earlier years. This byproduct of reversal was slow to take shape in his mind, and it is interesting to watch the development of the fictionalized elements of his past into accepted factual events: by dint of repeating them, as Weiss suggested, Charles came to believe in his own fabrications as history. As time progressed and the embroidery became more ornate, Charles grew increasingly impatient of contradiction and stubbornly defended the veracity of his inventions. With *Thérèse Aubert* (two editions, 1819) Nodier had not yet reached this stage of his personal mania, the events being ascribed to a certain Adolphe de S. Still, the details recounted in the opening page of the novel, the alleged study of Greek with the terrorist Euloge Schneider, of music with composer Edelmann, will appear again with slight variation—Nodier is sent by his father to study Greek with Schneider in Strasbourg where he meets the abovenamed composer—in the later *Souvenirs de la Révolution*.[6]

Aside from being a new departure in Nodier's conception of the novel, *Thérèse Aubert* is unique in its mournful requiem-like tones. As Nodier stated in the preface, "I have little to say of *Thérèse Aubert*, although it is the only one of

my books that I love. . . . It is the only one that was written
. . . out of moral necessity; the only one on which I shed
some tears and which I cannot reread even today without
weeping." But it was not the sentimental events of the novel
that urged the author to tears; it was the remembrance of the
loss of his son that this novel was to aid in dissipating by
repeated rationalizations of death. "It is better to lose a
loved one through death than to be deceived by him." "Death
is such a little thing." "So many of those who were dear to
me have enriched death that the prospect of losing the remainder no longer frightens me."

To a sorrowing father death can be more appealing than
life, and for once the eternal union of Adolphe and Thérèse
in death, the oft-repeated medieval theme here given Church
blessing by a compassionate priest, is appropriate to the
occasion. In the pages of this novel Nodier found a new tone,
a kind of pre-Stendhalian sensitivity to the burgeoning of
young love, an awareness of the little insights that instinc-
tively betray young lovers to each other without the aid of
the spoken word. Full advantage is taken here of the mutuality of suggestion created by a look, of a light surreptitious
graze in a narrow passage to which the lovers are uncon-
trollably drawn and of the communion of unuttered desires.
The descriptions of dramatis personae are less stereotyped,
less generalized than in Nodier's former efforts: Thérèse and
Adolphe have bodies, faces, and psychological traits that are
personal and precise. The accuracy of the view of the
scenery in the neighborhood of *Le Mans*, another stylistic innovation, Charles remembered from his trip to Normandy
to gather notes for the *Voyages pittoresques*.

Thérèse Aubert marked the transition between the *Werther*-
inspired novels of Nodier's youth and the "autobiographical"
studies, with historical background, of his maturity. We are
now in a position to examine the elements of the old manner
he was about to slough off and evaluate his contribution to
early French romantic literature. Ingredients: Purity of the
heroine, tissue-paper-thin sensitivity of the hero, external and
internal hindrances to consummation of their love, and the

promise of the bliss of eternal union in the hereafter. This was the leaven of German sentimentalism which Nodier gleaned from the writers of Central Europe.

To the examples of creative writing Nodier added a journalistic campaign in favor of romanticism in the pages of the *Journal des Débats*. This was not easy. The *Débats* was staffed with writers of a classic bias who abhorred romantic manifestations in literature, including Nodier's. In the early days of his collaboration with that newspaper, Charles was careful to advertise his adherence to the literary ideals of his colleagues and to decry the invasion of a *sensibilité niaise* in the clearheaded literature of France. He even begged forgiveness for the part he had played in bringing about this deplorable invasion.

"It would be too harsh to judge a writer on the basis of a few novels in bad taste he wrote in his youth. At twenty, one is easily the dupe of a mistaken talent, even though that young writer may bear the seeds of real talent. Moreover, unless he is an extraordinary person, it is almost impossible for a young novelist to avoid being seduced by the prevailing mode and to remain firm in the classic ideal." After the apology, the renunciation: "Since the appearance of this book [*Werther*] we have been swamped with novels without titles, without action, without plan, and without personality, ridiculous monuments to insanity and bad taste, of exaggerated passions and silly sensibilities, of mad acts typical of the Bicêtre and ravings fit for the Grève."[7]

After the death of Geoffroy and a consultation with the liberal editor Bertin, Nodier, emboldened by the security of his position, began to express opinions favorable to the "new school" and to its German models, reprinting the articles on "Slavic Literature" and showering praise on Goethe and Schiller.[8] Then came the three articles on Madame de Stael's *De l'Allemagne* championing the romantic cause and extolling the German poets.

Since its establishment soon after the 18 *Brumaire* by Louis-François Bertin, commonly known as Bertin *l'aîné* to distinguish him from his younger brother and associate, Bertin de Vaux, the *Journal des Débats* had supported a liberal view of politics. Unable to cope with Napoleon, whom it had initially hailed as the saviour of France from the threat of anarchy, the newspaper passed over to the opposition, whereupon the editor was arrested, locked up in the Temple prison, and later exiled to Elba. In the meantime the newspaper had become the official organ of the Empire, *Le Journal de l'Empire*, staffed by Fouché's henchmen. Traveling with a fake passport, Bertin was able to reach Italy and gradually make his way back to France, arriving in Paris in time to claim his property at the fall of the Empire. As in the case of Napoleon, the reclaimed *Débats* at first supported Louis XVIII; but when it became evident that the monarch would insist on a *restauration intégrale* of the absolutism enjoyed by his predecessors on the throne of France, the *Débats*, true to its dedication to the liberal cause, again joined the swelling ranks of the opposition.

At this juncture, June, 1819, Nodier, feeling secure only when he was supporting the government in power, allowed himself to be persuaded to leave the *Débats* and join the ultraroyalist paper, *Le Drapeau Blanc*, founded by a former colleague on the *Débats*, the swashbuckling, loudmouthed bully, Martainville, who had barely escaped the guillotine during the Revolution and seemed determined to invite a violent end through his offensive articles and truculent editorial policy. The *Drapeau Blanc*, with its intransigent motto, *Vive le Roi! . . . Quand même!*, daily assaulted the enemies of absolutism, whether ministers, newspapermen, or politicians. Gone were the quasi-philosophical symposia presided over by Bertin *l'aîné* in his quiet office in the narrow Rue des Prêtres just behind the church of Saint Germain l'Auxerrois. No longer did they gather each afternoon to thrash out editorial policy in an atmosphere of mutual respect and tolerance. Instead, Martainville held court in the noisy Café Valois, where, surrounded by his *ultra* friends, he boomed his invectives in a manner that patently encouraged no rebuttal. Such an attitude was not one to hold Nodier captive.

To make matters worse, Martainville insisted Charles write political articles in line with the newspaper's policy. After one such effort, a short story entitled *Liberté, égalité, fra-*

ternité ou la mort, anent his arrest and interrogation at the
time of the *Napoléone*, Charles refused to pursue this vein
on the grounds that he did not care to offend friends and hurt
the memory of the dead. Relations cooled between Nodier
and the director of the extremist newspaper. Whereas in 1819
from June to November we find sixteen articles by Nodier in
Le Drapeau Blanc, in 1820 only four, and in 1821 only one, appeared there over his name. Finally, in 1822, an abusive
attack against his friend Benjamin Constant drew Charles'
wrath. In a letter to Martainville published in *La Foudre*,
October 26, Nodier remonstrated that his name had been
illegally used in support of the attack on Constant, an act
of unscrupulous journalism he could not condone.

After 1820, Charles preferred to free-lance in the lucrative
field of conservative journalism, contributing articles to the
ultraroyalist *Quotidienne*, *La Gazette de France*, and *La
Foudre*, of which last he was one of the founders and principal contributors. The first issue, May 10, 1821, contained
two articles by him, one over his own name and the other over
a pseudonym, Matanasius. However, *La Foudre* was headed
in the same direction as *Le Drapeau*, and the French government, which had at first subsidized its publication, had
to step in and put an end to its scandalous attacks on the
leading liberals, November 30, 1823.

Charles published an article in Chateaubriand's ultradissi-
dent *Le Conservateur* which gave rise to a good deal of
comment then and still makes the reader wonder today.
Chateaubriand had been under fire from the liberal party
for some time when Charles came to his defense in an
article published in *Le Drapeau Blanc*. For this gesture Nodier
received a note from the statesman and author expressing
his gratitude and inviting him to come to see him often.
The diplomat promised to help Nodier in his search for
a librarian's post if he came to power, and opened the
columns of *Le Conservateur* to his writing. Charles submitted
an article entitled *Méditation*—the alert reader will immediately see in this title an allusion to Charles' earlier acquaintance with the *méditateurs*, where Chateaubriand's
"glory was eclipsed by Maurice Quai"—which was an obvious

imitation of Chateaubriand's florid literary style. Everyone thought Nodier was mocking the great man—the Bibliophile Jacob termed it "a remarkable reverie à la Swedenborg"[9]—and Count O'Mahony, in a review of the first volume of the *Voyages pittoresques*, quietly censured the piece. Even those in Chateaubriand's immediate entourage were sure Nodier was spoofing, but the editor of *Le Conservateur* paid handsomely for the article and their relations ended there.

Did Charles wish to recall his satire of twenty years earlier against the literary giant in the anonymous *Le Parnasse du jour*, was this a real conversion or merely a literary tour de force? At any rate, Charles continued to furnish material for the successor to *Le Conservateur*, *Le Défenseur*, a religious paper stressing rapport between altar and throne—notably *l'Apocalypse du solitaire*, January, 1821, one of the first manifestations, long before Lamennais, of the revival of apocalyptic literature in France. But by this time Chateaubriand had nothing to do with the newspaper, having surrendered the editorship with the demise of *Le Conservateur*. For his unstinted support of the monarchy in the Paris press Charles was awarded the Cross of the Legion of Honor, August 25, 1821. So Nodier stood, Janus-like, looking backward in politics and forward in literature.

The second in the series of pseudoautobiographical novels, *Adèle* (1820) is presented in the form of an exchange of letters between Nodier's alter ego, Gaston de Germancé, and a friend, Edouard de Millanges. Against the backdrop of the magnificent scenery of the Juras, where Charles had spent a good portion of his exile, we are faced with another story of unrequited love, far below the caliber of *Thérèse Aubert*. Yet the short novel is important for the definition, in the *Introduction*, of the *vague* in literature, a centripetal word of French romanticism which recurs often in *Adèle*.

Our curiosity has become blasé to the extent that we seek something outside the sphere of positive ideas; we are naturally interested less in facts than in passions, less in the material circumstances of a story than in the indefinite sentiment it gives rise to, less in the true or false adventures

of a hero than in certain *idealities*, which, though having no
precise character, correspond more or less to the needs, the
affections and the illusions of the majority in these unhappy
times of social change. This *vague* in literature results from
a general vagueness in morality, of which literature is the
written expression.

The significance of the impact of society on literature enun-
ciated here and attributed by Nodier to de Bonald was to
enjoy quite a vogue throughout the nineteenth century.

The other significant revelation contained in this novelette
provides the key to the mystic-union-after-death theme, an
idea Charles may have remembered from his *méditateur* days
while under the influence of Gleizes.[10] "The love of a woman,
of a mortal!" Gaston exclaims in the letter of April 21. "What
do you understand by that? A smile . . . a tone of voice . . .
the touch of a hand. . . . But this hand and this heart will
become dust which will not mingle with my dust." For dust
which has been scattered belongs to no man. "That kind of
love is only the figment of vanity. Real love is not a thing
of this earth, but the first conquest of resuscitating man."
Hence the reaching out for eternal union, which could be
achieved, according to Nodier's thesis, only beyond the grave.
That theme, which was to haunt opera composers from Bellini
to Verdi, had received its first expression in *Jean Sbogar*. At
the end of chapter XVI, when the bandit has escaped the
police by plunging into the ocean, his sweetheart Antonia tells
them, "Paix, il est allé le premier au lit nuptial." Similarly, at
the end of Verdi's *La Forza del Destino*, the moribund Leo-
nora sings:

> Lieta poss'io precederti,
> Alla promessa terra

Nodier's thoughts were again turning to his first love, the
theater.

An unsuccessful attempt to mount a dramatized version
of *Jean Sbogar* by Cuvelier and Léopold (Chandezon) at the
Gaieté on October 24, 1818, may have alerted Nodier's interests to the potentialities—not the least of which would be

the financial aspect—of the drama. In any event, after an absence of nearly twenty years, Nodier returned to the theater, collaborating with Carmouche and Jouffroy d'Albans in the presentation of the blood-and-terror melodrama, *Le Vampire.* Long an admirer of "Monk" Lewis and Anne Radcliff, Charles had already introduced the fantastic in his occult short story, *Une Heure ou la vision,* fourteen years earlier. In emulation of his boon companion, the successful melodramatist Guilbert de Pixerécourt, Nodier had been seeking a proper vehicle with which to invade the popular theater. He found it in the obscure novelette, culled from the English of Dr. Polidori, *Lord Ruthwen, ou les vampires,* by "Cyprien Bérard."

The story went that Lord Byron began the *Vampire* in 1816 in Geneva. His doctor, G. G. Polidori, took it up when Byron abandoned it and published the work under the title of *The Vampire* in *The New Monthly Magazine* over Byron's name (1819). Nodier, who had already discovered the vampire legends in Illyria and discussed their influence in an article for *Le Télégraphe Officiel,* April 11, 1813, No. 29, was supposed to have urged "Bérard" to approach the publisher Ladvocat with a French adaptation based on the translation of the Polidori work by H. Faber, and tell him that Charles would be glad to write an introduction to it. But Ladvocat was not convinced that the novel would sell, so he reduced to fine print the name of the unknown Bérard on the title-page and used bold-face type for the equivocal attribution, "published by the author of *Jean Sbogar* and *Thérèse Aubert.*" For this flagrant infringement of the publisher's code Ladvocat received a terse letter of disapproval from Nodier, for no writer of the time was more sensitive to literary fraud than the author of the *Questions sur la littérature légale.* Yet on the backflap of Volume I of the second edition, 1820, an advertisement of *Romans nouveaux* lists *Lord Ruthwen ou les vampires, by Mr. Charles Nodier, author of Jean Sbogar and Thérèse Aubert.* Since this edition is further embellished with Charles' *Note sur le vampirisme* (II, 194-208), we must conclude that he was at least a silent party to the publisher's artifice and had very likely written the novel in the first place.

Cyprien Bérard, Nodier's friend and director of the Vaudeville Theater, has only one other publication to his credit, a
routine report on theater management.

On July 1, 1819, Nodier reviewed unfavorably Faber's
60-page translation of Byron's (Polidori's) *Le Vampire* for
the *Journal des Débats*. In it, after two paragraphs of praise
for the author, who he thought was Lord Byron, he had this
to say of the translation: "I admit the reader must make quite
an effort to judge the merit of this work through the veil of
lead with which the translator has covered it. The reader will
not be able to enjoy its worth unless an author worthy of
the pen of Lord Byron—and I am told that such an author is
at present busy with this work of translation—repairs the
unflattering homage that the French press has just paid him."
He then suggests that the translator should be a Frenchman
and concludes, "[The translator] then will offer all these
trappings of melodrama to one of the boulevard theaters; and
what success will be in store for him!" Did not Nodier fulfill
all of these requirements?

The play, the earliest expression of the Dracula theme in
France, was a success. From the première on June 13, 1820,
Charles was a regular spectator at the Théatre de la Porte
Saint-Martin. Everyone has read the spirited passage in the
Mémoires of the elder Dumas in which the fabulous author of
The Three Musketeers has wittily recorded his first meeting
with Nodier at a performance of *Le Vampire*. Dumas found he
was seated next to a bookish gentleman avidly reading the
Elzevir *Patissier français*. Dumas, no enemy of eating, thought
he was in for an evening of succulent recipes; instead he was
treated to a disquisition on Elzevirs before curtain time.
Throughout the first act, he was amused by his neighbor's
mumbling against the bad French and the poorly written
dialogue, especially since he seemed more interested in his
Patissier than in the performance. Between the acts Dumas
received another lecture on the intervention of supernatural
beings in the works of Shakespeare, Molière, and Goethe. The
second-act curtain interrupted a flight into the future in
which Nodier—the great enemy of progress!—outlined à
la Jules Verne all that man would achieve when he had

mastered all of nature's secrets. More grumbling punctuated the unfolding of the second act. At intermission Nodier resumed with a fantastic account of his stay in Illyria where he had actually seen a vampire, and followed this up with learned references to the vampire story in Dom Calmet, *Traité des apparitions*, II, p. 41 *et suivantes*, as well as other verified and witnessed accounts. After a development of the history of the claque from Nero's time to the present, Nodier got up to take his leave. "Aren't you staying for the third act?" inquired the overwhelmed Dumas. "No," replied Nodier wearily, "I have seen the third act numberless times and I think it is terrible; you stay and see it." "But, sir," insisted Dumas, "if the play is so bad, how does it happen that you have seen it so often? Do you know the author?" "Intimately," rejoined Nodier, "it is I." The play is not really bad; it is rather well written, as *mélodrames* go, and succeeds in holding the attention. Of all the treatments in novels, plays, and cinema of the vampire or Dracula theme *Le Vampire* is certainly not the worst. Pingaud suggests that in *Le Vampire* and in the play he translated a year later in collaboration with Taylor, *Bertram ou le château de Saint-Aldobrand*, Charles was emulating the successors to Diderot's bourgeois drama (Mercier for dramatic theory and Pixerécourt for technique), and adds that for this reason Nodier could enjoy the plays of the elder Dumas, but was never blind to the shortcomings of Hugo's drama respecting style and credibility of character and plot.[11]

However that may be, we are more concerned here with Nodier's borrowing from foreign models to invigorate the theater, the actual locus of the French romantic revolution ten years later. Nodier and Taylor's adaptation of C. R. Maturin's *Bertram* was as great a success as the original had been in England; it had two hundred performances and had the additional merit of bringing the French romantic poets into contact with the macabre author of *Melmoth*, the English Faust, whose influence was to be felt on French literature for more than half of the nineteenth century.[12] In assimilating this English author previously unknown in France, Nodier indicated at the psychological moment the precise course the new romantic drama was to follow. The ill-fated 1822 performances of Shakespeare in English by the Penley troupe, at the same theater which had held *Le Vampire*, indicate that the new director of the Théâtre de la Porte Saint-Martin, his friend J. T. Merle, may have been under Nodier's influence. The 1827 performance of Shakespeare by the Kemble troupe simply provided impetus to a movement already set on foot by Nodier. It is especially important to stress this point of *rapprochement* between Maturin and Shakespeare, for, as we have seen, Nodier thought that Shakespeare's tragedies were essentially *mélodrames*.

Besides Alexandre Dumas, Nodier was meeting other young writers who were to form the vanguard of the romantic corps. At the February 28, 1821, session of the *Société Royale des Bonnes Lettres*, founded by Fontanes and Chateaubriand to encourage sound literary productions by royalist authors, he met the brothers Hugo, in whose honor this meeting had been called. Charles was very much taken with Victor, who was also born in Besançon, though his family did not come from there. (In Franche-Comté the inhabitants make a nice distinction between natives who originate in the area, the Bisontins, and those who are merely born there in transit, the Besançonnais.) In any case, the identity of birthplace was an added attraction between the forty-year-old journalist and the budding poet of nineteen, and Victor soon joined the group of young writers with monarchical sympathies that began to collect periodically in Nodier's house in the Rue de Choiseul. Over these gatherings Charles presided like a father and an enlightened leader, and thus established the first *foyer* of romanticism in France.

For them Charles drew up the thesis of romanticism as a continuation of classicism through evolution. In the words of Pingaud, this evolution was to be effected through *le féerique* and *le fantastique*, and not through the extreme *le frénétique*. In short, this transformation of classic into romantic ideal was to take place gradually, without revolutionary impetus.[13] By holding the hostility of the entrenched classicists to a minimum, Charles hoped to bridge the gap between them and the "new school" with the least possible friction. *Mauvaises langues* such as Madame Ancelot were to say later that Charles got along with both camps, counting friends among the classicists, the romanticists, the liberals, and the royalists, because he "didn't give a fig" for any of them; having lost all convictions of his own, "he only asked to live happily with as much money as possible in the middle of all that turmoil."[14]

But Nodier's roots reached back into the eighteenth century by date of birth and education, and his studies would never permit him to deny his debt to the past. He also demonstrated extreme sensitivity to new currents in literature abroad—he was the first influential critic writing for an important newspaper to analyze a novel by Sir Walter Scott, *The Puritans*, in *Débats*, November 28, 1817—and took up the cudgels in favor of the "new school" in the conservative *Débats*, a campaign he was to continue in the widely read *Quotidienne*. The view of romanticism Nodier exhibited to his young circle was an honest credo of conservatism in politics and liberalism in art which he had worked out for himself in the difficult years of his apprenticeship as a writer.

According to this thesis, Nodier held that the Revolution of 1789 had irrevocably shattered the bonds of political and artistic slavery. As a result, a new society had come into being which demanded a limited monarchy and a fresh literary orientation based on Christian ideals. Having liberated itself from the divine right of kings, was it so surprising, he asked, that this generation should desire to be free of cumbersome classic rules devised under the authoritarian régime of Louis XIV? Fixed tenets in literature were a logical appendage of fixed laws in government: now that the French had thrown off those laws it would be ridiculous to cling to those tenets, an anachronism which he could lay at the door of the liberals in politics who were the most adamant defenders of the literary ideals of the *ancien régime*. To the royalist classicists who favored the status quo of France before 1789, Nodier could only shrug his shoulders and point to the clock. To the liberal classicists who claimed that, after all, the Revolution was French and the sources of the new literary school of romanticism were not, Nodier could answer that the kernel of classicism, the drama, was based on unities drawn from Aristotle,[15] and that the French classical dramatists had drawn their plots from Greek and Roman antiquity. Indeed, how could it have been otherwise, he argued, since the educational system of the *ancien régime* was based on Greek and Roman models—another anachronism, since it meant having a republican or democratic educational system within the framework of a monarchy—in other words, French seventeenth- and eighteenth-century children were trained as if they were going to be citizens of Athens, Rome, or Sparta.

It may be asked, why did Chateaubriand not spear-head the romanticists' drive toward national recognition? Aside from the fact that Chateaubriand was absent from France on his many political missions at this crucial period in French literary history, the answer may be found in the difference in the character of the two men. A reading of the *Mémoires d'outre-tombe* reveals a convinced egomaniac who could be interested only in his own works. In this vast repertory covering 3,000 pages one finds a brief mention of Nodier and Hugo, none of Vigny and Musset; the three scant references to Lamartine are more political than literary in nature and serve to remind that Chateaubriand was probably more concerned with his political activity than with his literary productions. All of the above citations from the *Mémoires*—except the quotation from Nodier—are adduced by Chateaubriand to buttress his political position.

On the other hand, at forty Nodier had reached a stage of maturity which permitted him to be serviceable to his fellow men. The epigraph quoted at the beginning of Chapter III shows that Nodier had lost the idea that he was called upon to do big things. In its place he found a precious virtue, one that was to be of inestimable value to the romantic movement in France: he reached out a helping hand to *all* aspiring young writers; to the Hugos, Vignys, and Mussets must be added hundreds of names which never reached such literary prominence. His published and unpublished correspondence numbers hundreds of letters written in their behalf. His services opened to them the pages of the newspapers and magazines, the doors of the theaters, the pocketbooks of the philanthropists, and publishers' contracts. His worry about their welfare extended beyond literary recognition to the well-being of their families. Knowing from hard experience that even artists must eat, he carried on an unrelenting activity in favor of authors who had been forgotten and abandoned in their old age, like Bonneville, or neglected in their youth, like Millevoye. The most admirable facet of this trait of Nodier's later life was that he continued, even increased, his efforts on behalf of others long after he had achieved the relative security of the Arsenal Library.

One example of this type of activity will suffice. Shortly after the restoration, an obscure novelist in his twenties, Alexandre Pierre Barginet, came to Paris from his native Grenoble. Having been an ardent Bonapartist, this young man had difficulty finding remunerative employment of a literary nature until he met Nodier, who got him odd jobs as a free-lance writer and set him classifying his own articles in the press according to subject matter. The result of this rather needless occupation was a two-volume edition of Nodier's *Mélanges de littérature et de critique, mis en ordre et publiés par Alexandre Barginet de Grenoble*, 1820. Besides classifying the articles, Barginet contributed a three-page *Avertissement* in large print, mostly devoted to his system of grouping the articles. It is clear that this was one of Nodier's many philanthropic gestures on behalf of the starveling author. However, in 1822 there appeared an invective against the Decazes ministry entitled *Histoire véritable de Tchen-Tcheou-Li mandarin lettré, premier ministre et favori de l'empereur Tien-Ki, écrite par lui-même et traduite du chinois par Alexandre Barginet*. For this effort he was awarded fifteen months in prison and three thousand francs fine. Chateaubriand, under appeal of another unhappy author, Saint-Edme, succeeded in keeping Barginet in the Saint-Pélagie prison, where he could presumably still carry on his literary activity, thus nullifying the order to have the unlucky writer transferred to the malodorous central detention house of Poissy.[16] That was in 1823. After his release the following year, Barginet happened to meet Nodier in a café in the Rue Saint-André des Arts. His wretched condition so wrung Charles' heart that he immediately wrote to his influential young friend, Alcide de Beauchesne, chief of section of the beaux-arts department and gentleman of the king's chamber, the following lines intended to stir the young courtier to compassionate action:

My dear Alcide,

You know with what obliging and humane ardor our friend Jules Maréchal pleaded the cause of an old, unfortunate poet, who without his help, would have starved to death; and I know you well enough to fear that you were not a little jealous of that act. Unfortunately, there is no lack of opportunity to console yourself for the theft committed against your ready spirit of charity on that occasion. Here is one: The bearer of my letter, who does not know what it contains, and who sees in you only a protector in expectation, is a young man of much talent and loyalty whom circumstances too long to relate here have reduced to the lowest degree of misery.

Mr. Barginet (for that is his name) has made a false first step in politics. For that he has been persecuted, or at least too severely punished for some thoughtless peccadillo. The bad treatment he has received has not warped his character. He has matured without showing any sign of the bruises he has received, and I know no one who at present judges more equitably both men and events.

This state of mind is not one conducive to the seductive voice of parties, much less of factions. He has therefore no help from the cause for which he suffered, nor will he appeal for any.

Nevertheless he must live. His talent would be used to write in favor of the constitutional monarchy, against the stormy claims which threaten it. He is possessed of a good deal of verve, logic, and facility, but he also has a wife and a child who do not eat very regularly. Some help nobly given, as M. de la Rochefoucauld [Beauchesne's superior, Sosthène de la Rochefoucauld, directeur du département des beaux-arts] knows so well how to do, may preserve for France a writer who can render important services.

I have nothing to add to that, except that I must love you well since I dare ask you so much.

Your devoted,
Charles Nodier[17]

Little enough is known of Barginet's remaining career except that it ended in 1843 when he was only forty-six. Consequently, we do not know whether this letter achieved the desired result; what matters is that Charles Nodier was willing to take time out of a busy life to help an unknown fellow author in distress.

When the weather turned nice in the spring of 1821, Nodier started on his romantic journey to Scotland in company with Taylor, Cailleux, and the painter Isabey, to pay homage to the land of Ossian and the home of Scott. About to board the packet at Fécamp on Wednesday, June 11, Charles stopped to write to Désirée, who had been left behind with their newborn son, Amédée, to tell her that the view of the Channel had discouraged the young painter, who begged to be allowed to remain on terra firma in France. After an extremely rough crossing that took 36 hours, the little party arrived at Brighton, Friday, June 13, where they put up at the *Ship in Distress*. In London they stopped at the Hotel Chedron in Leicester Square just long enough to plot their itinerary in Scotland. Leaving Edinburgh on June 25, the group set out for Glasgow; then on to Ben Lomond, the real destination of the romantic trio, to visit the home of their idol, Sir Walter Scott. The Frenchmen were to be disappointed, as the poet was not at home when they called. Nodier's friend, Amédée Pichot, who was more successful when he visited Scott later, reported that Lady Scott was upset because Nodier had stated in his *Promenade de Dieppe aux montagnes d'Ecosse*, an account of the trip Charles published soon after the return to France, that the Scotch girls went barefoot.[18]

The *Promenade* is a journal, a sort of tourist's guide, of his seven-week trip from Dieppe to the highlands of Scotland. In this short space of time Nodier collected enough impressions, descriptions, and ethnological and entomological lore to fill 334 pages. The book, illustrated by Thompson and Isabey, and containing two plates by the naturalist Bory de Saint-Victor, was severely treated by the *Edinburgh Review*. However, a review of Clifford's English translation of the *Promenade* published in Blackwood's Magazine expressed surprise that a Frenchman could describe Scotland as seen through the eyes of a great poet. In France, the book was imitated by a spurious *Voyage en Ecosse* wherein "jolly wine" is translated *joli vin* and "plum pudding" as *pouding de plomb!* Nodier, at least, was not guilty of that. The travelogue contained a stimulating paragraph on the difference between classic and Gothic architecture, the result of a comparison between Westminster Abbey and Saint Paul's Cathedral in London:

"Saint Paul imposes by its grandeur, but, if I may be allowed the expression, it is a physical and material grandeur, an empty grandeur which has neither quietude nor sadness, neither obscurity nor secrets. Now in the smallest Gothic chapel there is a depth, a *vague*, an infinity of which there is no suggestion in this majestic but uniform vastness, flooded with equal light, and whose perfectly symmetrical exactitude leaves nothing to the imagination, nothing to thought."[19] These romantic terms lead him to muse on the fate of famous Gothic churches in France which are allowed to fall into ruin or be destroyed by *la bande noire;* would it be unpatriotic, he asks, to wish that a magic wand could transport them to England? So Charles learned in England that other countries cherished their heritage and took care of the national monuments; when he returned to France, he redoubled his efforts to preserve the memorials to medieval architecture that were still standing.

Nodier next published an amazing work, *Smarra* (*Nightmare*), which went beyond romanticism or any other *ism* of the nineteenth century. Purportedly a classical *pastiche* or miscellany of extracts from ancient Greek and Roman authors, *Smarra* bears a surface resemblance to Chateaubriand's prose epics with its division into *Prologue, Récit, Episode, Epode,* and *Epilogue.* If we make abstraction of the epigraphs from classical authors and Shakespeare—and the proverbially misleading prefaces—the remainder is a highly original fantasy, a prose poem loaded with classical and personal allusions of a psychoanalytical nature on bad dreams. The Sanskrit word for love is *smara*; it is derived from *smar*, to recollect; the same root has supplied the German *schmerz*, pain, and the English *smart*. The subtitle, *The Demons of the Night*, contains the key to an interpretation of the new page Nodier had turned in the history of literary creation; not until the hallucinations of his admirer and disciple Nerval or the automatic excursions of surrealism was the dream again to play so profound a role in literary expression. Once and for all Charles got rid of the terrifying recollection of the Ornans executions, when as a boy of thirteen he was forced to watch the decapitation of the rebellious peasants from a position close to the guillotine; by closing his eyes he could still see the head of one of the unlucky rebels bouncing through the crowd, the eyes flashing and the lips, forever silent, yet twitching in terrible unspeakable imprecations against the mob of sadistic onlookers.

Smarra was the last of the "Slavonic" novels to come from Nodier's pen. Perhaps the vein begun with *Jean Sbogar* three years earlier had dried up, or perhaps the boomerang of his recent division of the romantic writers into *acceptable* (Goethe, Schiller, Chateaubriand) and *bad* (*les frénétiques*) persuaded him to give up vampires and ghouls for gnomes and fairies. In a review of a translation of Speiss' *Petit Pierre* for the *Annales de la Littérature et des Arts*, Charles proclaimed, "It seems to me we should severely thrust aside those rather sacrilegious innovators who distort our pleasures with the foolish exaggerations of a fantastic, odious, and ridiculous world; . . . I am referring here neither to the classic nor to the romantic school, but to an unnamed group that I shall call, if I may, the frantic school." And in a review of *The Complete Works of Walter Scott* for the *Quotidienne,* December 17 and 31, 1821, he further defined this specimen as "that romantic type of author who draws his compositions outside of true nature and in a category of facts and sentiments which can never exist, or which can exist only as a monstrous exception." He hastened to add that Walter Scott did not fit that category, for he represented nature as he saw it, thereby joining the ranks of the *acceptable* romanticists. But what were *Le Vampire* and *Smarra* if not the depiction of monstrous exceptions? It could very well be that the failure of *Le Délateur* at the Panorama Dramatique Theater on October 30, 1821, which he translated from the Italian of Camille Federici, temporarily soured the critic against that violent phase of early romanticism he had tried to nourish with examples.

Meantime the death of Amédée, the unlucky Nodiers' second son whose life span covered but a brief part of 1821, caused the little family to desert the Rue de Choiseul for an apartment at No. 4, Rue de Provence, where they had as a neighbor the marine historiographer and librarian Auguste Jal. Toward the end of the year, a sudden illness attended by considerable loss of weight, which Nodier diagnosed as a slight stroke, brought friend Weiss posthaste from Besançon. To this accident we owe the closing of the gap between these two who had not seen each other in seven years; shortly thereafter, when Charles was in possession of the Arsenal Library, Weiss was to be an annual visitor to the brilliant circle that was forming around Charles Nodier, visits duly recorded by the provincial librarian on his way home in the pages of his notebooks, a faithful if somewhat amused account of the literary doings in Paris of his old friend, who had finally achieved his lifelong dream of prominence.

With the novelette *Trilby* Charles introduced his "Scotch" stories early in 1822. Many have seen in *Trilby* an attempt to rival Nodier's new literary hero, Sir Walter Scott; but *Trilby*, "the imp of Argyle," is more reminiscent of *Lear*'s Flibberti-gibbet than *Kenilworth*'s, and admits more kinship to Puck than to *The Black Dwarf*. Actually, aside from the descriptions of the Scottish countryside which Charles had just visited, *Trilby* is another of the impossible or unrequited love affairs in Nodier's earlier manner, without the sentimentality of *Les Proscrits* or of *Thérèse Aubert*. The story was a publisher's success, however, and for some reason gave rise to a vogue of Trilby hats for the ladies, an indication that the novel was more appreciated for its *bizarrerie* than for its beautiful symbolism. In 1823 three different stage versions of *Trilby*, presented in the space of eleven days—March 13 at the Gymnase by Scribe and Carmouche, March 20 at the Vaudeville by Dumersan de Courcy and Rousseau, and March

24 at the Variété by Theaulon, Lafontaine, and Jouslin—bear witness to its high popularity.

Very little notice was taken, on the other hand, of a slim collection of horror tales published anonymously under the general title of *Infernaliana*. Despite Nodier's anglophilism, these stories owe more to his literary ancestor and family friend Jacques Cazotte than they do to *Otranto* or *Udolpho*, as their recurring theme of a Faustian devil constantly demanding his due bears witness. Even the cavernous "che vuoi?" of *Le Diable amoureux* is repeated with infinite variation in these stories. Unlike *Trilby*, these tales represent a step backward in Nodier's literary art as they are neither symbolic nor genuinely fantastic, but a kind of facile, contrived terror fiction dear to chambermaids and coachmen.

In a curious preliminary notice of Amédée Pichot's French edition of the works of Lord Byron,[20] Nodier credits that poet with revealing the frantic side of the new poetic school, complete with ruins, melancholy and death. The new poets objected to the stale imagery of ancient mythology and since "the gods are dead," he continues, these romanticists, mythless, and Christless, invented a new *merveilleux* which was at the same time "the expression and the symbol of the great social malady which had produced it." They looked for the marvelous in "the dark images of Erebus and the night and in the mute and formless emanations of the tomb." Another aspect of this innovation, according to Nodier, was *le vague des passions*, of which Chateaubriand's *René* would be the classic type.

All this presents one of the most dread aspects of the contemporary social revolution: the ability to take thought has become a torture to man; as the old stand-bys fell away and he became more individualistic, a wave of doubt concerning his ability to know and understand swept over him, and in the succeeding chaos man experienced a kind of voluptuousness in plunging into nihilism. Romanticists, wanting to pierce to the reality of things, ripped away the veils of Isis in the horrible expectation of finding a corpse. Such is the idea upon which is founded those romantic fictions which belong to an order of seething passions unknown to the ancients, but too real and too exalted not to be poetic. . . . In ancient literature the hero's struggle was against the gods who represented moral ideas everyone believed in; modern man struggles only against himself, his passions, his mistakes, evil inclinations and prejudices, . . . because our sterility and our egoism have left the poet no other agents of sympathy. That is the basic idea of Lord Byron's principal poems.

If Chateaubriand and Byron were guilty of lapses into frantic romanticism, could he be blamed for *Le Vampire, Le Château de St. Aldobrand* and *Smarra?* Having failed in attempting to transplant this aspect of the new writing to France, Nodier was busy seeking fellow culprits at the fountainhead and apex of romanticism to console himself and excuse his straying from the true path. Or better, the frantic aspect was part and parcel of the new literature and had to be accepted along with its soberer moments as the fullest expression of postrevolutionary society in Europe.

Evidence that the romanticists were gaining ground may be gleaned from Charles' review of the frenetic novel *Han d'Islande* for the *Quotidienne*, March 12, 1823: "The classicists are still holding their own in the newspapers, the academies and literary circles. The romanticists succeed in the theater, at the bookstores, and in the salons. We pledge allegiance to the former, but we read the latter; and the most distinguished effort that could issue from the *good school* nowadays would not share for a moment the irresistible wave of the sometimes extravagant reveries with which the *bad one* swarms."

This nine-year period ended as it had begun, with Nodier intensifying his compaign in favor of romanticism. He contributed articles to the obscure and friendly *Oriflamme* and to the struggling romantic organ *La Muse Francaise* as well as to the powerful *Débats* and the popular though conservative *Quotidienne.* This catholicity strengthened his position as the initiator and herald of the romantic movement, and now his enthusiasm embraced all of its phases, *acceptable* or not.

In his articles on Scott, at the end of 1821, Nodier came out more boldly in favor of a total romanticism, which in his eyes had the advantage of filling a void left by the Revolution. In the immutable series of changes that society goes through, when religious and political institutions lose their hold and the mind wanders in a bog of doubt and despair, are we to reject, he asks, a creative new school that pulls us out of this trough, because its adherents do it violently? Here Nodier touched upon another pivotal point that was to cause much learned and bitter comment in the years ahead: "Christianity and morality, driven from the church, took refuge in literature." So romanticism became a stabilizing and chastening force in helping to bring order out of chaos. In the beginning of the year 1823, in a review of the *Mémoires de Jacques Fauvel* by Droz and Picard for the *Quotidienne*, January 12, Nodier carries this idea a little farther when he states that modern man is more moral than his ancient counterpart, and thanks to romanticism, he declares in an article on Millevoye for that same journal, March 19, 1823, morality and religion reentered literature.

This interjection of the role of romanticism in the resuscitation of religion—everyone already knew that Nodier's royalism was closely allied to the new school—was another of the ingenious author's paradoxes, not to say a tour de force, intended to throw confusion into the classicist ranks. How could they attack with impunity a school of literature that espoused both church and throne? The paradox, that the romanticists were at the same time violent and frenetic, yet supported the monarchy and religion, the two strongest influences for stability and order, and the tour de force—this was much easier—that ancient Greeks and Romans, i.e., the classicists, had no religion in the sense that christianity is a religion, permitted Nodier to accept the freneticism of *Han d'Islande* as an "irreparable" but "inevitable" byproduct of romanticism. However unfortunate, this aspect, according to him, was a valid manifestation of young Hugo's world view, conditioned by the upheaval of the late Revolution and determined by social forces prevailing in the post-Napoleonic restoration period.

The accolade to the twenty-one-year old author of *Han d'Islande,* laudatory in the main, must have meant a great deal to Victor Hugo. The day after the appearance of Nodier's review, Hugo came round to thank the critic for his encouraging remarks; from that day relations between the two men were established on a firmer basis and Nodier never missed a chance to praise Hugo's works. Thus a review of the works of James Fenimore Cooper for the *Débats*, November 21, 1823, contained a paragraph in praise of *Han d'Islande*. The publication of Hugo's *Nouvelles Odes* elicited another flattering review from the pen of the mature critic in the *Quotidienne*, March 8, 1824. Hugo was on his way to Nodier's with a copy of the poems when the publisher Ladvocat told him the *Odes* were already in the critic's hands, and that the latter had agreed to write a review of them for the *Quotidienne*. Thereupon, Hugo began a letter explaining this to Nodier, and asked in wonderment, "Would the eagle consent to judge the flight of the sparrow?" At that moment the March 8 *Quotidienne* was brought to the young poet, who interrupted his writing to read the review. He then concluded the letter saying, "Words fail me to express my thanks, and the hope you give me at the end of your too kind article overwhelms me completely."[21]

The warm and affectionate friendship with Lamartine began in much the same manner. On October 4, 1823, the *Quotidienne* carried a sympathetic article on the *Nouvelles Méditations* signed Charles Nodier. It was in this essay that Nodier resumed his theme that "In ancient times poets created religion, today religion creates poets." After the turmoil of the Revolution, he goes on, people sought comfort in Christianity, and poetry was born again with *Les Méditations*. Verse had fallen into such disrepute, he concludes, that publishers would not touch it, preferring a musical picturesque prose; but *Les Méditations* changed all that immediately.[22] Lamartine thought so highly of this review that he used it as the preface to the eleventh edition of *Les Méditations* in 1824, and dedicated the edition, "To Charles Nodier from the author, his admirer and his friend. St. Point, December 30, 1823." The cordial relations begun in the fall of 1823 were strengthened three months later, when, in a review of the *Mélanges poétiques* by Ulric Guttinguer for the *Quotidienne*,

January 4, 1824, Nodier placed Lamartine between Shakespeare and Byron.

Toward the end of 1822, Taylor, General d'Orsay's aide-de-camp, was called to the army in Spain. When he returned to Paris a year later, he learned that the Abbé Crozier, librarian at the Arsenal for the king's brother, the Count d'Artois, had just died. Both he and Alphonse de Cailleux, who had been aide-de-camp to General Lauriston and had just been created secretary of the royal museums, combined their efforts to have Charles appointed in the Abbé Crozier's place. In the meantime Charles had been in correspondence with Duke Fitz-James, first aide-de-camp of the king's brother, Monsieur, the Count d'Artois, recommending his friend, the painter Alaux. This letter brought him close to the Marsan Pavilion of the Tuileries Palace, which housed the various chiefs of departments of French bureaucracy. Thanks to this concurrence of influence exerted in the right quarter at the opportune moment, Nodier's nomination to the post of librarian at the Arsenal was signed by the Count d'Artois, whose property it was, January 3, 1824, and approved by the minister de Corbière on April 3. Nodier's official installation as director of the Arsenal Library took place on Friday, April 14, 1824.

V

Charles Nodier and Victor Hugo

All the elements of revolution are now present; there only wants a man, a signal. Who will begin? As soon as a point of leverage is offered, everything will be set in motion.—
Bonaparte

(Hugo, *Han d'Islande,*
epigraph to Chapter
XIII)

It is an amazing commentary on literary fortunes that when Nodier succeeded to the directorship of the Arsenal in 1824 Victor Hugo at half his age was already on his way to being an established author, with two collections of poetry and a novel to his credit. At twenty-two Hugo had seemingly accomplished with a few pen strokes what it had taken Nodier forty-four years of hesitation and failure to achieve. It is equally amazing to learn that Nodier accepted Hugo as a brother-in-arms from the very start, proclaiming him the shining light of romanticism while he was still in the process of developing.

It is therefore surprising, not to say shameful, that Hugo, who was to become France's greatest poet, was ungenerous in his attitude toward Nodier in his later years. "Not for an empire," writes Constantin-Weyer in his *l'Aventure vécue de Dumas*, "would Hugo have admitted that he owed much to Nodier."[1] After 1828, Hugo erased one by one the dedications to his older friend, studiously omitting the epigraphs he had borrowed from his early mentor; having used Nodier to climb to the top of the romantic movement, he cast him aside. What were the reasons for this apparent ingratitude? In the present chapter that debt is revealed in the Nodier-Hugo relations, a study which should contribute to a better understanding of both men.

They met at the second weekly *séance publique* of the Société Royale de Bonnes Lettres, dedicated to the brothers Abel and Victor Hugo, *hommes de lettres*, February 21, 1821. Abel, the older of the two boys, who had become deeply interested in Spanish literature while their father, the general, was stationed in Spain, read an excerpt from a projected work on that subject. Victor, just turned nineteen, read his ode, *Quiberon,* which was warmly applauded. After the meeting,

145

the royalist-Catholic society took these two youngsters to its heart as the members crowded about the speakers' platform. Charles fell into conversation with the young poet and soon discovered they had a common birthplace. Talk of Besançon led to an expression of dual admiration for the last great champion of Franche-Comté independence, the seventeenth-century brigand Lacuzon, about whom they lightheartedly agreed to do a biographical novel. Two weeks later, March 13, Hugo read another ode, *La vision*, to the society; but it was not until the end of the following year, December 10, 1822, that he achieved his greatest triumph there by reading to these ultraroyalists his ode on Louis XVII.

Then Hugo published the fantastic novel, *Han d'Islande*. With its epigraphs drawn from Maturin's *Bertram*, one borrowed from Nodier himself (the idea of heading each chapter with epigraphs taken largely from foreign literature was certainly an imitation of *Jean Sbogar*), and its reminiscences of *Smarra*, this was clearly a *roman frénétique à la Nodier*. Recognizing his brainchild, Nodier was the only influential critic writing for a newspaper with wide circulation to hail *Han d'Islande* in a review for *La Quotidienne*, March 12, 1823. The other critics either ignored the young poet's first published novel or attacked it viciously. Léon Thiessé, writing for the *Mercure du Dix-Neuvième Siècle*, called it the work of a genius, if genius could be equated with dementia, or a four-volume nightmare, and Victor Vignon parodied it under the title *OG*, tracing its parenthood back to *Jean Sbogar* and *Le Vampire*.[2] Hugo was thankful for Nodier's epithets of "erudite and witty, a lively, picturesque style, a delicacy of tact and a finesse of sentiment"; of course Nodier did add that the above virtues contrasted strangely "with the barbarous fantasies of a sick imagination."

In the preface to the second edition of *Han d'Islande*, written but a few weeks after Nodier's review, April, 1823, Hugo showed his appreciation by taking public notice of the critic's strictures on the preface to the first edition, saying that those four or five hapless pages of introduction "had already attracted the anathema of one of our most honorable and distinguished authors (Mr. C. Nodier, *Quotidienne*, March 12) who accused him [Hugo] of taking the bittersweet tone of the illustrious Jedediah Cleisbotham, schoolmaster and sexton of the parish of Gandercleugh."[3] Nodier's actual words were somewhat less playful. "I have said nothing of a preface," he wrote in the concluding paragraph of his review, "in which the author imitates rather skillfully the bittersweet manner Sir Walter Scott employs in speaking of his confreres. He will sense that an author who tries to stir similar emotions and who has probably not succeeded without a great deal of difficulty is not free to use it. What does not sit well in an aging Sir Walter Scott is still less appropriate in a very young man to whom an unquestioned merit has accorded certain privileges. The first duty that talent imposes is that of not abusing one's rights." Yet, on the whole, no one could say that Nodier's article was not laudatory in the extreme and sincerely meant to encourage a young novelist in his first venture, when everyone else was advising him to stick to poetry.

In 1823 the future of the novel in France was not so clearly indicated as it was to be twenty years later; so Nodier showed considerable acumen in perceiving the gold among the dross of *Han d'Islande,* and uncommon foresight in observing that Hugo could turn his creative gifts to prose fiction as well as verse. Finally, Georg Brandes, who held Nodier to be "a forerunner of greater men than himself," praised his review of *Han d'Islande* as "a little masterpiece of criticism, sympathetic and acute. . . . The appreciation of Hugo is so marvelously correct that in reading it today one can hardly believe that its writer was unacquainted with all the master's later works. It required no small amount of cleverness to foresee them in *Han d'Islande.*"[4] It was as a result of this demonstration of goodwill that acquaintance grew into friendship between these two men and "le cher Victor" became a constant visitor at Nodier's house in the Rue de Provence.

In July they both published verses in the first issue of the *Muse Française,* a shortlived magazine dedicated primarily to poetry of a romantic cast. Nodier's increasing influence on the young poet may be seen in the publication of Hugo's finest ode, *La bande noire,* in the September issue of *La Muse Française.* Prefaced by an epigraph drawn from Nodier, this poem was inscribed by Hugo as an unmistakable tribute to Charles' crusade against the vandals, *les démolisseurs* of architectural masterpieces of the past. By thus identifying himself with one of Nodier's prime romantic facets and by making common cause in print against the enemies of the new school, Hugo signified his endorsement of Nodier's leadership of the romantic movement in France. Early in 1824 they were both contributing articles and poems to *L'Oriflamme*, a short-lived daily with royalist tendencies and romantic sympathies. Then came Nodier's brief but admiring article on Hugo's *Nouvelles Odes* in the *Quotidienne*, March 8, which evinced the letter of thanks from the young poet quoted in Chapter IV.

Romantic forces suffered a severe jolt in their allegiance to the constitutional monarchy of Louis XVIII when Chateaubriand fell from power in June, 1824. Politics was an integral part of the romantic program. Briefly summed up, it called for loyalty to the constitutional monarchy, since that form of government represented as much of an advance over the absolute kings of the *ancien régime* as romanticism in the arts represented over the rigid doctrines of classicism. In Nodier's words, with time and patience more liberty would be envisaged in both government and art as an ideal aim for the future; but for the present, one must be practical. Accept and consolidate the gains already achieved, was his slogan. As long as Chateaubriand remained at his post of Minister of Foreign Affairs, the royalist romanticists felt they had a pledge of representation and progress at court. They took the fall of their representative as a personal affront. Victor Hugo protested vigorously in his *Ode à M. de Chateaubriand*, written three days after the destitution of his hero, and the romanticists launched a campaign in the public press against that archvillain, Prime Minister Villèle. The death of Louis XVIII in September probably halted momentarily further division and defection among the ranks of the romantic royalists, for Villèle was instituting a series of repressive measures which threatened the very heart of the romantic revolution: the freedom of the press. By muzzling all the newspapers of the opposition, Villèle hoped to induce an atmosphere of harmony in which the régime would appear to be unanimously supported. Where there are no critics, there can be no dissension.

Meantime it was a question of crowning the new king, Charles X, at Rheims. On May 20, 1825, Victor returns from a visit of reconciliation with his father at Blois, where he has left his wife and infant daughter as a token of *rapprochement* with the general, and finds a note from Charles Nodier asking him to call at the Arsenal. They have both been invited to the coronation; Victor has written from Blois to thank Charles for his congratulations on receiving the coveted *Légion d'Honneur* and to tell him that he will be delighted if they can travel together.

At his entrance next day Victor finds Nodier grieving over the death of his mother-in-law, Madame Charve. Since last winter, the Arsenal has become a sort of hotel for the distaff Nodiers: besides Désirée's mother the family now includes Charles' sister, Elise, and her daughter, Francine, aged seven. Victor is used to the lively, populated, and talkative atmosphere of the Arsenal. He has brought his wife, Adèle, blooming with youth and beauty, to meet the genial hostess of the place, whose natural grace has captured her immediate friendship, and he himself feels like an older brother toward the charming Marie, only nine years his junior. Now he steps up to the table, where, instead of the interminable game of *écarté* that is Nodier's passion, he finds three men silently bent over maps and plans seriously considering ways and means of getting to Rheims. They are all going to the coronation, Charles as a sort of historiographer of the event, Hugo as the poet laureate to mark the ceremony with an ode, Alaux (nicknamed "le Romain" because he had won the Prix de Rome) to fix the pomp and parade in color, and the other, Alphonse de Cailleux, in his capacity as general secretary of the royal museums, to bring back documents. How to get to Rheims? Since all public conveyances will be overcrowded (the diligence had all seats reserved three months ago), Charles suggests striking a bargain with a coachman he employes on his trips to the surrounding countryside, who has offered to put a rather large carriage at their disposal for 100 francs per day or 400 francs ($100) round trip. Much relieved, the others decide to leave the arrangements to Charles.

Early in the morning of Tuesday, May 24, the group sets out by easy stages, since the coronation is not to take place until May 29. The weather is fine, everything is green, but the carriage is not nearly as spacious as had been promised, seating only four and leaving little room for baggage, which is squashed into corners and suspended somehow from poles on the top and sides of the vehicle, and there is a lot of it, for these men must appear in the ceremony *à la française*, the standard court dress of buckles, breeches, and doublet, complete with the side-arms of the time, an unwieldly sword, perhaps a bit rusty at that. That night they reach the village of Létignon, where they sleep poorly on four hastily improvised cots. At 4:30 they are off again. After lunch in Soissons, Nodier, ever on the prowl for old books, makes a real find in an old junk shop; one of the few extant copies of the complete *Romancero*. When they stop along the roadside to refresh the horses, Charles finds a five-franc piece. "For the poor," he announces holding up the shining new coin. Then he finds another and another. The party is off on a treasure hunt. Someone conjectures that the new king has strewn his path with largesses. Then Victor finds the cross of the Legion of Honor he was awarded a month ago; it is his baggage that has burst and spread his belongings over the last mile or so of the journey. Laughing, the travelers resume their places. That night they sleep in Braine.

Eager to resume their journey, they get a 3:30 start on the following day and cover the remaining distance without incident. But when they reach Rheims in the afternoon of the twenty-seventh, there are no more rooms to be had. In fact, all the rooms have been let for several days in advance. Travelsore and weary from the bumpy ride, the four men look at each other, wondering why one of them had not thought of reserving lodgings two weeks ago. They wander aimlessly about the streets, in no mood to visit the town. After many more rebuffs, Charles, who has been lucky on this trip, sees a familiar face; it is the director of the local theater, Solomé,

who perhaps owes Charles a favor. "Where are you staying?"
in his first question. "In the street," answers Charles. Though
unfortunately he himself has no room, the director knows
that one of his troupe, a Miss Florville, has rented large
quarters; perhaps she might be willing to give up half her
apartment to the stranded four. Charles again takes charge
of arrangements and within a short time they are more or
less comfortably housed in the actress' parlor. The next
evening, they are having trouble with Victor. Mademoiselle
Florville has prepared a gay dinner for the guests, but Victor
is nowhere to be found. Finally, Charles comes upon him,
sulking in a dark corner of the room. "What's the matter?"
Victor, the prudish young husband and father, not wanting
to slight even in thought the chastity of his vows, is disturbed
by the bare shoulders of the actress. They finally overcome
his priggishness and drag him to the dinner table. Later, Victor
gives Charles his academician's medal from the *Jeux floraux*
as a token of friendship.

The next day, Sunday, May 29, the day set for the coronation of the king, rain began to fall from the early morning,
but by noon it cleared and the sun came out. At one o'clock
the ceremony, full of pomp and tinsel, pageant and symbol,
affected the spectators variously. The cathedral was too
crowded, protocol was too rigid, the ceremony was not as
impressive as they had expected and it took too long. Chateaubriand had wanted the king to enter an undecorated cathedral
on horseback. Hugo found the walls painted blue and the
statues decorated with gold and tinsel in bad taste; but he
claimed as a sign of the progress of romantic ideas that the
ornaments, except for the throne itself, had all respected the
Gothic style. In the evening, instead of going to the Duke of
Northumberland's ball, Nodier and Hugo read to each other.

During the long coronation, a M. Hémonin had placed a
volume of Shakespeare's works in Nodier's hands. From this
he translated as he read for Hugo passages from *King John*.
For Hugo, this was a revelation: "The first time I heard the
name of Shakespeare," he states in *Choses vues,* "was at
Rheims from the mouth of Charles Nodier. . . . This revelation of Shakespeare moved me. I found it great."[5] Later,

when Hugo wished to minimize Nodier's influence upon him, he went through his essay on Shakespeare and removed the reference to this reading, but apparently forgot that he had already let the cat out of the bag in the new series of *Choses vues*. (The definitive edition of this work, Ollendorf, Paris, 1913, also omits this passage.) In any event, Emile Henriot has found an unpublished chapter of Hugo's manuscript essay on William Shakespeare in which the poet recalls that "being at Rheims in 1825 for the crowning of Charles X with his friend Charles Nodier, the latter having found at a bookseller's a volume of the great Will, gave a word-for-word translation of several passages from it to Hugo, who was dazzled."[6] Thus is the poet confounded by his own words. Though this was certainly not the first time he had heard of Shakespeare, we know that before the session with Nodier at Rheims Hugo entertained a low opinion of the great dramatist. In 1820-21 he rated him below Corneille and Racine in the pages of *Le Conservateur Littéraire*. In 1821 he had accompanied Adèle to a performance of *Hamlet* in translation, but the young lovers were more interested in looking at each other than in what was happening on the stage. What Hugo meant in the above excerpt from *Choses vues* was that he had his first glimpse of the real Shakespeare athwart Nodier's *viva voce* reading of the original text followed immediately by a good translation into French.

Of his trip, actions, and thoughts Nodier wrote every day to his wife. The crowded conditions of the town's hotels and dining facilities, the coronation, the meeting with friends, all came in for review; but mostly he wondered if he should have asked for a promotion. All the pomp and glitter had gone to his head and he would have liked to come back a baron in the company of that other newly created baron, Victor Hugo. When he got back to Paris, however, the real trouble began, as he had difficulty collecting expenses from the budget set aside for the coronation. On July 8, he began bombarding the Minister of the Interior, Count Corbière, an old friend, with letters asking for reimbursement. Victor Hugo had, upon returning from Rheims, been reimbursed upwards of 700 francs (about $175) for expenses incurred while attending the coronation. Nodier wondered why he had not been similarly reimbursed, since he shared the vehicle, the rooms, and the meals with Hugo, who had drawn up identical expense sheets for both of them. Two days later, Charles brought this all again to the attention of the minister, suggesting that perhaps his account was trailing about the office in some dossier. After more than two weeks of waiting, Nodier again importuned the count with a letter, this time in scathing terms:

"M. de Cailleux has been good enough to inform me that *one of these days* I shall receive an order indemnifying me to the last farthing, after they have checked the figures at the inn and post, pretty much as one would pay for the hire of a horse. This *kindness*, which I am to expect *one of these days*, will postdate by two months full reimbursements made to my honorable and honored friends." It was bad enough to neglect this account, he continued, but now he was being humiliated into the bargain. He therefore expressed his desire to withdraw as historiographer of the coronation. "The coronation budget does not need me and I do not need it. Perhaps I spent some *louis* at Rheims without having recourse to the king's treasury. That was no doubt foolish. . . . *I no longer belong to the historiography section of the coronation;* just let them pay me the *useless* expenditures that they think are my due." This letter apparently brought results, for two days later Charles was thanking Corbière for settling the affair in his favor and for assuring him that no slight was intended. Considerably placated, he stated that he would not have been so bitter about the evident injustice in the way funds were allocated to the various individuals attending the coronation at the king's invitation if he had not thought he perceived another more serious inequality of consideration and respect. Thoroughly satisfied and reassured, he now had another favor to ask of the minister. He was leaving for Switzerland on Monday; since the account had already been settled, could not the funds be made available to him before his departure? The next day, Saturday, Nodier received full satisfaction, as we learn from a note of thanks to de Corbière written July 30.[7]

This fresh excursion was something dreamed up entirely

by Nodier as an excuse for the two authors to visit Lamartine at Saint-Point. While they were still at Rheims, Hugo, disappointed at not seeing Lamartine at the festivities, expressed a desire to visit the famous château of Saint-Point, the poet's residence near Lyons. On his visits to Paris Lamartine had spoken so glowingly of his home and had so intrigued the Parisians that they eagerly sought an occasion to take advantage of his hospitality. He had repeatedly invited them to come to him. Nodier, who was in the mood for more travel, put forth a plan by which the trip would cost them nothing. How? After they left Lamartine, they would continue on to Switzerland. Well? Well, then the three authors, if Lamartine was willing, would write about their travels, a sort of anthology, verse by Hugo and Lamartine, prose by Nodier, and sell this *album de voyage* to a publisher. They might even interest Taylor in joining the enterprise as an illustrator. And Nodier knew just the man who would support such an undertaking, Urbain Canel.

Upon returning to Paris they easily secured the support of Taylor and Canel for their project. Taylor was to provide an artist who would receive 2,000 francs for eight drawings; Hugo, 2,250 francs for four odes; Lamartine, 2,000 for four meditations; and Nodier, 2,250 for the text. Both Hugo and Nodier received 1,750 francs advance from the publisher. This tidy sum, together with the proceeds of the Rheims trip he had just received, put Charles in a splendid humor. But this time they would need two carriages, since they were both taking their families. On Tuesday morning, August 2, Nodier, Désirée, Marie, and the artist Gué in a *calèche*, and Victor, Adèle, the infant Léopoldine and her nursemaid in a *berline* joined forces at the *barrière de Fontainebleau* and took up stations side by side so they could converse across the road on the leisurely journey to Saint-Point.

During lunch at Essones Nodier told one of his tall tales. "You have no doubt heard of fathers who were not sure their children were their own, but I'll wager you have never heard the story of the twenty mothers who could never be certain they were the real mothers of their children." "How can that be?" "What nonsense!" "Where did that take

place?" and similar shouts of disapproval greeted the speaker's
opening statement. "Right in this hotel on the billiard table
in the very next room," countered Nodier. "Two years ago
a vehicle carrying children and their nurses from Paris to
Burgundy stopped here for lunch. In order to be more at
ease the nurses deposited their charges on the billiard tables
and went to lunch. In the meantime some local characters
came in for their daily game of billiards, and finding the
tables encumbered with babies placed them on the floor and
on benches pell-mell about the room. After lunch the nurses
came to pick up their charges, but found they were at a
loss to recognize the infants, all newborn babies look alike,
don't they? They resolved the problem by arbitrarily assigning
the children to various names involved, having regard only
for their sex. And to this day there are twenty mothers who
are tenderly saying 'my daughter' and 'my son' to what is
very likely someone else's child." "Come now," objected the
levelheaded Mrs. Nodier, "surely the clothing was marked?"
"Oh, well," retorted her husband, "if you seek probability,
you will never find truth!"

Much has been written about Nodier's charm as a racon-
teur, how, for instance, at the Arsenal he would hold the as-
sembled company spellbound while for minutes at a time,
his tall, somewhat stooped frame backed against the mantel-
piece, he would tell off the beads in the chaplet of his memory,
freely rearranged to suit his fancy. In this connection it is en-
lightening to translate a perceptive paragraph from *Victor
Hugo raconté par un témoin de sa vie* commenting upon the
above anecdote. "Mr. Nodier was an exquisite conversation-
alist. His lively and colorful wit contrasted with his sleepy
drawl. He possessed that extraordinary faculty of combining
the wide grasp of the philosopher with the naive graciousness
of the believer. The stories he told more often from imagination than from memory had in their fiction the sincerity of
ıeality and in their truth the charm of the impossible."[8] What
more convincing proof could be adduced that the gifted
witness was no other than the great poet himself? If such
was the case, then we can say with some justification that
Hugo's admiration for Nodier at this time was unbounded.

Thus diverting each other, the travelers continued on their road to Saint-Point. At Vermenton there was an embarrassing delay caused by Hugo's impulsiveness. Leaving the coach to enjoy the beautiful view up ahead, Victor forgot momentarily that he had left his passport in Paris. Dressed in a light gray suit bearing the ribbon of the *Légion d'Honneur* in the lapel, he was accosted by the local constabulary, who, suspicious of the youthful appearance of the poet, desired to know what that ribbon meant. Upon being informed that it meant the Legion of Honor, the gendarmes scoffingly retorted that it was not customary to grant that high honor to children, and, their suspicions now thoroughly aroused, demanded to see the papers confirming his right to the decoration. When poor Victor could not even produce a passport to establish his identity, the young poet was in danger of being taken to headquarters for questioning when fortunately the others drove up. Springing from the *calèche*, Nodier asked these gentlemen why his friend was being detained. After hearing their apparently all too well grounded suspicions he blurted out, "Why, gentlemen, this is the famous Victor Hugo!" as if everyone should already have been familiar with the poet's great future reputation. Not wishing to seem uninformed and having established that the older man's papers were in perfect order, the policemen released Hugo with sheepish apologies for not having recognized him sooner.

The next news we have of the travelers is their detour at Dole to lunch with Nodier's old friend, now Mayor, Dusillet. It is strange that Charles did not extend this little detour to include Beasançon and Quintigny close by. From 1818 to the end of his life Nodier returned to Besançon only twice: in 1826 for his mother's funeral and in 1835, when, as an official of the Académie Française, he had to be present at the unveiling of a statue to Cuvier in Montbéliard. Even on those occasions, Pingaud tells us, he stayed close indoors as if he were afraid of running into his old enemies, the ex-Abbés Dormoy and Proudhon.[9]

Lamartine was waiting for them at Macon. Besides the château at Saint-Point, he owned a house in the city, about an hour's drive from his country seat. Lamartine was for starting immediately for Saint-Point, but Nodier felt they had traveled enough for that day and the ladies had to have a chance to rest up a bit before pushing on. Moreover, the prefect, hearing of their coming, had placed his theater box at their disposal. After dinner they went to the theater where Léontine Fay was performing in *La Petite Soeur;* but an even more exciting spectacle for the Maconnais was the presence of Hugo, Lamartine, and Nodier in the same loge.

Next morning the party set out for Saint-Point with Lamartine as outrider on horseback showing the way. At the door they were met by the poet's mother, Madame de Prat, his wife and her mother, Mrs. Birch. Inside, in the great salon, were the poet's sister and her husband, the Cessiats, another brother-in-law, M. de Montherot, and a visiting female cousin. Later, Lamartine's daughter Julie, a golden-haired child of six, was introduced to the new arrivals. The dinner that followed the reading of several poems by the master of the house was rather too formal for the taste of Désirée, who was not used to being dressed to the teeth from morning until night. She and Adèle had only brought one silk dress each for rare occasions and now they had worn them on consecutive days. They were both put out at dinner with the finery of the other ladies, but Désirée made up with wit what she lacked in chic. Even so she found the stiff atmosphere very trying and suggested they leave that evening. Lamartine regretted he could not go with them, but he escorted them part of the way, put the ladies on their road, and showed Victor and Charles a short-cut through the woods. Though they were on foot, the men reached town first and impatiently awaited the arrival of their families, who, finding the evening enchanting and wishing to enjoy the glorious scenery, had driven at a slow pace.

Years later, commenting upon one of his *Harmonies, La Retraite, Réponse à Victor Hugo*, Lamartine recorded his reaction to Nodier:

Nature has made few men so charming and so different. In him were to be found traces of the peasant, the gentleman, the *émigré*, the republican, the knight-errant, the man

of letters, the savant, the poet, and especially, of the
lazy man. . . . You could have created ten men out of the
elements present in his makeup, yet the way they were
arranged in him they did not form a consistent whole, but
the fragments were admirable.[10]

This is as just an appreciation of the essential Nodier as
could be found anywhere.

At five o'clock the next morning they continued on their
way to Mont-Blanc and Geneva. At noon, because the drivers
had missed a turning, instead of the hearty lunch they antic-
ipated they had to be content with an omelette of four eggs
for seven people taken in a wretched inn lost by the wayside.
They spent the night at Bellegarde and left France the next
day in such a heavy fog that they could hardly see where
they were going. Suddenly the fog lifted and they were
presented with a dazzling vista of Mont-Blanc. Hugo was
so taken with the Lake of Geneva that he wanted to dine
in a restaurant with a view, but Nodier, in whom the four-egg
omelette divided among seven people still rankled as an
insult to gastronomy, remembered an inn facing a great gray
wall he and his family had visited the year before. When Hugo
protested, Charles told him that he did not judge restaurants
by the view, but by the cuisine, and that he was going to the
one that had the best food. Hugo begrudgingly gave in, but
had to admit Nodier was right when he tasted the fresh-caught
lake fish accompanied by an elegant sauce.

Registering at a hotel in Geneva in those days was as much
of a bore as it has become practically all over Europe, involving the filling out of endless forms requiring answers to
such impertinent questions as the reason for the traveler's
visit. Nodier was so exasperated by this last question that
he wrote "To overthrow your government" in answer to it.
The grandeur of the view of Mont-Blanc they had caught
at the entrance to the city began to fade in disillusionment
when they found themselves constantly thwarted by the
stringent regulations the city fathers had instituted to keep
Geneva a clean, almost clinical, modern city. They made one
excursion to Lausanne for a festival in honor of William Tell,

but they found the town too small to accommodate the many spectators drawn there. So they returned to Geneva, which they found even more forbidding than on their first contact, and they decided to leave the next day. But the next day was a Sunday and the travelers suffered a whole skein of frustrating events. They were not allowed to visit the churches, since they might disturb the faithful at worship; on the other hand, they were prevented from leaving town while the services were in progress. Finally, the last hymn having been sung, the gates of the town swung open and the unwilling visitors rushed toward Sallanches and freedom.

The following day they visited the Alps at Chamonix. At lunch they ate up the last of the publisher's advance so they had to abandon their plan of going on to Italy. A headlong retreat to Paris to get down to the business of writing was in order. But a collaborative effort bearing the names of Hugo and Nodier as co-authors was not to be. At first, Nodier, the master procrastinator, said he would wait until the artist had finished his drawings. Then Urbain Canel went bankrupt and there no longer was any pressure on them to write at all.

From Nodier, the prime mover of the idea for the book, *Voyage poétique et pittoresque au Mont-Blanc et à la vallée de Chamonix*, only a fragment, *Les bosquets de Maglan*, describing that part of the trip from Geneva to the Bosquets, was published two years later in the *Annales Romantiques*, accompanied by the explanatory footnote: "This fragment is extracted from a work under press entitled, *Voyage aux Alpes*, by Messers Charles Nodier, Victor Hugo, and Baron Taylor, to be published next January by the publisher of *Les Annales Romantiques*." The publisher of the *Annales* was none other than Urbain Canel, realizing at last some return on his investment.[11]

The years 1825 and 1826 may be taken as the high point in the Nodier-Hugo entente, years in which Hugo admired Nodier as an older brother, a fount of knowledge and a source of constant inspiration. Upon their return to Paris, the famous Sunday nights at the Arsenal had resumed with the Hugos in constant attendance. Not only was Victor an intimate of Nodier's Sunday dinners for his old cronies, Taylor, Cailleux, and the painter, Dauzats; he also dropped in frequently and sat down to lunch during the week. The many hastily scribbled notes that passed between these two friends, of which unfortunately only a few have seen print, attest to this familiarity.

Meanwhile the violent attacks continued against the beleaguered romanticists in the form of articles, pamphlets, and speeches. The fulminations against romanticism Auger pronounced in his speech at the Academy April 24, 1824, had elicited approval from such members of the old guard as La Harpe, Artaud, Viennet, and Népomucène Lemercier, from the turncoats Alexandre Soumet and Baour-Lormian, another resounding speech by the master of the University of Paris, Frayssinous, a flurry of supporting articles, mostly anonymous or signed only with initials in the *Journal des Débats*, *Le Constitutionnel*, and in the conservative press generally, which professed to represent public opinion, and finally, an unusual number of unsigned pamphlets, a specialty of the conservative attack. Only Stendhal, in his second part of *Racine et Shakespeare*, March, 1825, and Emile Deschamps, in *La Muse Française*, took up their defense.

Help came unexpectedly from a new quarter when a very important newspaper took the field in favor of the new school. This was the recently launched *Globe*, founded in 1824 by Pierre Leroux and Paul Dubois and staffed by such eminent writers as Jouffroy, de Remusat, Duvergier de Hauranne, Ludovic Vitet, and J. J. Ampère. At first dedicated exclusively to literature, this paper recommended a kind of middle ground between the romantic royalists, who espoused foreign models, and their opponents, the liberal conservatives, who denounced the influence of foreign literature. In recommending that local authors remain French while accepting ideas from abroad, the *Globe* easily aligned itself with the romantic camp on literary grounds, though maintaining aloofness on the question of politics, in which it was liberal, thus splitting the romantic party into two factions, royalists and liberals. A sort of coolness had reigned between these two factions until the end of 1825 when an unsigned article, probably by Dubois, defending their common interest, brought a deputation composed of Nodier, Hugo, Emile Deschamps, Augustin Soulié, Saint-Valry, and Guttinguer to the editor's office to thank him for his eloquent defense of their cause. Dubois remained very reserved throughout the interview, but stated that he would continue to support the new school as long as it backed Chateaubriand, who had just joined forces with the liberals against the Villèle ministry.[12] Although this brought them closer together, the two factions did not merge until a bridge was thrown up between them by another liberal newspaper, *Le Mercure du Dix-Neuvième Siècle*, which, rapidly gaining in romantic sympathies, published an article by H. de Latouche urging coalition against the common foe (late 1825).

By closing their ranks, they spread alarm throughout the conservative forces; but they were split too. Alongside the diehard monarchists of the old school, who with characteristic xenophobia repulsed everything foreign—and everything new, for that matter—there had grown up a powerful group of liberal conservatives. These were the sons of the Revolution and Empire, who, while they rejected the monarchy and pursued republican politics, hated the foreigner who had scotched their revolution and clung tenaciously to the literary ideals of the seventeenth and eighteenth centuries. The rallying points of these two diametrically opposed political factions were hatred of foreign influence and belief in the superiority of French culture. They both feared that along with the importation of foreign literary models would come an invasion of Protestant religious philosophy. In the minds of the old-line monarchists, this would disperse not only absolutism in government firmly founded on Catholic approval but that very Catholicism on which it was grounded. Paradoxically, their parochialism caused them to cling to a neoclassical literature based on pagan models, because it was typically French and part and parcel of the *ancien régime*. Clearly, this position, espousing Catholic ideals in religion and government and at the same time encouraging the imitation of pagan literary models—had not Boileau ostracized the treatment of religious (Christian) themes?—was untenable. It left them cruelly open to Nodier's quip, "Is it true . . . that I must be a pagan in order not to be called a heretic?" But they somehow sensed that, more serious than the Revolution of 1789 which they finally put down (with foreign help, it is true), these romanticists would incautiously bring in the more insidious cosmopolitan Protestant revolution which would eventually sweep everything French before it. Founded in the spirit of inquiry, one of the sources of their own hated revolution, they feared this religion would surely and inevitably lead to universal anarchy and atheism. It is no wonder that they made friends among their erstwhile enemies, the liberal conservatives, who were also disturbed at the prospect of the disappearance of everything that was typically French from the world. These thought that their revolution had been homegrown and that if there was to be republicanism, socialism, atheism, or communism, it must first of all be French.

The linking of literature and politics which characterized the romantic movement in France may seem strange to the student of romanticism elsewhere, but from the very beginning hardly an article or a critical review of a literary work appeared that was not used as the springboard for a political tract. Perhaps Nodier had a good deal to do with that, since after 1817 he seized every opportunity to introduce political argument, whether it was appropriate or not, into his literary criticism. Romanticism became identified as a manifestation of the overall political revolution which was slowly engulfing western Europe and as such considered either a boon or a danger, depending on where the writer stood. In many ways this confusion of literature and politics was unfortunate in that it did much harm to the romantic movement in terms of aesthetic ideals. The romanticists had to take the political picture into account, though perhaps they could have solved their literary problems much more quickly and achieved their artistic revolution more quietly and easily had it not been for the constant irruption of this unwelcome intruder. It was on this rock that Nodier and Hugo eventually split.

Nodier had accepted the progress made by romanticism in literature and had reconciled himself to a slow-paced and rather unsatisfactory political situation. Thus he stood with one foot in the future and the other mired in the past. It was not long before Hugo became impatient with this awkward posture. Since literature and politics were so hopelessly tied together there was nothing for it but to be consistent and admit that you could not go forward in one and lag behind in the other. When he wrote, "Le romantisme n'est autre chose que le libéralisme en littérature," he had already made up his mind to take the next step and admit, to himself at least, that to be logical, romanticism meant liberalism in politics as well. It was some time, however, before he was to state triumphantly that the currents of liberalism in literature and liberalism in politics had met in him. For the moment, Nodier had no idea of the changes taking place in the young poet at his side. It was perhaps natural that Nodier, always indolent and now very tired, should have made do with the unhappy politics of the time and perhaps just as natural that the young and energetic Hugo should have sought a more dynamic platform. Hugo's new position certainly was more logical and more consistent, one that clearly pointed the road a robust and productive romanticism was to travel in the immediate future; he was to be amply justified.

But Nodier was also unaware of Hugo's overweening ambition, which would not let him play second fiddle to anyone. If Nodier had typified everything that Hugo wanted for romanticism, still Hugo would have insisted on nothing less than the leadership of the movement. One must admire the art of the caricaturist, Granville, in *Le Grand Chemin de la postérité*, where he shows Hugo leading the onrush of the romantic cohort, a harebrained looking crew. Hugo's leadership of the movement, while it was dynamic, overlooked, half understood, or neglected many of the subtle nuances Nodier had been introducing into French writing—ideas and techniques which did not receive attention again until a century later. Moreover, much of the name-calling and unpleasant publicity romanticists drew upon themselves by their antics would have been avoided under Nodier's guidance; a check of the roster of visitors at the Arsenal will show that an attitude of friendliness, tolerance, and mutual respect prevailed there, since the master's cordiality was extended to members of both camps, and to those that belonged to neither. Later, when the more fiery romanticists moved to the *Cénacle de Joseph Delorme*, only the most sanguine of the faithful, i.e., those who believed that Victor Hugo *was* the romantic movement, were admitted. The congenial atmosphere of the Arsenal was not conducive to organizing and mounting a sustained drive to launch Hugo's version of the movement.

But all that was not yet—and Hugo was still under the spell of Nodier's lighthanded guidance. A notable publication event of the spring of 1826, Vigny's historical novel, *Cinq-Mars*, brings to light this accord between master and disciple. Vigny, another denizen of the Arsenal, expected Nodier to do a critique of his novel for the *Quotidienne;* but Nodier was ill throughout that spring and summer, the doctors not diagnosing muscular inflammation until September. On June 1 Nodier wrote to Vigny—probably in answer to a discreet query—excusing himself for not having taken part in the reception of *Cinq-Mars* because of ill health; otherwise he certainly would have done a *compte-rendu* for the *Quotidienne*. In any case, he continued, the article that did appear there (anonymous, probably by Soulié, May 30, 1826, an *article de fonds*) was "written in a better style than anything I could have done, but with a less deeply felt enthusiasm for the beauty of this work."[13] On July 8 Sainte-Beuve attacked *Cinq-Mars* in the pages of the *Globe*. An answer from the romantic camp was called for. Since Nodier was indisposed, an anonymous defense of the novel was published in the *Quotidienne*, July 30. Vigny's letter to the editor, Augustin Soulié, thanking him, reveals that the author of the article was Victor Hugo.[14] Now Augustin Soulié was Nodier's friend of long standing and future associate at the Arsenal; moreover, it was Nodier who had been contributing literary reviews to the *Quotidienne* since 1821. This defense of *Cinq-Mars* was the only article Hugo ever contributed to that newspaper, which was generally inimical to him. What other conclusion can be drawn than that Hugo was substituting for Nodier in defense of their friend and cause?

Another incident of the year 1826 serves to confirm the master-disciple relationship of Nodier and Hugo. As the head of one of the more important libraries of Paris, Nodier thought his position eminent enough to secure him a seat in the French Academy. He had tried twice unsuccessfully in 1824, at the instigation of editor Soulié, who pushed his election in *La Quotidienne*, in June for the seats vacated by Aignan and Bausset and in September on the death of Lacretelle. Charles decided to enter the lists again two years later, supported again by the advertisements of Soulié in *La Quotidienne*, January 3 and April 3, 1826. In April, 1826, we find him writing to Hugo asking him to plead with Guiraud to withdraw from the field of applicants, then thanking him for having run the errand. Féletz, Guiraud, and Brifaut were elected in that year, but not Nodier. In his pique, he wrote to Hugo suggesting the formation of a new Academy.[15]

In October Hugo published his third collection of poetry, entitled *Odes et ballades*. Of the twenty-three poems comprising this edition at least seven are traceable directly to Nodier's influence. The ballade, *La ronde du sabbat*, imitated from *Smarra* and perhaps from Goethe's *Faust*, is dedicated to Nodier. The ballade *A Trilby, Le lutin d'Argail*, needs no comment. Miss Schenck has satisfactorily revealed the Nodieresque echoes in *La fée et la péri*, *Les deux archers*, *A un passant*, and in the ode, *Aux ruines de Monfort-l'Amaury*.[16] Furthermore, another ballade, *La fiancée du timbalier*, bears a striking resemblance to the first part of Bürger's *Lenore*, one of Nodier's favorite poems. Hugo's advice, in the Introduction, that a poet should study only two books, Homer and the Bible, was an idea gleaned from Herder. Prior to Hugo's meeting with Nodier, his knowledge of foreign literature seemed to be limited to Latin and Spanish; it was on the trips to Rheims and Chamonix that Nodier communicated his enthusiasm for English and German literature to the young poet. René Canat noticed that Hugo's poems written under Nodier's influence were so imitative that they reflect even Nodier's ironic style, and Léon Séché states that Hugo might never have written any *ballades* at all if it had not been for Nodier, so inextricably was his conception of this form bound with ideas of the fantastic borrowed from Nodier's works.[17]

As might be expected, Charles reviewed *Odes et ballades* in

La Quotidienne, February 10, 1827. But first he inserted a preview encomium of it in an article written earlier for that same newspaper. In discussing the poems of Madame Amable Tastu, one of the Arsenal habituées, October 23, 1826, he had occasion to compare her poetry to that of other romanticists, notably to "the fantastic charm of the ideal creations of Victor Hugo . . . whose inimitable productions will be one of our best titles to glory in the eyes of posterity." In his appreciation of *Odes et ballades* Charles leans naturally toward the "delicious ballades wherein the poet proves so well the astounding flexibility of his talent—which lends itself without effort to handling all forms—and that he has songs for the tenderest as well as the most solemn thoughts." As to the faults, inequalities, weaknesses and imperfections of the poems in this collection, he more than anyone is sensible of them because of the "brotherly friendship which binds him to the author." The reader feels that this publication is almost a family affair and that Nodier, as a brother, can be critical without in any way detracting from "the brilliance with which this young poet is developing."

Hugo was not behindhand in expressing his thanks; that same day he wrote a letter echoing the critic's effusions:

> Yes, Charles, let us proclaim our friendship, this *brotherly friendship* which binds me to you as it united Thomas Corneille to the great Pierre, this friendship of which I reap all the advantages and you the cares. Take me under your wing and I will be as invulnerable as you.
>
> How beautiful your article is and at the same time how good! I want to come and thank you for it with a thousand kisses. You cannot know, illustrious friend, how much pride and joy I derive from being thus praised by genius. For you to experience this emotion you would have to write an article on one of your own works, which would be impossible.
>
> As for me, whatever the future may hold in store, I am satisfied now; my name is sealed under yours. Ensconced in your article, my name is like one of those ephemera preserved into eternity in pearls gilt with amber. What can

I fear now? Am I not attached to the column of your glory by the *iron-knot?*

This last was the pun Hugo had derived from Nodier's name by translating it into Spanish: *nodo de hierro,* and which he used later as the password among his supporters during the famous *bataille d'Hernani.*

Nodier's warm appraisal of Hugo when he was only twenty-four goes deeper than reading into his future, as Brandès mentioned earlier in reference to *Han d'Islande.* It is rather an appreciation of his own past, an acknowledgment that Hugo was realizing all the hopes and ambitions that he, Nodier, had wanted to see fulfilled in French poetry. His share in Hugo's success was more than just a vicarious partnership, it was that of an older brother observing with satisfaction the implementation of his teaching by a younger brother; *adducite mihi psaltem,* the poet had finally arrived. All his life Nodier had been seeking a kindred spirit who would help him to find himself, to realize his full potential. Lacking that, he hoped to be loved by a great man whom he would accompany into posterity, like La Boétie, Montaigne. In his *Souvenirs de jeunesse,* Nodier claimed that his hopes had been surpassed, since "Chateaubriand has called me his pupil, and Hugo, his brother."[18] As a boy, he worshipped Oudet, whom he made leader of the Philadelphes; as a man, he admired Hugo, whom he made leader of the romantic movement. Not being a leader himself, Nodier became a kingmaker. "Nodier had a genius for recognizing talent in the arts in very young men (Hugo, Dumas, Musset, etc.) and encouraging it," wrote Delacroix in 1830, but the great painter did not guess the deepseated need that lay behind Nodier's genius for recognizing talent; after the break with Hugo, Nodier was still looking for the great man he could accompany into posterity.

Though antiromanticist attacks had lost some of their violence in 1826 and the *Mercure du Dix-Neuvième Siècle* had rallied solidly to the side of the new school, the movement had reached a sort of impasse and even the well-disposed *Globe* ruefully complained that no romantic writer of the stature of Byron, Schiller, or Goethe had appeared in France. Hugo, Vigny, and Lamartine had given only a promise of great things to come, and then had begun repeating themselves.[19] Authors with any pretension to national significance in France had always written for the stage. Since Corneille, Racine, and Voltaire had called attention to their artistic excellence by a series of successes in the theater, romanticists sensed that to capture the national imagination a resounding triumph of a romantic play would spell the victory of their revolution in literature in a most striking manner. But how were they to approach the boards of the *Comédie Française* whose direction was anything but friendly toward them? Of course, there were other theaters, but these did not carry the prestige of *the* Théâtre Français.

A thoroughly unforeseen event, brought about largely through the efforts of Charles Nodier, opened wide the doors of the traditionbound theater to the romantic cohort; this was the appointment of Baron Taylor, whose title dated from the coronation of Charles X, as "commissaire royal auprès du Théâtre Français" on July 9, 1825. In the language of those days it meant that Baron Taylor was to assume direction of the royal theater. The romantic camp had succeeded in placing a friend and sympathizer at the head of an impregnable classic fortress. An admirer of Nodier and an habitué of the Arsenal, Taylor had met there all the romantic coterie with whose enthusiasms and platforms he had become familiar and to a generous degree had made his own. If Nodier had done nothing else on behalf of the romantic movement in France, his urging Taylor's appointment among powerful friends in the Pavillon Marsan should have earned its undying gratitude.

Almost immediately young romantic hopefuls set about writing plays. Victor Hugo, busy with *Cromwell*, was in the forefront. Of all the subjects open to romantic dramatists, the career of the Puritan dictator seemed to appeal most. Balzac's year of trial to prove to his family that he was a writer was spent under penurious circumstances in which he underwent untold deprivations of nourishment and comfort to compose an unsuccessful play about Oliver Cromwell. One of Mérimée's earliest, and unsuccessful, attempts at playwriting also concerned Cromwell. If, as Ludovic Vitet had said so succinctly in the pages of the *Globe*, romanticism was nothing more nor less than Protestantism in literature, then it was appropriate that the romantic revolution should achieve recognition by dramatizing the life and deeds of this Protestant rebel. That of all these efforts nothing more should have survived than Hugo's famous *Préface* as the romantic manifesto par excellence is an irony.

Early in 1827 Sainte-Beuve had written a masterful critique of *Odes et ballades* for the *Globe*. Author and critic exchanged visits and verses and were soon fast friends. Hugo was intrigued by Sainte-Beuve's liberal ideas and this new orientation spelled the end of his allegiance to the romantic royalism of the Bonnes Lettres society. It also meant that political preoccupations were to give way to literary ones. The romantic movement, divested of its anachronistic baggage of political loyalty to the crown, was ready to move out confidently under the leadership of its new master, Victor Hugo. In February Hugo invited Sainte-Beuve to a reading of selections from *Cromwell* at his father-in-law's house in the Rue du Cherche-Midi. This reading, which included the first four acts of the play, was considered a great success by the young romanticists grouped around their new leader. In the same month, Hugo made public his *Ode à la colonne*, a slap at the reigning ministry for the rebuff Napoleon's old marshals suffered at the Viennese ambassador's reception. If Nodier was not alerted by this signal of the defection of his protégé, he must have taken umbrage when Hugo spirited the enthusiastic audience away from the Arsenal to hear the reading of the fifth act of *Cromwell* at his home, March 12, 1827. The reason for this move was that Hugo wanted only the purest of the pure, only the most sanguine of his followers to hear him reading his play. The Arsenal was a common meeting ground where classicists and romanticists learned to respect each other. This atmosphere was not charged with enough electricity to suit Hugo's dynamic needs. René Bray says that Nodier was distressed by the violence exhibited by the newly formed Cénacle. "His intelligence was too open to accept the exclusiveness necessary to the foundation of a school. His friendliness lost its influence on men who were being increasingly suborned by boldness."[20] On the same page, however, he says that Nodier could have been the leader of the romantic movement; but the very elements outlined above, his easygoing amiability, his horror of violence, and his aversion to narrowness, precluded that possibility.

Two actions are indicative of Nodier's pique with Hugo at this time and have hitherto gone unnoticed by students of Nodier-Hugo relations. The first was the announcement in a letter of March 18, 1827, to Weiss that he had resumed work on the novel *Lacuzon;* this was symbolical, in view of the fact that Nodier never completed the novel. He seemed to be saying that he had given up all hope of collaborating with the defector Hugo. The second was the publication of his *Poésies.* Perhaps even more meaningful than the resumption of the unfinished novel, this thin volume represented Nodier's entire poetical output, some of it going back to his earliest literary efforts. Steeped in the *Fables* of La Fontaine and the witty poetry of Parny, there was little here that could be termed romantic. Why did Nodier wait until June, 1827, to publish these poems? He obviously did not wish to compete with Lamartine and Hugo; this would have had the effect of one who, knowing three or four words of a foreign language, suddenly wishes to appear fluent in it. Rather, since these poems represented the hopes and dreams of his youth, love, and friendship, probably he wished to restate a literary ideal, however poorly realized in his verse, to bequeath a poetical testament of protest to those who would assume all the credit for launching the new school.

Another fortuitous event of the year 1827 was to help prepare the ground for a favorable reception of a romantic drama by the French public. This was the arrival at the Odéon, on September 6, of the Abbot-Kemble troupe with its repertory of English plays. Remembering the unfortunate experience of the Penley players five years earlier, Abbot, the director of the latest arrivals, had booklets printed with the original text and a suitable French translation facing each other, so that the French could follow the progress of the drama more intelligently. The first performance, Sheridan's *The Rivals* teamed with Allingham's *Fortune's Frolic*, was a great success. Five days later, *Hamlet*, with Kemble in the title role, and on September 15, *Romeo and Juliet*, with Harriet Smithson, completely captivated the French audience. On October 4, the troupe moved to the Théâtre Italien for a performance of Rowe's *Jane Shore*, which was received with bravos. December 10 was to have been their farewell performance, but public clamor kept them in France, moving from theater to theater until July 21, 1828. It is difficult today to stress sufficiently what a momentous share the arrival of these English players had in the succeeding annals of romanticism in France. Not only did their performances pave the way for another kind of theater than the one consecrated by time and ferociously defended by classicists in France, but they also provided a spur to the romantic poets, painters, and musicians in the audience—and there were many of them—who were especially enthralled by the magnitude of Shakespeare's genius. Out of this first brush with the actual, live Shakespeare an imposing bibliography of poems, plays, articles, paintings, and musical compositions was to result.

Perhaps not the least of these in momentary impact was Nodier's article for the *Mercure du Dix-Neuvième Siècle* entitled "Sur le théâtre anglais à Paris." It was with a sense of great satisfaction that he hailed the successful tour as an event bound to have important repercussions on both English and French literature. Before their arrival, he continued— setting aside the well-intentioned but imperfect translations of Ducis—*Hamlet* and *Othello* were known to us only through the cynical derision of Voltaire, who mocked everything, "like the damned spirit of Faust." We had no conception of the vast universe that is Shakespeare's theater before our eyes were opened by these English actors. Thanks to them, the French have finally conquered Shakespeare, an event of the highest import to France. Nodier praised the acting of Charles Kemble, Abbot, Chippendale, Bennet, Miss Foote; but especially "the natural acting, so true, the touching sensitivity and passionate energy of Miss Smithson." With characteristic thoughtfulness, he even praised the attitude of the audience, attentive throughout to a foreign language.[21]

If the French could be receptive to plays in a foreign tongue, then they were ready for plays in French based on foreign models. Between the arrival of the English troupe and December, 1827, Hugo composed his epoch-making *Préface de Cromwell*. The heavy debt this romantic manifesto owed to Nodier both in spirit and content is discussed in Miss Schenck's excellent thesis entitled *La part de Charles Nodier dans le formation des idées romantiques de Victor Hugo jusqu'à la préface de Cromwell*. We need only add, as Jensen has pointed out, that some of the ideas of the *Préface* were already presented in the 1826 preface to the *Odes et ballades*.[22] So this was no impulsive outburst, but a consistent program that had been formulated in the shadow of the Arsenal for two years.

If Nodier was present at the readings of *Cromwell*, as his daughter claims they were in her *Episodes et souvenirs de la vie de Charles Nodier*, he did not join in the general acclamation of the play. Or again, we may attribute his apathy to poor health. The illness that had plagued Charles since the preceding summer came to a crisis in those months of February and March, 1827. In a letter of this latter month to Weiss we learn that he had been unable to eat meat, vegetables, or bread without vomiting; the eruption of a veritable "volcano of sulphurous bile" remedied that condition.[23] But the attack left him weak and emaciated, so that for weeks he hardly had enough strength to leave his bed.

Another striking proof of Nodier's lack of enthusiasm for *Cromwell* is the fact that, since *Han d'Islande*, Charles had greeted every new work of Hugo with a published appreciation, but in this instance, even after the publication of *Cromwell*, Nodier remained strangely silent. We do have Hugo's letter to his friend Victor Pavie thanking him for his glowing article on *Cromwell*, which he has already shown to David d'Angers, Sainte-Beuve, and Paul Foucher, and promised to bring to the attention of Charles Nodier. Whether or not Hugo carried out his promise, he recorded the ecstatic response of approval Pavie's first article on *Cromwell* had elicited from the abovenamed gentlemen:[24] of Nodier's reaction, not a word. It would seem, then, that the cooling of relations between Hugo and Nodier was begun by the latter.

On June 28, 1827, Hugo sent Sainte-Beuve to Nodier with a note of introduction. Sainte-Beuve had been collecting material for his critical volume, *Le Tableau historique et critique de la poésie française et du théâtre français au XVIe siècle*. When Hugo became aware of Sainte-Beuve's interest in the poets of the *Pléiade*, remembering Nodier's edition of *La Satire Ménippée* and of his enthusiasm for Ronsard, he suggested Nodier as the man of letters in Paris who was probably most knowledgeable on this subject. "It is a task," Hugo's note ran, "which requires a high order of talent and a profound science. He has the talent; you can open up for him new sources of knowledge."[25] This cannot be interpreted as anything less than a friendly note. As it turned out, Nodier helped Sainte-Beuve materially: the *Tableau*, begun as a classical study, became a retrospective apology for romanticism, a sort of second manifesto.

But the fact that Hugo went on treating Nodier in a friendly fashion after the slight offered his mentor in the celebrated *Préface de Cromwell*, in which he mentioned his name only twice—and then as if by chance to identify a couple of quotations from Nodier he wished to acknowledge—does not excuse him from the charge of ruthlessly brushing the older man aside in assuming leadership of the romantic movement. Nodier felt keenly too Hugo's total lack of consideration in sweeping the young audience away from the Arsenal to set up the *Cénacle de Joseph Delorme*. The pseudonym of the poet Sainte-Beuve was used as the banner of Hugo's new allegiance, a clear indication to Nodier that Hugo, in changing the focal point of romanticism from the Arsenal to Rue Notre-Dame des Champs, wished to symbolize the transfer of its tutelage from Nodier to Sainte-Beuve. With Hugo as its major poet and Sainte-Beuve as its chief critic, the new school faced the future without cloying alliances and unhampered by embarrassing obligations to forerunners and pioneers, whom they sought to renounce or at least set aside. How else was Nodier to interpret Hugo's assertion, near the end of the *Préface de Cromwell?* "We are approaching the moment when we may see a new criticism prevail, based on a broad, solid, and deep foundation." This "strong, frank, learned" criticism would displace all criticism that had come before the *Préface*, including, of course, Nodier's. Not content with having sloughed off Nodier as guide and tutor, Hugo had to cut away the very ground on which he stood. Is it any wonder that Nodier was hurt, retreated into silence and sulked? And that, when he broke his silence, he occasionally grumbled and discreetly sniped at Hugo's taking the romantic movement entirely to himself?

In June, still convalescing from the effects of his illness, Charles decided to take his family for a vacation in Italy. Instead, we find him in Catalonia in July. This was the second of his projected trips to Italy that aborted, the first brought to an end for lack of funds at Geneva, this one for reasons of health; he doubtless thought of the rigors of crossing the Alps in his weakened condition. Then, too, the presence of Baron Taylor on this excursion would imply they were collecting material for the section on Languedoc for the interminable *Voyages pittoresques.* After a three-day visit to Barcelona cut short by the heat (the temperature was 34 degrees Reaumur or about 85 degrees Fahrenheit), the Nodiers retreated to the coolness of their apartments in the Arsenal, now rather quiet.

That Nodier was chagrined at the desertion of the young romanticists in that season of 1827-28 may be seen in a letter to Weiss of February 13, 1828, in which he bitterly reports that "Victor Hugo no longer appears in the very limited circle in which we live."[26] But if he harbored any illusions as to Hugo's estrangement, if he still had any doubts concerning the poet's increasing megalomania, they were quickly dispelled when he saw his name disappear from the dedication to "La bande noire" in the fourth edition of Hugo's *Odes* which was published in August, 1828. This gratuitous act of discourtesy proved beyond all doubt that Hugo was determined to eradicate systematically from his works all references which would tend to betray the new school's indebtedness to any previous writers, so that romanticism in France would seem to stem exclusively from him.

In September Weiss appeared for his annual visit to Paris and stayed almost two months. In all that time he did not see Hugo at the Arsenal and when he returned to Besançon he wrote his friend a letter which contains a very revealing paragraph concerning Nodier's relations with Victor Hugo at this time. "You should make my excuses to Victor Hugo. If I did not see him on my last trip, you are partially to blame. Every time I mentioned that I wanted to go to see him you would say: 'We'll go another time, Victor is coming Sunday.' Thus weeks and months passed waiting for him to come to the Arsenal and I left without seeing him."[27] A clearer documentation of Nodier's pique with Hugo would be hard to find. We can picture in it Weiss' bewilderment at Nodier's conduct toward Hugo, whom he formerly showed off with pride as his dearest protégé. And now this sudden aloofness, an unwillingness to follow the romantic crowd that was beating a path to Hugo's house in the Rue Notre-Dame des Champs and away from the headquarters of romanticism Nodier had established at the Arsenal.

Perhaps not so much to "revindicate his own," as Schenck and Pingaud suggested, but to clarify his position, Nodier made some covert protests to the course the new school was following under Victor Hugo. His rambling essay entitled "Quelques observations pour servir à l'histoire de la nouvelle école littéraire," intended as a preface to a new edition of *Les Dernières Aventures du jeune d'Olban*, was published separately in the *Revue de Paris* for October, 1829. In this article Charles traced the development of romanticism from German and English sources, stressing its heavy debt to *Werther*.

Meanwhile other romanticists and sympathizers of the new school were resenting the Hugo–Sainte-Beuve takeover. On April 30, 1829, J. B. A. Soulié, editor of the *Quotidienne* and Nodier's associate at the Arsenal since the preceding year, in reviewing Nodier's *Examen critique des dictionnaires de la langue française*, draws attention to his friend's claim as founder of the romantic movement. "We will add without fearing contradiction that it was perhaps the first poetical works of Charles Nodier, containing as they did innovations little known until then, which opened the way for the young literary school whose triumphs are daily proclaimed in our newspapers." In October, Henri Latouche, a former adherent of the young movement, published a scathing article in the newly launched *Revue de Paris* entitled "La camaraderie littéraire." Without actually mentioning their names, Latouche accused the members of the romantic clique generally, and Hugo and Sainte-Beuve understood they were meant in particular, of patting each other on the back in their critical appraisals of romantic works. The mounting wave of disapproval was swelled by the colorful prose of another young journalist, Jules Janin, who concentrated his attacks on Victor Hugo.

Nodier chose this moment to give vent to the pent-up rancor of the past two years. The occasion was a projected edition of the poems of Byron and Moore translated into French by Amédée Pichot, Henrion, and Stendhal's correspondent, Louise Belloc, to which Nodier was asked to write a preface. Though the work did not appear until January, 1830, Charles inserted his preface in *La Quotidienne* for November 1, 1829, under the title, "Byron et Moore." Speaking of the pseudo-oriental poetry of Byron and Moore, Nodier attributed their appeal, as well as their success, to the Britishers' contact with the Orient, thanks to the Empire. "In truth, our orientalists," he continued, "if they have produced anything, have yet to write a poem in this vein which approaches the admirable compositions of those great geniuses." Hugo's *Les Orientales* of that year, the first three editions in January, February, and April, had received a mixed press, to say the least. Reviewers in the *Globe, La Revue Française,* and *Le Mercure du Dix-Neuvième Siècle* all thought it a step backward, or in the wrong direction. So it is understandable that the young poet was stung to write Nodier the following letter:

And you too, Charles!

I would give anything not to have read yesterday's *Quotidienne.* For it is one of life's most violent shocks to root out from the heart an old and deep-seated friendship.

It has been some time since I gave up looking for your support of my works. Yet I did not complain about that. But why did you continue to compromise yourself in public friendship with a man who brings to his friends only the contagion of hatred, calumny, and persecution? I noticed you were withdrawing from the melee and, loving you for yourself, I found that proper.

Little by little, from silence and indifference toward me, I saw you pass over to praise, enthusiasm, and acclaim of my enemies, even of the most ardent, bitter and odious ones. Nothing strange about that either, for after all, I realize that it is merely a personal matter that I should resent their attacks and I concede that my enemies may not lack wit, talent, and genius. I say all that is very understandable, far be it from me to complain about it for an instant. I didn't love you less and (you would be in error not to believe it, Charles) from the bottom of my heart.

I had not foreseen, however, and from this ignorance stemmed my perfect tranquillity on the matter, that it was a natural transition, perhaps irresistible for you, to join the field against me. So there you are with them too; last night's attack was, I admit, veiled, obscure, ambiguous; but it nonetheless cut me to the quick and, like an electric shock, alerted twenty other persons who came to commiserate with me.

And what a time you chose for that attack! When my enemies gathered from everywhere more numerous and more unrelenting than ever are busily spinning around me a web of hatred and calumny, you chose a moment which finds me alone pitted against two equally ferocious antagonists; the government, which is persecuting me [the authorities had just banned his play, *Marion Delorme*, because of alleged irreverence to Louis XIII] and that stubborn cabal which has posted itself in all the newspapers. Ah, Charles! In such a moment I thought I could at least count on your silence.

Have I done something to displease you? If I have, then why didn't you tell me about it?

I am not taking exception to your criticism, which is just, solid, and true. There is a great gap separating *Les Orientales* from Lord Byron; but Charles, weren't there enough enemies to say it at this time?

You will perhaps be astonished to find me so susceptible, but what can you expect? A friendship like mine for you is frank, cordial, deep-seated, and does not break without a cry of pain. Anyway, I am like that. I don't mind the dagger-thrusts of my enemies, but I feel deeply the pin-pricks of a friend.

When all is said and done, I don't hold this against you; tear up this letter and don't think any more about it. What you wanted to break is broken; I will always suffer from it, but what does it matter? If anyone mentions it to me again, I will defend you as I defended you yesterday. But believe me, this is a sad business for me, and for you too, Charles, for in your whole life you never lost a friend who was more tenderly and profoundly devoted to you.[28]

What did Nodier think of this jeremiad, with its guileless question, "Have I done something to displease you?" We have no direct response, but Nodier's presence at the preparations for the campaign that was to launch *Hernani*—it may be useful to recall that the password among the faithful supporters of the play was to be *hierro* (iron); earlier, Hugo, the Spanish scholar, had jokingly suggested that Nodier derived his name from *nodo de hierro*, the iron-knot—the frequent *consultations à trois* at the Arsenal concerning that same play involving Hugo, Taylor, and Nodier as the principal strategy board, and finally, his appearance at the première of *Hernani* only eight days after Marie's wedding, serve to convince us that he had decided to adopt Hugo's cavalier attitude toward slights and differences and act as though he had never received the letter. So there was no open break and Nodier, considering the rebuff to his pride as having been amply repaid, could let bygones be bygones. The two men continued to visit each other and seemed on the best of terms, but the perfect entente had been destroyed and the hostility, though driven inward, was nonetheless ever seething between them thereafter. Ten years after Nodier's death Hugo was to recall with bitterness this thrust of his former friend in the midst of composing *Les Contemplations* and he could not resist rhyming this parting shot:

"Horreur! et vous voilà poussant des cris d'hyène,
A travers les barreaux de la Quotidienne!"

an undeserved and venomous reproof, if it was aimed at Charles Nodier; for of all the quirks in his peculiar makeup, not one of them could have been likened to the ways of the hyena.

On Friday, February 26, the press was unanimous in its acclaim of *Hernani*. But neither Nodier nor Sainte-Beuve was responsible for any of the rave notices it received. It is true that Nodier was busy making a serious readjustment in his life necessitated by the marriage of his daughter. Sainte-Beuve was on the spot when, after the *première*, Charles Magnin was writing his review of *Hernani* for the *Globe*. Sainte-Beuve tells us himself that, in the general anxiety prevailing among staff members as to what attitude the paper should take toward Hugo's drama, it was not he who resolved Magnin's hesitation by shouting, "Allons, Magnin, lâchez l'admirable!"[29]

Although, as Eggli has pointed out in his monumental *Schiller et le romantisme français*,[30] Hugo got more than one idea for *Hernani* out of a dramatized version of *Jean Sbogar* (off-stage crowd noises, during a love scene on stage between Antonia and Sbogar, indicative of a battle between bandits and regular troops), Nodier was not enthusiastic about the play. He confided this in a letter to Lamartine, January 11, 1830, in the midst of preparations for the *première*. After having invited the poet to Marie's wedding, he casts an anxious eye on the forthcoming battle for *Hernani*:

I doubt that you are taking much interest in our literature, which has never been more stationary, not to say retrograde. Your confrere Lemercier has just given his *Clovis*, which they say is of a piece with all the classical tragedies with which they have been plaguing us since Lemierre and company, and with like success. We're awaiting *Hernani*, which will certainly make more noise, but the cabal has already prepared its downfall in its vaudevilles and newspapers. It is a play, moreover, done entirely according to Hugo's system, in which, as usual, his theories are carried to the ultimate expression of boldness. My

friendship for him causes me to deplore the hazardous courage with which he risks his peace of mind and his happiness
in this chancy whirl of stormy publicity, which this time
threatens to take on the aspect of a minor civil war. Whatever his strength of character may be, I do not see how he
can avoid becoming embittered in this polemic in action,
wherein the hatred of the factions passes so easily from the
work to the man. Happy the poet who, like you, can enjoy
his creations without being obliged to make of them a war
chant. I tell you all this because it is one of the bitterest
preoccupations of my heart, which has never more than
now needed to confide in you. I would have told it to Victor,
if my serious friendship had the same sway over him as it
did ten years ago; but when one has formed a literary sect
at twenty-seven, it is rare that one can still listen to the
voice of reason. The enthusiasm of his young admirers must
produce on him the same effect as the songs of the sirens.
This is one of the sweetest fruits of glory. May the future
spare him its trials![31]

It is plain from the above that Nodier had begun to take
a neutral stand with respect to the belligerent young romanticists; he was still in favor of the revolution in letters he had
presided over for so many years, but he viewed with trepidation the course the new leader had taken. In the tone of his
remarks concerning the current state of his relations with
Hugo, we sense the regret and a little of the bitterness of one
who is being pushed aside. His attitude toward *Hernani* did
not suit its fiery author. Nodier did not like *Hernani*, nor,
generally speaking, Hugo's subsequent romantic dramas, because they did not realize his ideals of romantic aesthetics,
which he found much more tangibly attained in Lamartine's
Méditations and in Hugo's *Odes et ballades* on one hand, and
in the latter's novels on the other. And history has proved
Nodier right in his preferences; for it was not on the stage,
though that was the locus of its showiest manifestation, but
in lyrical poetry and in the novel that romanticism was to
reveal its most lasting and most fruitful contribution to French
letters.

When Hugo had achieved the notoriety of *Hernani* he was

Portrait by Garnier, about 1825, at the time
of his appointment to the Arsenal Library

Nodier in his fifties, head of the Arsenal Library, respected author and critic, and mainstay of the Bulletin du Bibliophile

one day short of his twenty-eighth birthday and the father of a growing family. On July 28, 1830, a fourth child, his second daughter, Adèle, was born, and this event Hugo joyfully announced in a note to his "cher Nodier." Was this a first step toward a reconciliation with the master of the Arsenal? As we have seen, Hugo took for granted all the praise heaped upon his works but never forgot a slight offered his vanity. In this case, however, as undisputed master of the romantic movement, he could afford to be generous to a man who had sponsored his earliest efforts and who posed no threat to his present literary eminence. Patching up his differences with Nodier cost him little, and Nodier was still an influential critic whose benevolent offices could aid him materially in his stormy career.

But if Nodier accepted this new *modus vivendi* he nonetheless clung tenaciously to his ideas. In an essay which appeared in the *Revue de Paris* for September, 1830, entitled "Des types en littérature," he mentioned Hugo as creator of the type *obi* and *anthropophagus*, namely the fantastic character *Han d'Islande*, which fell squarely into the tradition initiated by Nodier; he says nothing of Cromwell or Hernani as representing types; these Hugo found on his own. Two months later, in still another article for the *Revue de Paris*, "Du fantastique en littérature," Nodier went into greater detail in a study of the source of this particular aspect of romanticism in world literature. Again Hugo is mentioned favorably as the author of the psychological novel, *Le Dernier Jour d'un condamné*, and ten pages later he is grouped with the "great masters," Byron, Scott, and Lamartine, as an exponent of *la vie idéale* in contrast to eighteenth-century authors who pursued *la vie positive*. But Nodier is here concerned primarily with establishing the fantastic as the only new contribution of romanticism to the world of letters. He seems to take notice exclusively of the works which followed his stripe of romantic writing. Nodier firmly believed that romanticism was the progeny of Odin, an epithet he used to sum up the heritage of northern Christian literature. At this time he was writing souvenirs and short novels for the *Revue de Paris* in which he referred to himself as Maxime Odin.

A year after the July revolution, the more lenient and less

squeamish government of Louis Philippe lifted the ban on
Marion Delorme, which was performed on August 11, 1831,
at the Porte Saint-Martin Theater. On Sunday, September 5,
we find Hugo writing to Marie, now Madame Nodier-Mennessier, thanking her in advance for her father's proposed
article on *Marion* to appear in the recently founded newspaper, *Le Temps*.

> You overwhelm me, Madame, and Charles too. An article
> by Charles on *Marion* would be more than glory for me,
> it would be good luck. My poor comedy has been singularly
> flattered and gilt by the critics. I have great need of a hand
> like my friend's, your father's, to peel away some of that.
> It would be very nice of him if he would also inform
> *Le Temps* that he is going to do the article on *Marion*, the
> book, if there is to be one. I am ashamed to add this task
> to all the trouble he is already undertaking on my behalf;
> but his voice in *Le Temps*, as indeed everywhere else, must
> have more credit and authority than any other, especially
> mine.[32]

Nodier did write two articles for *Le Temps* on *Marion
Delorme*, October 31 and November 2. Laudatory in the
main of Hugo's dramatic procedures, Nodier cautioned the
dramatist against seeking novelty for its own sake. A closer
inspection revealed to Hugo that his former patron and champion was reading him a lesson on dramatic art. After a pref-
atory paragraph extolling Hugo the poet, Nodier turned the
remainder of the first article over to an examination of Hugo
the dramatist. He points out immediately that Hugo is trying
to introduce a new kind of theater to which the French audience is unaccustomed, but he hastens to add that it is not at
all certain that Hugo has hit upon the right form with his
first stroke. This will be decided only after a long process of
trial and error in which the author will explore the resources
of his art and the dramatic needs of the local spectator, for
it is only when this mutuality of understanding and interest is
built up that the dramatist can lead his audience and impose
his particular form of the art upon them. Nodier then passes
on to a consideration of the aesthetics of the dramatic art as

opposed to those of the lyrical poem; in the latter, an ejacula-
tion of the inspiration of genius from his experience and sensation may be a sufficient basis for creation; it is all his entirely personal view of the world. But the needs of drama are
something else again. The play is a living and speaking epic
in which the poet must remain invisible, like God behind his
creation. (Could Hugo fail to understand that this was a
direct slap at his *Préface de Cromwell* in which he maintained
that the dramatist must be *visible?*)

Drama is not the spontaneous song of enthusiasm by the
genius who fulfills his mission; it is rather, asserts Nodier,
the faithful representation of a domestic action developed by
the dramatis personae involved in that action and its style
must be adapted to the various personages according to their
age, condition, experience, and motivating passions. This function of the art was admirably respected by Shakespeare, Calderón, and Molière (*read* "but apparently not by Hugo,"
though Nodier does not say that). The function is one the
French have never respected, at least not in the tragedy. Once
the dramatic poet forgets the basic law of the diversity of
his characters and shows himself, the illusion is lost. As for
style in dramatic verse, Hugo is attempting to break the
stranglehold that the twelve syllable Alexandrine line with
its caesura after six and its slight pause at the hemistich has
exercised over the French drama for two centuries. Who
would say that this innovation was not long overdue? Who is
not bored by the monotonous fall of the voice after each
couplet, read them as you will? As to the run-on line, if the
pseudoclassicists of the nineteenth century took the trouble
to read the real classics of antiquity instead of the neoclassicists of the seventeenth century, they would see that Horace
did not shrink from this so-called fault; indeed, he even di-
vides words syllabically at the end of a line, so that half or
part, sometimes one letter, of the word appears in one verse
and the remainder in the next.

Nodier continues flaying the prosody of the French neo-
classic *tragédie* in the second article on *Marion Delorme*, but
by and large this part of his critique was intended as a guide
to the young dramatist. With the precipitance of youth, Hugo

was guilty of being "more in a hurry to strike hard than careful to strike justly." There follows a three-paragraph manual of do's and don'ts for the dramatic author, in which Nodier cautions Hugo against seeking novelty for its own sake, against flying in the face of his audience and riding roughshod over their needs. He ends by warning Hugo about his abuse of metaphors, "which only amplify the thought without lending it power" (a pivotal point of romanticism, this horror of metaphoric saws, which Nodier had been preaching for more than twenty years, beginning with his *Dictionnaire des onomatopées*) and to be wary of his tendency to show off his vast erudition. Although the beginning and the end of these two articles were highly complimentary, the matter in between was hardly meant to give Hugo comfort; their lessons, however, could have been put to use by a less egocentric dramatist.

In December Charles gave a magnificent critique of Hugo's latest volume of poetry, *Les Feuilles d'automne,* in the *Revue de Paris*. After successfully paring away the political pretensions from the poetry in this collection, the critic artfully congratulates Hugo on his return from the pseudo-Orient to his natural habitat.

And what has Victor Hugo accomplished by opening up this new mine of poetry which he exhausts as he passes through it? You will no longer see him sleeping in the shelter of the Pasha's tent, wandering with the desert Klephte along the mountainsides, smoking with the dust and blood of battle among the flying squadrons, or stirring with a bold hand the bubbling bronze of La Colonne. You will see him now in the heart of a happy family, surrounded by artists and poets encircling him like a richly decorated belt, abandoning himself, like us, to the simple pursuits of a simple soul. Perhaps you had been waiting for him to return there from the strange worlds he was visiting—so had we.

And Nodier ends this reconciliation speech in good form, styling himself the patron and herald of Hugo and Lamartine.

The Hugos' next move, to 6 Place Royale, in October, 1832, brought them within easy walking distance of the Arsenal and Victor renewed his Sunday night visits, as we learn from a letter he sent Sainte-Beuve on November 13: "I would be very happy to see you one of these Sunday nights chez Nodier."[33] The *Witness* tells us that Hugo moved to the Place Royale to be near Nodier,[34] an unmistakable sign that the reconciliation was complete on both sides. From this point very little seems to have disturbed relations between these two henceforth diametrically opposed romanticists. Hugo continued with the series of romantic dramas that was to end only with the next decade. Nodier dissented less and less with his former disciple, but he never abandoned the stand he had assumed since *Hernani*. He continued to praise Hugo's poetry —*Les Chants du crépuscule* drew from him an admiring letter, November 12, 1835[35]—and to snipe at the dramas. As late as 1841, in his preface to the collected plays of his dear friend Pixerécourt, we find him classing the tragedies and dramas of the new school as "nothing more than melodramas dressed in the artificial pomp of lyricism." This practice of praising him by name and damning him by implication was to be the trademark of Nodier's attitude toward Hugo to the end of his life.

After many failures Nodier was finally elected to the French Academy, October 24, 1833. Two days later, Hugo, who was rehearsing *Marie Tudor* at the Porte Saint-Martin Theater, sent him a congratulatory note, "C'est une gloire qui entre à l'Académie, chose rare! Aussi voilà que nous applaudissons l'Académie, chose non moins rare!" But this did not prevent Nodier from carrying the fight to the floor of the Academy when he delivered his reception speech the following January. Departing from the conventional form of these harangues, which usually include the recipient's thanks followed by a lengthy eulogy of his predecessor, Charles used the first part of his speech to call to his side all present members who had aided or encouraged him.

Nodier used the brief eulogy of his predecessor, the dramatist Laya, as a subtle transition to the main subject of his oration, his fostering of a type of romanticism based on two sources of inspiration: the long-neglected literature of the Middle Ages in France and contemporary literature abroad. This was Nodier's specific contribution to French romanticism and for this he was being honored by membership in the Academy.

He disowned all other forms of romanticism and in a none too veiled allusion slapped at the "erring genius" who must be set right, recalling that Icarus had been punished for approaching too close to the sun. Not wishing to mar the happiness of his day of triumph, Charles mused aloud that it was an admirable thing to have gone near the sun and that, after all, the sea into which Icarus fell still bears his name. However, when Hugo came to announce his candidacy in 1836, Nodier refused his vote and read the younger man a lecture on his play, *Lucrèce Borgia*, which had ruffled his religious sensibilities—in 1833! How could Nodier have nursed this grievance against Hugo for three years without saying anything about it at the time? Especially was this argument weak in view of Charles' warm appraisal of *Les Chants du crépuscule* of 1835. The real reason for Nodier's refusal lay in the fact that he had already promised his vote to Dupaty, who was supported by the powerful liberal Jouy, to whose influence Charles owed his own election. However, at the end of 1836 and again in 1840, Nodier voted for Hugo.

Meanwhile, on the eve of his departure for Germany, August 29, 1840, Hugo informed his wife that he had invited Madame Mennessier, Nodier's daughter, to visit her in his absence. Victor had always been on the best of terms with Marie despite his differences with her father; nevertheless, we are impressed with his solicitousness on her behalf in the midst of his wanderings up and down the Rhine. From Mainz on October 1 he wrote to inquire of Adèle whether she had received Marie's visit; then he continued with this insistent appeal: "Have you written to her at least? Have you invited her? Do not forget, my dear, to make a friendly gesture in that direction; after all, these are friends of seventeen years standing!"[36] Was Hugo worrying about Nodier's support in his fourth attempt to enter the Academy, and was he merely using Adèle's hospitality as a skillful diplomatic move to insure Nodier's good wishes? In any event, though the *Witness* says nothing of this, we know that it was thanks to Nodier's maneuvers that Victor Hugo was elected on his fifth try, January 7, 1841.[37]

So they were brothers-in-arms again. Hugo, Nodier, and

Lamartine formed the nucleus of a growing bulwark of romanticism in the heart of the Academy. Their friendly relations continued without interruption until Charles' death in 1844; Victor was one of the pallbearers at his funeral. At Marie's request, he agreed to complete the preface Charles had been writing for his *Journal de l'expédition des portes de fer,* an account of the Duke d'Orléans' Algerian campaign Charles had been commissioned to write using the Duke's diary.

Romanticists had hoped Vigny would succeed Nodier in the Academy. Instead, Mérimée was elected to his seat. When the incumbent uttered some disparaging innuendos anent his predecessor's credibility, Victor Hugo set the record straight the following year in his *Réponse à Sainte-Beuve,* February 27, 1845. In welcoming Sainte-Beuve among the immortals, Victor Hugo said:

> By your researches into the language, by the suppleness and variety of your mind, by the vivacity of your ideas always fine and often fecund, by this mixture of learning and imagination which makes it impossible for the poet in you to disappear completely behind the critic and the critic to rid himself entirely of the poet, by these qualities you recall to the Academy one of its dearest and most regretted members, that good and charming Nodier, who was so superior and yet so gentle. You resemble him as much by the ingenious side of your talent as he resembled other great men by the carefree side of his. Nodier reminded us of La Fontaine; you remind us of Nodier.[38]

It was just and proper that Hugo should tartly mingle Nodier and Sainte-Beuve in the same breath, for the great critic, after having naively accepted everything Nodier told him at face value, had belatedly taxed Nodier with the "gift of inexactness." This *amende honorable* delivered before the distinguished assembly delighted Marie. When Alphonse de Cailleux, Nodier's friend, thanked him for it, Hugo answered with the following lines: "I took what was in my heart and I said it. You were as happy to hear it as I was to say it. The fact is, dear friend, that between us there is a secret bond of brotherhood; we love each other in Nodier."[39] That made up, to a degree, for some of the less noble phases of Hugo's conduct toward Nodier. The end of their association was in the spirit of the lines Hugo had penned during the early days of their friendship. At the bottom of a page on which Nodier had written the poem, *Action de grâce d'un classique,* Hugo wrote: "We owe these pretty verses to a man who occupied at the same time a high rank among our most eminent writers, our most courageous royalists, our wisest savants, our most enlightened critics, and our most inspired poets."[40] Perhaps it is best to remember, after all, only the good that great men say of each other.

VI

From the Arsenal to the Academy

I consented to march at the head of this brilliant general staff, not to help it, but to lead it.

NODIER, Introduction to *Les Environs de Paris*

VI

From the Arsenal to
the Academy

"Don't look forward to Nodier's promised visit to Franche-Comté next spring," Weiss wrote to his friend Pallu on February 19, 1823. "He says no more about it and I happen to know he's busy with an important work which will not permit him to leave Paris for some time. He has undertaken to publish the acceptance speeches of the members of the French Academy with biographical notices on all the writers who have composed that illustrious company. This collection should comprise twelve to fifteen volumes in octavo and could be quite interesting." What became of this project? Like so many others, Nodier allowed it to perish before it ever left the planning stage; but Weiss' note is important because it contains the first written hint of Nodier's interest in the French Academy, awakened by Count Pastoret the year before.

June 25, 1824, Charles made his first formal bid to enter the Academy in a letter addressed to its *secrétaire perpétuel*. In announcing his candidacy for the seats left vacant by the deaths of Aignan and Bausset, he was careful to minimize his participation in the romantic movement and put forward as his only titles to consideration his *Dictionnaire des onomatopées*, the edition of La Fontaine's *Fables* with his commentary, the first two volumes of the *Voyages pittoresques*, literary articles in "the most important journals" and his new *Dictionnaire de la langue française;* furthermore, he claimed he had "immense amounts of material on this language in particular and on all branches of philology." He took the liberty of pointing out in a final paragraph that the Academy had been founded to represent *toutes les hautes études littéraires* and that the seat of Vaugelas, Boindin, d'Olivet, etc., should not be left vacant in an association which had as its principal mandate "the preservation of rules and the discussion of the difficulties of the language." This is the only seat, he concluded,

191

to which he could lay any claim. Having failed to obtain either seat (one went to Alexandre Soumet, the other to the archbishop of Paris, Monseigneur Quélen) Charles wrote again on September 8, 1824, upon the death of Lacretelle, a short note supporting his application and urging the same titles as before plus the *Questions de littérature légale* and "a great number of unpublished works on philology known only to savants, especially an *Histoire philosophique des mots et de l'écriture,* of which the Academy has already received a favorable account."[1]

Needless to say, this attempt failed like the other. His compatriot and former teacher Droz was elected, but his claim to a seat in the Academy on the basis of his published and unpublished works on the language is revealing. It shows that he thought this was his most serious vein for consideration to membership in a law-making body whose authority did not extend beyond the French language at the time of its establishment. He even made himself eight years younger than he was when he published his *Dictionnaire des onomatopées,* which he brought out at the age of twenty-eight, and not at twenty as he had stated in his first letter, no doubt to convince the academicians that his preoccupation with language was his earliest and most enduring concern. (But Nodier's good genius was guiding him well, for it was as grammarian and lexicographer that his name was added to the Academy rolls nine years later.)

Stung by the Academy's refusal, Nodier swore he would never again enter the lists as a candidate, and this in a letter to an academician, probably Auger, that irreconcilable enemy of romanticism, dated November 7, 1825. Without going too deeply into the background of the letter—Baron Taylor had reported that the academician had felt slighted in some verses Charles had written in an album belonging to Adèle Hugo, and Nodier thought he should write to explain that the verses were not evilly meant—we may state that no one could have been more emphatic in his renunciation:

> You do not accuse me of lying, but you do not know that I am incapable of conniving and you imagine that this appeal for your esteem which I need covers a secret appeal for your

favor I will never use. The future will show whether this disclaimer is seriously meant. A covert plan set in motion by five or six over-zealous friends and which I brought to a halt an hour later, before the first visit [candidates for a seat in the Academy have to visit each member to solicit his support] caused my name to reach the file of aspirants to a seat in the Academy. It will *never* be found there again. *I give you my word of honor,* mon cher maître, that I will never invoke your support as a writer.[2]

From now on, each defeat will be met with like protestations of "never again." Yet Charles stood for the Academy in 1826 and was so disgusted with not having been chosen that he suggested to Hugo the formation of a new Academy.

What were his main claims to the Academy in 1826? He felt he was more deserving than most current members and he was a royalist. Alexandre Guiraud, his competitor, had come round to ask Nodier to desist from his candidacy, but had not found him at home. In a letter written in April, 1826, Charles begged Victor Hugo to run a similar errand *chez* Guiraud and listed his reasons for refusing to withdraw: he was older than Guiraud, who was 38; there were already too many poets in the Academy; Guiraud was healthy, he was ill.[3] It must be admitted that among the reasons advanced by Nodier none was compelling enough to impose his election; Charles must have been very naive to think that they constituted a serious platform. Guiraud was elected.

In his disappointment Charles was learning; he realized that getting into the Academy would be, for him at least, no easy matter. Applying for a seat that seemed tailormade for him was simply not enough. He knew of the factions that ran the Academy and that the powerful liberal party led by his onetime friend, Etienne Jouy, was inimical to him. Charles had more or less lost contact with Jouy since their happy relationship at Amiens and when they did meet they quarreled because Jouy looked askance at Nodier's royalist attachments after the restoration. As a diehard classicist he was put even more on his guard by Nodier's recent blandishments in favor of romanticism. So wooing Jouy back to a friendly attitude, a *sine qua non* of Nodier's campaign, became logically his first objective. Before entering the lists again in 1826, Charles wrote an exploratory letter to Jouy asking his support. The "hermit of the Chaussée d'Antin" and the collaborator, with Hippolyte Bis, on the libretto for Rossini's *Guillaume Tell*, must have responded rather tartly, listing his objections to Nodier's candidacy, for we find echoes of it in Nodier's letter to Jouy dated May 11:

My dear Jouy,

I have waited to answer your letter for the hour of *your decision,* because the event has already answered the first, the most pressing of your reproaches, the one which allied my pretensions to an intrigue and which I would not have understood if I hadn't thought that twelve years can efface a character as well as a face. I persist in believing that there are no intrigues in the Academy; but most of all I no longer fear that you will suspect me of taking advantage of any that might exist there. The friends who would have voted for me, if I had not withdrawn my name from competition and I had not imposed upon myself the decision never to try again, are such that you would never refuse to vote with them; but I will not place you in this predicament.

The reproof that hurt me most, *the one that vibrated on my heart like a death-dealing arrow,* was that I abandoned you after the Hundred Days, I who have remained the faithful friend of Mellinet, of Fayolle, of Montarlot and who have more than once left the gates of their jails in tears.

God is my witness that I expect nothing from you, Jouy, not even your good will, but I have done nothing to lose your esteem. I have been exalted in my sentiments and I admit this is unfortunately a defect in my character; but I cannot recall a single incident in which I abandoned my affections in favor of my opinions. There is in my life more passion than judgment; but I hope you will find in it neither egoism nor ingratitude. It would be awkward, not to say unfortunate, that one who has striven only to be *loved* should have unwittingly betrayed the *friends* he *loved* best. If I had put forth in my behalf, as so many others have done, titles of consideration which are considered important only by those who lay store by such things, you would know that I wrote in favor of *all exiles* a pamphlet which caused me to lose favor and fortune under the very ministry of M. Descazes; but what can men who judge me only by the efforts I have made to be known really know of me?

We separated, my dear Jouy, for other reasons; you are much in society, I keep to myself; you are *absolute,* I am timid; you are in the first rank of literature and society and I desire to remain obscure and forgotten. At the time *we separated* I often avoided you for your own good. At opposite poles, upon what and why should we engage in a thousand quarrels? We have had only one and it has led to an explanation.

If this explanation were to bring you back to me now that you can no longer suspect me of ulterior motives, I will have earned more than the hope of becoming your worthy neophyte; I would prefer a chair at Malherbe's to a seat in the Academy.

Yours always,
Charles Nodier[4]

We can well believe that this eloquent appeal somewhat pacified Jouy's animosity toward Nodier; but five more years were to pass before he capitulated and consented to support Charles in his candidacy.

On his part, Charles demonstrated in a letter to Weiss the following year, March 18, that he was not as naive as he would have his correspondents in the Academy believe: he was aware that august body was really shot through with intrigue and *l'esprit de coterie.* He had an academician's word that the main factions were so busy maneuvering for power that their very last concern in weighing the respective merits of an applicant was his talent. Charles related that the two most influential cliques sought to add members who would enable them to keep the upper hand, because an academic majority represented in Parisian social circles a real power. In order to obtain the support of either major party, he continued, one would have to give up his soul in advance. What were his chances without their support? He would have the backing of the real *literati*, such as Chateaubriand, Auger, Droz, Villemain, Delavigne, Michaud, and Soumet, but these votes were too few to bring about his election and the defeat would harm his literary reputation. "Be persuaded therefore, that common sense keeps me away from these honors, which could add little to my literary stature, already greater than I ever wanted it to be."[5] So Charles abstained from attempting to join the thirty-nine immortals until he had prepared firmer ground under his feet.

Despite his disappointment at not being created a baron like Hugo, at the crowning of Charles X, and the humiliation he endured in collecting expenses incurred at that event, Charles was still faithful to the restored monarchy. It was not until 1828, in the Preface to his *Examen critique des dictionnaires de la langue française,* that his profession of fidelity to the regime was tinged for the first time with a note of bitterness. He admitted in his notice that he had been deceived in his expectations of reward at the hands of the king, along with many other legitimate claimants to royal favor who had disdained to "publish their titles on the officious list in the antechamber." So their claims were passed over in favor of more wily courtiers and Nodier went back to work on his etymologies and dictionaries, a fortunate occurrence, as it turned out, since this tack provided at last the only practical basis on which the Academy could elect him.

For almost two hundred years the famous *Dictionnaire de l'Académie* had undergone little change and present members were most dilatory in bringing it up to date. As the journalist Feuillide said a few years later in an article pushing Nodier's election in *L'Europe Littéraire,* September 1, 1833: "We have lost [through your having failed to obtain a seat] the hope of ever bringing to a conclusion this famous *Dictionnaire de l'Académie,* which, in the language of these gentlemen, must fix the language. Alas! They are so slow . . . that the language is pleased to render obsolete on the morrow the words these gentlemen called new the day before, and to revive those they have classed as no longer current." What they really needed was a recognized *éplucheur de mots* who would take over direction of this task of revision and inspire the others with enough enthusiasm to bring the work to a happy and swift conclusion. Charles must have sensed that advertising his titles to leadership of the dictionary staff would afford the open sesame that would swing open the academic portals, for he initiated in the *Examen critique* a campaign of attack against the Academy's stranglehold on the language and its dictionaries.

All the elements that were to contribute eventually to Nodier's succession to a seat in the French Academy—the courting of the liberal party through a revival of Jouy's friendship, the publication of works advancing his claim as grammarian and philologist; i.e., a second edition of the *Questions de littérature légale* (1828) and the *Mélanges tirés d'une petite bibliothèque* (1829), the attacks against the Academy's *Dictionary* to show his qualification as lexicographer and the flow of letters to his friends denying his interest in a seat—all were inventoried by 1830 when he posed his candidature against Pongerville and Cousin. First he published a baffling *bluette*, as he called it, entitled *Histoire du roi de Bohème et de ses sept châteaux* (1830). Inspired by Corporal Trim's unfinished tale in Sterne's *Tristram Shandy,* this work may well have foreshadowed, as M. Jean Richer has suggested, "the boldest researches of Mallarmé, Apollinaire, Jarry, Joyce," in the use of language.[6] Whatever else speculation may reveal about this curious work—Weiss was not impressed with it, in fact he thought it idiotic—the *Roi de Bohème* is first and foremost a satire on the Academy under the thin gauze of "l'Académie de Tombouctou." As such it has a place in the documentation of Nodier's drive on that institution.

Unwilling to assume publicly the responsibility for appearing once again in the ranks of the hopefuls, Charles blamed Désirée for awakening him at one o'clock in the morning to write a letter to Madame Chassériau in support of his candidacy. "This is the hour when the mind is most impressionable," he wrote to that lady, "and perhaps I had the bad luck to be dreaming of the Academy, as good a nightmare as any other. However, I did not realize that entering the Academy constitutes a science more complex than any of those I have bothered my poor head about, and one could hardly ask that I start learning the elements of that science, at my present advanced age of forty-seven." (He was really fifty.)[7] Supported at last by a bonafide romanticist, Lamartine, who had succeeded in penetrating the Academy earlier that year, and sure of the votes of Chateaubriand, Droz, and his "friends of thirty years' standing," Jouy, Etienne, and Arnault, Nodier left no stone unturned. He wrote two weeks later to his friend Aimé Martin to help him solicit the vote of Lainé, "who I understand voted for me twice before when I wasn't even a candidate." Despite Lamartine's opinion that his ten center votes would not grow, Victor Cousin was elected to the seat left vacant by the death of Fourier. Nodier was sure the right would vote for Ancelot (whose name did not even appear; he was not elected until 1841) and that the left would favor Nodier since they could not muster enough votes to elect Benjamin Constant (who received nine votes), and that consequently both these parties would select Nodier as a sort of dark horse. He polled not a single vote.[8]

After the July revolution of 1830 Charles was more than ever convinced that he should persist in his elusive pursuit of a seat in the Academy. Always in need of money, he found the years 1829-30 especially disastrous. In letters to the banker Laffitte and to Weiss in August and September, 1829, Nodier claimed he had lost 9,000 francs "in the disastrous events affecting the book trade." So that debt of 30,000 francs contracted *chez* Laffitte in 1817, which had kept him solvent for the past dozen years and of which he had barely succeeded in paying the interest by engaging his literary pension as collateral, was increased by an additional 5,000 francs. At the end of the year he was obliged to sell his library, valued at 30,000 francs, to provide a dowry for his daughter, who married Jules Mennessier in January, 1830. The literary pension, cut in half by Montbel on January 1, 1830, was completely suppressed by Peyronnet on July 22, and Charles even feared the loss of his position at the Arsenal Library. He may have overplayed his hand in trumpeting his participation in the Revolution of '89—to gain the backing of the liberals in the Academy—in a series of articles he had published in the *Revue de Paris* (1829). This rendered him suspect to the minister Polignac, who dismissed Nodier from his post on

July 22. Luckily, the revolution that took place a few days later caused the fall of the Polignac ministry and Charles' dismissal did not take effect.

What role did Charles play during the three glorious days of the July revolution? The only clear fact is that he did not leave Paris. Assumably he did not view with equanimity his destitution at the hands of Charles X, his former patron and owner of the Arsenal. In his extremity, he turned to his cousin, the new governor of Paris, Lt. General Pajol. This gentleman had come out of his forced retirement to help drive Charles X into exile, thus automatically becoming *persona grata* with the new regime of Louis Philippe. In a reassuring note to his son-in-law, who had taken Marie to his family in Metz, Nodier counseled him to stay out of harm's way until the trouble blew over. As for the Arsenal, he added in a postscript, there was no danger; everyone in it was armed to the teeth.[9] After the fighting was over, Charles ventured out of the library and sustained a broken leg while attempting to protect an apple-woman from her brute of a son; though he deplored the long confinement, the accident served to keep him in bed for two and a half months, writing.

"There are only forty-two applicants for my post," Charles wrote ironically to his old friend, Jean De Bry, who had taken advantage of the revolution to return from his exile in Belgium, "many of them people who were out of favor under the last administration and whom I helped to be reinstated." There was one ray of sunshine in all this adversity, he went on; friend Roujoux invited him to take refuge in his prefecture of Lot if Nodier was dismissed.[10] But Charles' faith in Cousin Pajol was completely justified; the new administration did not insist upon his resignation.

Reduced to a base income of 4,000 francs as librarian of the Arsenal, nine mouths to feed—besides Marie's husband, Nodier had taken in the Tercys and the Tourtelles with their daughter Francine—and a debt of 35,000 francs hanging over him, his finances reached an acute stage of distress in 1830. Despite the redoubled literary activity forced upon him in his bedridden condition, he could not make up the deficit caused by the loss of his pension. More than ever he needed the

1,500 francs per annum afforded Academy members and, once inside, he could aspire to the post of *rapporteur du dictionnaire,* an appointment which carried an additional 6,000 francs per annum.

Arriving at the Arsenal shortly after the July revolution, Edouard Turquety found its master greatly perturbed. Nodier had just learned that the Academy had all but decided to accept him when someone innocently mentioned *Smarra.* From this slight demur there instantly arose a wave of protest against this ultraromantic work, and its author's name was set aside. In his agitation, Charles vented his spleen in a tirade against the Academy's complement for Turquety's benefit. According to this dissection, the Academy was composed of forty writers "more or less illustrious" who might be divided into three categories: the men of genius, always three or four in each group, such as Chateaubriand and Lamartine at the present moment; the men of recognized talent, about a dozen in number, who always formed the solid base or the durable element of the Academy's composition; finally, the twenty-five or more who escape classification, "academicians by the grace of God," Nodier termed them. No one knows how they got there, he commented, as there were just as many outside who had equal claim to a seat; only friend Balzac could describe the intrigues, political, social, and even conjugal, which brought them into the Academy. To sum up, the Academy was composed of three sections, of which the first represented genius, the second talent, and the third, just anybody.

Placated by this outburst, Charles enjoined Turquety not to repeat what he had just heard; after all, one who aspired to membership should not seem to run down his future colleagues.[11] Moreover, he did not want it known that he was aware of the shoddy intrigues that determined election. The interview, which Turquety wrote down soon after his visit, shows that Nodier's interest had developed into a preoccupation and that he was keeping a close watch on the Academy's doings.

In the very first issue of his friend Dr. Veron's *Revue de Paris,* March, 1829, Charles began publishing a series of monographs on the revolution and, later in the year, on the empire.

Conceived as a vast apologia and justification, not to say a whitewash, of the principal figures in that historical drama, including Robespierre and Napoleon, these fragments were issued prematurely to give substance to Nodier's claim that he had never abandoned the liberal party. When he collected them two years later under the general heading *Souvenirs, épisodes et portraits pour servir à l'histoire de la Révolution et de l'Empire,* it became clear that he had abandoned the original historiographical design in favor of a fictional one advancing his participation in these events. Appropriately dedicated to the liberal banker Laffitte, the *Préliminaires* to this edition show how fictional this history had become: "I honored the glory and genius of Napoleon even when I alone dared to proclaim liberty. An inclination fortified by time and by persecution did not permit me to lend the aid of my feeble efforts to the government which succeeded his by the law of the Charter, since this government, under a fatal influence, has divorced its interests from those of the country."[12]

Writing after the fall of the autocratic monarchy of Charles X, Nodier could say openly that he had never supported him; but how could he expect to get away with it? In 1822, after his first visit to the Arsenal, Weiss confided to his *Carnets de route* his disgust with Nodier for the latter's ultraroyalist attitude, his ridiculous claims to nobility, and his travesties of history to court favor with the monarchy.[13] Four years later Nodier was advancing his fidelity and service to the king as his principal claim to a seat in the Academy. Then, suddenly, in the beginning of an article published in January, 1831, in the *Revue de Paris* entitled "De la république," he discovered this formula of self-exculpation: "By birth, education, sentiments, doctrines, and morals I am on the side of liberty. I never wandered from this principle even in my sincere devotion to the restoration; which is, according to my conscience, in all written history THE ONLY SOCIAL SYSTEM within which the organizing ideas of liberty have been converted into laws." Thus, in supporting the restored monarchy, he thought he was serving the cause of liberty; anyone might have made the same mistake.

In a letter to Weiss on July 6, 1831, Charles was more

frank in his vindication. He says, in effect, that he had served
the restoration as long as he saw in it a guarantee against two
execrable forms of slavery, the Parisian democracy and the
Empire; but the high centralization of the government drove
him away. Having washed himself clean of royalist attachments, Nodier proceeded to lay the ghost of romantic engagement: "One can hardly place in circulation these days a work
however slight without stating to which literary school he
belongs or claims to belong. It is a question which in certain
quarters goes hand in hand with political considerations and
in others takes precedence. There are *romanticists* so hungry
for novelty that they style *classic* pedantry everything that is
simple, natural, and reasonable; there are *classicists* so limited
in their scholarship that they proscribe under the title of
romantic everything they do not understand, a principle of
exclusion which covers a wide ground. These discussions seem
to me to be rather otiose when they are no more than that."[14]
Having lost the leadership of the romantic movement, Nodier
was willing to occupy the middle ground; as he had suggested in discussing politics in this essay, perhaps both sides
were wrong.

Disclaimers of Nodier's newfound solidarity with the revolution and especially with the Girondists began to reach him
from different quarters. Bibliophile Jacob reported that Martainville, who had remained ultraroyalist *quand-même,* twitted
him once publicly: "Really, Charles, aren't you rather over-
doing that bit about having been beheaded with the Girondists?"[15] And Jouy, who had been reading with a good deal
of skepticism the articles in the *Revue de Paris,* chancing to
meet Nodier, challenged: "You speak of Saint-Just, of Vergniaud, and the Girondists as though you had lived with them.
How old are you? You must have been a child during the
Revolution!" Unperturbed, Nodier made answer, "I don't
know how old I am and I don't care; however, I am certain
that I was in direct contact with Vergniaud, for instance."[16]
This was not true, but Jouy was fascinated by Nodier's narrative and wanted to believe him though he knew better. In token
of his appreciation of Charles' brilliant rehabilitation of the
Girondists Jouy sent a note of thanks and Vergniaud's watch.

This watch was the last item Vergniaud had bequeathed to Adèle Sauvan—later Madame Legouvé; she in turn left it to Jouy—before mounting the cart that was to take him and the other Girondists to the guillotine. "It is a memento," Jouy's note ran in part, "that you are more worthy than anyone else of wearing, since you honor so well the holy martyr of liberty it recalls to us." Charles was overjoyed with the gift and the letter and hastened to seize the opportunity to seal the rapprochement here offered. His answer is dated June 13, 1831:

My dear Jouy,

Yesterday my heart was so full of gratitude that I did not have the strength to express it. I thought I would never again weep for joy. This is a happiness that I owe to you, and please do not do me the injustice to think it is the possession of a priceless jewel that had this effect on me. It is much more than that: it is the testimony, so consoling in my loneliness and abandonment, of the friendship of one of the men I have most consistently and sincerely cherished and admired, of one whose affection is a source of glory which amply fulfills all the fondest dreams of success and fame I entertained as a silly youth. How happy I was to see Emma [Jouy's daughter, married to Colonel Bondonville. She probably delivered the watch.] whom I always loved, whose sweet and angelic face recalled to me the happiest days of my unhappy existence. Let me hope that this will not end here and that you will come back at my call. I'll write you about that next week. I want you to see Jean De Bry whom you do not know as you ought. I'm sorry to hear you spent some time together without speaking of me.

Goodbye my dear friend. Please believe in my thanks, my inviolable attachment, and my unending devotion.

                                                    Charles Nodier

Charles could well afford a shout of triumph; he had won over a most stubborn adversary and had taken a giant stride toward the Academy. From this day forward Jouy always supported him and obtained for his "candidate of the Girondists," as he styled him, the votes of his friends.

The conquest of Jouy permitted Charles to concentrate on

the other half of his campaign: the attacks on the Academy, its members and its dictionary. Sniping at the Academy had become Nodier's favorite sport since 1829, as his remarks on Richelieu and the founding of that institution testify, "The fact is that the Academy was essentially a body detached from movements in language and politics, an institution that one would have thought had been established by the uncanny foresight of Richelieu, to *immobilize* the human spirit and petrify words; it represented the state of our literature in precisely the same way as the court represented our social posture."[17] In short, it lagged behind the times and defended rules of classical drama more militantly than the ancients themselves would have done. Aristotle, in his profound knowledge of things human, would have revolted against these *exigences académiques* which hampered Corneille and Racine but aided the mediocre, the *genus academus,* who could always cry out against the barbarity and the stupidity of innovators and take refuge "au milieu des honneurs de l'Académie."[18]

The publication in 1831 of the sixth edition of the *Dictionnaire de l'Académie Française* provided just the target Nodier needed. Earlier, Charles had taken occasional notice of the *Dictionnaire de l'Académie Française* to damn it. In the first two *Miscellanées, variétés de philosophie, d'histoire et de littérature extraites d'un livre qui ne paraîtra point,* Nodier warned that "the grammar and lexicology of a language are best studied at the beginning, at its foundation, or after it has lost currency and become a dead language. That is why the *Dictionary of the Academy,* which came *medio rerum,* is such a pitiful work." In the second *Miscellanée,* Nodier cut even deeper:

At the time of the founding of the Academy there were only two men in France who could have cooperated with real efficacy in the composition of the dictionary, the principal reason for establishing that institution; they were Ménage and Furetière.

Toward the end of the eighteenth century there were only two men in France whose profound knowledge of language mechanics could have introduced into that great work the philosophical spirit which it lacks and will continue to lack: they were Court de Gébelin and President des Brosses.

Pascal, Molière, J. B. Rousseau, J. J. Rousseau, Diderot, Beaumarchais, Mirabeau, Court de Gébelin, and President des Brosses did not belong to the Academy.

Ménage did not belong to the Academy; Furetière was kicked out.

Cassaigne and Cotin belonged.[19]

He might have added more names to his list of great men passed over by the Academy—Descartes, Arnauld d'Andilly (he was invited to join, but refused; visits were made obligatory after that), Bayle, Vauvenargues, Le Sage, l'Abbé Prévost, and André Chenier; but he was courting, not crushing.

When the long-awaited sixth edition came out, Nodier dedicated two articles to it in *Le Temps,* June 23 and July 3, 1831. Borrowing a leaf from the *Letters* of Madame de Sévigné, Charles announced with fanfare and suspense the appearance, at last, of the new dictionary; but where he had expected to find a "progressive, emancipated," up-to-date work, he found the same old "backward, refractory, lagging, retrograde" dictionary. You cannot blame academicians such as Corneille, Bossuet, Montesquieu, Buffon, Jouy, and Lamartine for the poor quality of this dictionary, he added, since they never read it. Richelieu had imposed the task of drawing up a dictionary at the founding of the Academy [actually it was his secretary, Charpentier, who suggested it], but the first lexicon did not appear until sixty years later; this is the only one of our national charters, Nodier reflected, which has never been reformed. The mistake was thus committed at the very beginning by confiding this task to forty nondescript immortals. If the Academy had understood its mandate aright, he continued, a man of genius aided by two or three efficient secretaries would have been selected; these would have erected a monument for all the world to admire, instead of mutilating Nicot and copying Richelet as the forty had done. Nodier, the fervent etymologist, wanted the dictionary to group words around a common root, e.g., sense, sensation, sensibility and so on. But in the Academy's version, in order to find *non-sens* and *contre-sens* you had to leaf through the entire work, "unless you are willing to stop at the first *non-sens* or the first *contre-sens* you meet, in which case you will not have to look very far."

In the second article he concentrated on specific faulty definitions, such as "embrasement, un grand incendie," and "incendie, un grand embrasement." Then he concluded that the dictionary seemed to have progressed backwards, "by a procedure which grammarians term pejorative and of which the Academy makes no mention, with reason; thus, the seventh edition will not be worthy of the sixth, which was not worth as much as the fifth, which did not match the fourth, which was worse than the third, which fell short of the second, which was not as good as the first, which was worth nothing." But he held out hope for the future, since the Academy had the happy office of renewing itself by the election of new members; waiting in the wings were Benjamin Constant, Chênedollé, Lamennais, Ballanche, Victor Hugo, and Béranger (not to mention Nodier, who, it is quite clear, was the only lexicographer among the candidates). These may tell the Academy that it must march to prove movement, and when it begins to march, the first move, according to Nodier, would be to burn the sixth edition of the dictionary.

In the first five months of 1832 Charles continued to worry the Academy and its dictionary. Thus, in a review of Delphine Gay's novel *Le Lorgnon* for *Le Temps*, January 12, he stated that no dictionary told him what this instrument was, not even the *Dictionnaire de l'Académie* "which contains necessarily all the words in use, and even those which will never be used, except in the Academy." He then referred to a group of academicians, who looked at him through their *lorgnons;* upon his identifying this instrument, Michaud, Duval, and Jouy, surprised, reminded him that it was never called anything else. "Well, then," rejoined Nodier, "don't forget that when you get to the seventh edition."

Discussing Raymond's *Dictionnaire général de la langue française* in *Le Temps*, March 10, Nodier declared that the Academy's dictionary was bad because it tried to fix language usage, whereas a good dictionary should try to follow usage and change with the changing language. He then went on to explain more fully the reason for his implacable hatred of the *Dictionnaire de l'Académie Française:* every time an academician died a great hue and cry arose in the newspapers that Charles Nodier wanted to succeed him. Only forty people knew that was not true, i.e., Nodier and the thirty-nine immortals. In order to reveal this to the rest of the world, he attacked the *Dictionary* viciously and constantly, so that everyone could see he was not courting. Ten days later Charles developed this thought more intimately in a letter to Lamartine in which he wrote that he was *sui generis* and must maintain his independence at all costs.

> When I was younger, Dame Fortune occasionally crossed my path and may have even smiled upon me; but she thought me too extravagant to give me anything. So I, who have never hated anything, made believe I hated her as a defense against the insolence of her disdain. For the same reason I have unceasingly attacked the Academy in my articles and books. I have amounted to little on this earth, but I have never been anyone's second best.[20]

This explanation of his stand, intended for the approval of an intelligent friend, was much more plausible than the one aimed earlier at the general public.

In a second article on Raymond's *Dictionnaire* for *Le Temps,* April 9, Nodier essentially repeated his claim—clearly a case of protesting too much—that his bad humor grew every time a seat became vacant in the Academy to show he was not interested in becoming a member. Finally, in a third article, dated May 4, Charles got down to the business of reviewing this work, but first he gave a historical survey of the better dictionaries of the French language. They were notably Borel's *Thrésor de la langue françoise,* Nicot's *Dictionnaire de la langue françoise* and Richelet's *Dictionnaire de la langue françoise.* As for Ménage's *Mercuriales littéraires,* they must be used by etymologists with caution, though Ménage himself was not lacking in instruction. Furetière's *Dictionnaire* was bad, but no worse than that of the Academy. Elaborated by others later, it was much improved as the *Dictionnaire de Tré-*

voux. Charles Laveaux tried to remedy the Academy's dictionary and was prosecuted for his efforts. Other dictionaries, by Restaut, Wailly, Gattel, etc., were plagiarisms of the big three mentioned earlier. Boiste, in his *Dictionnaire universel,* tried to encompass too much. Raymond profited from the mistakes of his predecessors and was more careful, complete, and exact, but he left many gaps. Clearly, then, the Academy still had a duty to perform for the French language and its dictionary.

On March 26, 1832, the cholera which had broken out in India fifteen years earlier reached Paris. In five days there were 300 cases in the capital. In April, the peak month of the epidemic, there were as many as 860 deaths in one day. After a period of abatement in May, new waves of the disease hit Paris in June and July when 300 deaths were recorded in a single day. In all, the epidemic lasted six months and carried off 18,406 Parisians out of a population of 645,698, or 23 per thousand. At the height of the plague Charles took refuge with his son-in-law's family in Metz, relatively free of the death-dealing cholera. From there he wrote a long letter to Weiss, dated April 24, containing, in the words of Dr. Paul Fabre, "a complete theory of cholera from pathogenesis to treatment."[21]

But Nodier's understanding of the malady was sketchy, to say the least; he obstinately considered cholera as "a pulmonary disturbance," thus taking an effect in an advanced case for a cause, and recommended "five or six inhalations of pure oxygen" as a specific. Dr. Fabre collects evidence to show that Nodier did not claim to be a doctor of medicine; yet at the onset of the epidemic he sent his view of its treatment mentioned above to his friend Dr. Koreff.[22] It is hard to believe anyone would be playing games with medical practitioners at such a time of crisis. Dr. Fabre simply lacked the insight into Nodier's method of denying publicly or in print the very thing he stood for or wanted most. His flirting with the Academy is a good case in point. Moreover, we have the evidence of Weiss' letter to Mérimée to prove that Charles actually fancied himself strong enough in medical knowledge to pass himself off as a doctor. "On one of his last trips to Besançon," Weiss wrote, "we happened to be seated in a café where the principal doctors of the town used to congregate for a chat over a glass of beer. The conversation turning by chance on a medical topic, Nodier treated it so brilliantly that his auditors expressed some surprise. 'What is so surprising about that?' Nodier retorted. 'Don't you know that I studied medicine and that I also have the honor of being an accredited doctor of the imperial faculty of Vienna? Ask Weiss, he has seen my diploma.' I nodded my head by way of affirming that I had seen the diploma and to this day you will find twenty people in Besançon ready to swear that Nodier was a doctor of the faculty of Vienna."[23] Weiss told Mérimée this story to show that occasionally he humored Nodier in propagating his harmless fibs; but Charles' medical degree was as groundless as his conspiracies. The essential point in both cases is that Nodier, surrealist *avant la lettre*, was willing to *believe* or *be* anything he could convince himself he *was* in the hearing of others.

Nodier recognized this at his personal property when he copyrighted the idea in the *Préface* to his first masterpiece, *La Fée aux miettes*, which Renduel brought out as Volume IV of the *Works* of Charles Nodier in 1832. "The fact is, to interest anyone in a fantastic tale you must be believable, and in order to bring others to believe something you must first believe it yourself. Once you have accepted this condition, you can boldly say whatever you like." In the beginning of his short story, *L'Amour et le grimoire,* published that same year in the *Revue de Paris,* Charles said that he had always dreamed of being the hero of a fantastic tale. Well, why were all the escapades he related for the delectation of his guests at the Arsenal invented, if not to make him the hero of the fantastic tale he dreamed his life should have been, could have been and, on occasion, when he was in particularly good vein, was?

The elder Dumas put his otherwise heavy finger with uncanny deftness on Nodier's extraordinary capacity for believing his own inventions when he wrote in the preface to *La Dame au collier de velours,* "For him, *Thérèse Aubert, La Fée aux miettes, Inès de les Sierras* really existed. They were his daughters as much as Marie; they were Marie's sisters." And Weiss, who knew Nodier better than anyone else, paid tribute to the latter's ability to convince others of the veracity of his fabrications about himself when he reported in his *Carnets de route* (October 23, 1832) that despite his intimate knowledge of Nodier's past, he was forced to admit he was spell-bound. At a dinner given by M. de Magnoncourt that autumn (besides Weiss, Hugo, Théodore Jouffroy, Pouillet, and Gustave Fallot were present) Nodier, heated by frequent potations of champagne, monopolized the conversation. "We formed a circle around him," Weiss wrote, "and listened to him tell anecdotes in his own inimitable style about Casimir de Montrond, Colonel Fournier, etc., until midnight. We all laughed till we choked, especially Jouffroy and Victor Hugo, who was seated on the corner of a table. We were all like children listening to capital stories of which we did not want to miss a single word. It was simply because everything must have an end that we separated, and then only with great regret." And he concluded, "In listening to him one must admit that if the events he is narrating did not take place exactly as he tells them, it is as he relates them that they should have happened."[24] Under the happy inspiration of this narrative mood Charles produced his two best works: *La Fée aux miettes* and *Le Dernier Banquet des Girondins*.

Recently Nodier's masterpiece has evoked a good deal of critical comment,[25] but in 1832 *La Fée aux miettes* went practically unnoticed; only his friend Fontaney gave an intelligent interpretation of it, along with the other novels that had appeared in the first five volumes of the Renduel edition, for the *Revue des Deux Mondes*. In Vienna, the poet Grillparzer found it "clever but dull." At fifty-two and at the height of his storytelling powers, as one of the outstanding men of letters of his time, Nodier was entitled to more critical acclaim than he received on this occasion. That he resented this neglect may be seen in his review of Boiste's *Dictionnaire universel de langue française, Le Temps*, November 15, 1832: "For the past five or six years I have been trying to compensate for my political and social nullity by composing romanesque stories in the manner of Madame de Tencin and little fairy tales in the style of Madame d'Aulnoy." This gave him the opportunity to talk more about his own works, "since no one else wants to write an article about them, as I did for others, young promising authors, who did not suffer for my having greeted and crowned them!" Of course, Nodier was no longer young and promising, and despite the bantering tone of this mock-serious charge there is an overtone of bitterness that there was no return for all the acknowledgments he had lavished, in print, on his contemporaries.

At least faithful Weiss was not slow in writing his appreciation of Charles' masterpieces in a letter dated from Besançon, June 7, 1833.

My dear friend,

I have just spent a morning the like of which I have not enjoyed in a long time and I must thank you for it, because you are responsible for the pleasure I took in it. I had told Deis [their mutual friend from boyhood days, who had become a bookseller in Besançon] to bring me your *Girondins* as soon as he received it. Once I had the volume in my hands, I began page one and did not stop till I reached the last page. I shed quite a few tears while reading it too. I only find one fault with it, it's too short; the remedy for that is to start all over again when one has finished, which is exactly what I intend to do. Your *Girondins* is a beautiful book but your masterpiece, in my opinion, is *La Fée aux miettes*. I don't know of a single work that I would rather have written. What good sense and reasoning Michel's narrative contains! What wonderful philosophy in his teaching! And what perfection of style! There are thirty or forty pages in this little volume that would be the most beautiful in the language if *Emile* did not exist; even so I am not sure I would not give the palm to your Michel. Since I no longer read the newspapers, I don't know what they said about your book, but rest assured that it is a man's work.[26]

Whatever else may be said about *Le Fée aux miettes*, there is little doubt that it opened up new vistas in European literature, from the novels of Gérard de Nerval, an avowed disciple, to the works of the surrealists of a century later, who never mentioned (perhaps never knew) their debt to Nodier. Whether it be considered a *roman à clef,* in which Charles would be Michel, the hero, or a symbolic novel cast in the

framework of masonic initiation like Mozart's *Magic Flute,*
wherein the trials that beset Michel would be seen as a test of
steadfastness and fidelity to an oath, or as the first psychoanalytical novel in which Charles sublimated his vaguely
sensed incestuous leanings toward his daughter, Marie, all
these and many more possible interpretations indicate that
Nodier had written a masterpiece of universal moment, one
of the most original inventions in world literature. The enig-
matic ending, suddenly shifting the locus of the novel to Italy
so that *La Fée aux miettes* could be hawked about as a penny-
dreadful in the best tradition of the Commedia dell'Arte, or
as a nostrum à la Dulcamara to cure the world of all the ills
that beset it (its moral being that one should take life as it is)
is not the least ingenious touch of this masterwork. Reader,
"ceci est un livre de bonne foy," as Montaigne said; if Nodier
had never written anything else it would have served to keep
his name before the public for a long time to come.

But in less than a year Charles produced another capital
work of his maturity, *Le Dernier Banquet des Girondins,* published as Volume VII in the Renduel edition. This rehabilitation of the martyrs of liberty, combining the dialoguing verve
of Diderot's *Le Neveu de Rameau* with the philosophical de-
tachment of Plato's *Symposium* completely won over whatever skeptics still remained in the academic camp. Now it
could only be a question of time and convenience before the
Academy would accept him as a member. Whence came Charles'
intimate knowledge of the last hours of the Girondists? From
the Abbé Emery, according to Weiss, from Jean De Bry,
according to the bibliophile Jacob. But wasn't Charles merely
fulfilling another of his father's wishes, overheard in a conversation with the philosopher, Delisle de Salles, that historians
should write about the revolution as living history, like Plutarch, rather than reproduce the cold annals of contemporary
chroniclers? In any event, Charles enriched his *Banquet* with
copious notes paying tribute to *all* liberals, living and dead;
one note in particular, describing Vergniaud's watch, gave
him the opportunity to turn a deft compliment to his mentor,
Jouy.

Fortified by the appearance of *La Fée aux miettes,* an

Caricature in the Panthéon Charivarique, "Nodier Bibliophile." Accompanying verse runs in part, "il aime vivre en famille," probably a reference to the Nodier apartment in the Arsenal, occupied at one time by six in-laws as well as the immediate family

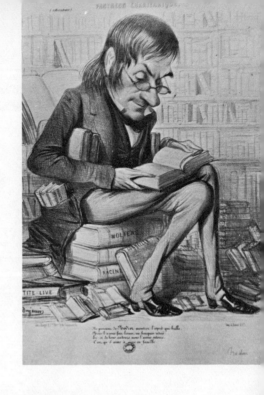

Weiss (Charles),
Biographe, l'un des principaux auteurs de la Biographie universelle.

Besançon Library

Charles Weiss, biographer, Nodier's lifelong friend

Marie Nodier-Mennessier, portrait by
Gigoux in 1833, shortly after her wedding

Mme MARIE NODIER-MENNESSIER

imaginative work which had the stature to impose him on the immortals, Charles renewed his application for admission to the Academy in March, 1833. He made no visits, received seven votes on the first ballot and only two on the second when Tissot, a classicist was elected. As he said in a letter of April 25 announcing the publication of *Le Dernier Banquet des Girondins* to Weiss, the Academy had taken its revenge for his criticism of the *Dictionnaire*. So the moment was not yet ripe. As René Doumic has said in his article, "Comment on devient un académicien," the question of timing is all-important for candidates running for a seat in the Academy. "If the moment is not ripe, there is no use trying to force the doors. On the other hand when the hour has struck, everything comes easy, all resistance has ceased and the doors open automatically."[27]

Nothing daunted, Nodier, who knew his election was imminent, submitted his name again May 15 for the seat vacated by the death of Andrieux. But his consternation was aroused by the entry of a formidable opponent in the person of the historian and minister, Thiers. From his bed of pain—Charles had fallen from a ladder while hunting some books—he dictated a letter to his wife for Emma de Bondonville, Jouy's daughter and Nodier's most ardent advocate before his friend and protector.

My dear Emma,

I had intended to pay you a visit and thank you for Mr. Jouy's charming book, which I read with a great deal of pleasure though something seems to be missing in Volume I, which ends on page 272. I hope to be able to complete it, for this is one of those books in which one does not want to miss anything.

I was crossed in my plans by the unfortunate accident suffered by your poor friend Charles, who was thus prevented from coming in person to solicit the good offices of Mr. Jouy in the forthcoming election. In submitting his name again he is merely following the advice of his many friends who could not vote for him in the last election because they had previously given their word to someone else.

But today came the announcement of the candidacy of
Mr. Thiers, who could be elected just about whenever he
wishes it, for the present vacancy. So Charles is certain not
to be chosen, though it is no great dishonor at any time to
be passed over for a minister. His only hope in the present
election is to gather enough independent votes to establish
his claim and his right to a seat. He thinks he is well
enough acquainted with your excellent father's noble frank-
ness to be able to count on his vote. Please consider this
letter as substitute for the visit he cannot pay as he is unable
to walk and in considerable pain.

In any case, I beg of you, my dear Emma, to preserve
your friendship for us, as I am sure it is more precious to
my husband than all academic honors.

Affectionately,
Désirée Nodier[28]

As Charles predicted, Thiers was elected, polling seventeen
votes against seven for Nodier. This was his last defeat.

In the summer of 1833 the revolutionary author and playwright Laya died; he had occupied *Fauteuil* No. 25 since
1817. This Charles learned from his friend Amanton. On the
same day he forwarded his application to the Academy, he
returned answer to Amanton. His letter ran in part:

You tell me of Mr. Laya's death and I am sincerely sorry to
hear it, though he did not like me, for what reason I never
knew. If I had to write his eulogy [a successful candidate
has to eulogize his predecessor in his acceptance speech] no
one would be more disposed than I to pay full homage to
the purity of his talent and the nobility of his character.
L'Ami des lois [a play on which Laya's reputation was
based] was one of the most heroic acts of the revolution.
But this honor is certainly reserved for another. My solitary
and rather savage existence has placed me in contact with
no more than a dozen academicians and I cannot count
upon the suffrage of those who know me only through my
works. What are the works of one who has never had the
leisure to undertake a great, strong book and who has
touched upon everything without leaving a trace anywhere?

I will nevertheless be among the hopefuls since they have placed me there, but it will be the last time. I have already given up too many days to personal vanity when there remain to me so few in which to contemplate the universal vanity of things. The only lesson I have learned from my literary and philosophical studies has been not to attach the least importance to their success.[29]

Nevertheless, on the following day he wrote to his sponsor, Jouy.

29 August, 1833

Dear and illustrious friend, this is the last test to which I will put your warm and faithful regard for me. They say I have a chance, but I will never forget that I owe most of it to you. If I fail this time I shall retire within my tent, which is not Achilles', and no one will ever hear speak of me again. There will always remain from my academic pretensions the consciousness of having obtained the votes of the men I esteemed most and this surpasses all my literary ambitions. And then, academician or not, I will always have the right to think that I was one in the eyes of Jouy. A man must be proud indeed who would not be content with that.

Please convey my respects to Emma and M. de Bondonville.

Your grateful and devoted
Charles Nodier[30]

And probably at the same time, though the letter bears no date, he took the precaution of writing to Victor Cousin, who had bested him in the 1830 election.

Mon cher et illustre maître,

I should like to invoke the good will of which you have given me such touching and flattering tokens. I should like to be bold enough to remind you that your very words encouraged me in the high ambition I dare aspire to today and whose success would be a thousandfold less meaningful to me if I did not owe it in part to your patronage.

Whatever the issue may be of this last attempt on the

portals of Corinth—I shall not renew my efforts if entrance is denied me this time—please believe that your judgment will be decisive in forming my opinion concerning my weak claims on the Academy and that the outcome will in no way affect the inalterable sentiments of respect I will always bear you. I hope I may continue to be worthy of being one of your sincerest admirers and the most devoted of your friends to the end of my life.

Charles Nodier[31]

It was at this point that C. Feuillide's excellent, all-embracing review of Nodier's works appeared in *L'Europe Littéraire* September 1, 1833. After a particularly exhaustive listing of Nodier's erudite contributions, Feuillide concluded, "In spite of all this, there are seventeen gentlemen who are licensed, privileged, organized, paid 1,500 francs per annum to have wit and taste who know all that about Nodier as well as you and I and yet do not believe that there is enough there to make an academician. Why insist?" he asked, turning to Nodier. "Didn't you know they would exclude the man who dared laugh at the Institut de Tombouctou in the *Roi de Bohème?*" Assistance even from this moribund journal did not hurt Charles.

Desiring to leave no fire untended, Charles began finally the publication of his "Notions élémentaires de linguistique, ou histoire abrégée de la parole et de l'écriture, pour servir d'introduction à l'alphabet, à la grammaire et au dictionnaire" in article form in *Le Temps,* September 13, 1833. By election day, October 24, Charles succeeded in bringing out four articles on the subject, about one every ten days, and became so engrossed with it that he set aside the ambitious *Roi de Bohème* in favor of the *Notions* for the last volume of his *Oeuvres* Renduel had been publishing since 1832. For the moment at least, Charles was eager the Academy should forget the aspersions he had cast upon it in the *Roi de Bohème* in favor of his present musings on philology. This the Academy did, giving Nodier seventeen of the eighteen votes cast on the first ballot to find a successor to Laya. After nine years of frustration and disappointment, Nodier had finally won with his pen a seat in the Academy.

In order to become a full-fledged member, the successful candidate, having been duly elected, must be received. To fulfill the formality of his reception, he must prepare a speech of acceptance in which he thanks the Academy for admitting him to its august company, eulogizes his predecessor, whose death has made his election possible, and makes a general statement concerning his aims, setting forth, as the French say, his titles of admission. Copies of the speech must be deposited one week before the reception with the general (perpetual) secretary and the director designated as sponsor, so that the latter may make some suitable rebuttal and the ears of the other academicians may not be offended. The date fixed for Charles' reception was Thursday, December 26. He began his speech by thanking first the men who were sitting there before him, in particular Arnault for seconding his brief teaching career, Etienne for recalling him from exile, and Droz for inspiring him with literary ambitions. Then he paid his respects to Volney, who fired his interest in linguistics, to La Harpe for criticizing his first efforts, to Chénier (Marie-Joseph) for correcting his poetry, and to Suard, for polishing his style. After a brief review of the works of his predecessor (he only expatiated on *L'Ami des lois*) Nodier launched into the main part of his discourse.

Nodier was the first militant romanticist to join the Academy. Chateaubriand, who had been there since 1812, was not technically a participating member, having failed to deliver his speech; he made only infrequent visits, appearing mostly at elections, and, from the day a stuffy director took the trouble to remind him of his irregular status, never spoke in the assembly. Soumet had turned coat to gain admittance. Lamartine had remained aloof from combat, although everyone had expected him to make a ringing statement in favor of romanticism. Despite the fact that Nodier's ardor for the new school had cooled considerably since he had lost leadership of the movement to Hugo five years earlier, he really tried to satisfy all parties so that his speech fell between two stools.

He did say that his position with regard to the Academy was an anomalous one, since he, the friend of innovations in literature, was being received by a company which was the natural guardian and conservator of forms and tastes consecrated by time; but a few moments later he severely weakened this stand by flaying the desire to renew at the expense of taste and good form. Jouy boisterously applauded these remarks as a sign of relief from the pill of innovation Nodier had made him swallow earlier, but the romanticists felt Charles had been too timid.

All in all, the speech was well received, as A. Guéroult, who reviewed the meeting for *Le Temps* three days later, indicated. Weiss exultantly confided to his *Journal* on the last day of the year that Nodier's speech had caused a sensation: "I hear from Paris that this séance was one of the most brilliant this illustrious company ever had. . . . Only Messrs Villemain and Dupin of all the members of the Academy seemed bored. The former, whom Nodier satirized in *Le Roi de Bohème*, was so visibly displeased that the newspapers mentioned it, and the latter in spite of his talent and fortune, is only a lawyer and Nodier has said somewhere that when the reign of the lawyers began it spelled the final dissolution of society. In any case, these were the only two pouters that were noticed, except perhaps the *Journal des Débats* which carries an article signed R. composed in a denigrating mood but without wit or color."[32]

More just than the jubilant Weiss, who may be pardoned for his credulous enthusiasm, was the report signed Guéroult mentioned earlier. He felt it was rather pointless to tell the Academy in 1833 that literature had undergone a revolution which everyone else had accepted as accomplished by 1827. Always ten years behind the times, that stronghold of conservatism still did not acknowledge the new movement in life and letters and had done nothing to help the renewal. If it had, he would be delighted to see the new school receive the stamp of approval in the person of Nodier: "No one is more qualified to represent the new school, no one has fought harder for it, no one has been more enthusiastic in his encouragement of it." He would even "applaud their choice of

Nodier as the negotiator between the new and the old"; instead, the Academy missed both golden opportunities of making literary history (by hailing Nodier as the champion of romanticism, or at least by welcoming him as a mediator) and was adding him merely as another "old hat," as may be gathered from the smug remarks of Jouy's *réponse.* "In his answer to the *récipiendaire,* Mr. Jouy was careful to place some of those expressions which assure the good health of literature, such as, for example, 'the language *fixed* by our great writers, etc.' so that, without positively damning the progressive theories proclaimed by M. Nodier, he seemed to be making large reservations and giving notice that he was not about to abandon his position."

Indeed, Jouy's speech made it clear from the start that he had made up his mind to accept Nodier on his own (Jouy's) terms; he would ignore or censure Nodier's straying from the path trodden by the classicists and approve such phases of his work as suited the sponsor's views of the good and the beautiful. Caressing with one hand and slapping with the other, he began by terming Nodier's criticism of the Academy's dictionary unjust, "but this did not prevent the Academy from appreciating the useful things in yours." After a few glowing remarks about the *Mélanges tirés d'une petite bibliothéque* and the *Dictionnaire des onomatopées,* he praised Nodier's style (mostly, one suspects, because it gave him a chance to repeat Buffon's saw about "le style, c'est l'homme") but then he rapped him for his "affectation néologique." To this blunder—Nodier did not affect neologisms, which he hated, but merely revived old words which in his estimation should never have lost currency—Jouy added another when he endowed Nodier with "l'esprit voltairien"! That must have made Charles jump.

Unfortunately the *récipiendaire* does not have a chance to rebut the director's response; Charles might have had something to say to that. Earlier, when someone asked Nodier why he quarreled so much with Jouy, he answered, "It's very simple: Voltaire is the damned soul of Jouy, whereas Rousseau is practically a god for me." And as this biography has shown, Nodier was anti-Voltaire from his student days, opposing him on orthography, Shakespeare, and philosophy, a position he never changed. Next, Jouy struck a happy note, warmly praising Nodier's zeal as a partisan of the freedom of the press, as a champion of liberty. "To be convinced of this, one has only to glance at the *tablettes* of *Jean Sbogar* where you expose powerfully and logically your theories of liberty, probably the boldest that have ever been written." Jouy was more in his element here and as a political liberal he appreciated at its true worth Charles' plea in favor of the exiles of 1815, but then he spoiled it all by inveighing against "la licence de la presse," complaining of its ingratitude towards him (Jouy). All this had nothing to do with Nodier, and he had probably ceased listening.

Jouy had finished his speech on this note. Not a word did we hear of Nodier's spearheading the romantic movement, encouraging and helping young authors, creating the *salon de l'Arsenal, the* literary salon of the 1820's and the cradle of the new school, nor of his recent masterpiece, *La Fée aux miettes,* which Jouy had probably not read. All this was foreign and therefore inimical to Jouy's nature, and he was pleased to pass over it in silence. This was the most he could bring himself to do; any consideration of Charles' real claims to academic distinction, or for that matter to any sort of distinction, might have prevented his sponsorship. Jouy had laid the large glass of the telescope to his eye and the image of Nodier that appeared at the other end was small indeed. Nodier was to live to deserve this diminution in stature.

In general, Weiss was right about the chorus of praise that went up from the Paris press. They all agreed that the reception caused a great flutter of curiosity and excitement among the public who flocked to the event to see how the champion of romanticism would conduct himself before the Academy. Three of the leading newspapers (*Le Constitutionnel,* December 27, unsigned, *Le Journal des Débats,* December 28, signed R., and *Le Temps,* December 29, A. Guéroult) thought Nodier's posture of modesty and humility in the exordium overdrawn to the point of irony. Most felt he had passed rather deftly from his classicist beginnings to his stand on romanticism "without abandoning any of his former attachments and without hurting anyone," but at least two saw his castigation of the wayward genius as shafts aimed directly at Victor Hugo; "though he did not name the contemporary author to whom he had liberally granted the gift of genius," ran the *Constitutionnel* article, "he would be much mistaken if he thought that his protests against the deviations of this genius . . . would entirely erase the memory of his immoderate praises of him. The more reason upheld his strictures, the more the audience showed it agreed with his critical reflections, the more certain he must be that he opened an incurable wound in the heart of the offended one. However, we are certain that the orator was animated by the most generous sentiments, that he was motivated by a desire to fulfill a duty by giving useful advice."

Etienne, the editor of *Le Constitutionnel*, who had often befriended Nodier and had a hand in his election, was Hugo's bitterest enemy. In his reception speech before the Academy, in 1829, he had characterized the new school as "a cabal that thinks itself a school." Nodier's invectives were aimed to please him. *La Quotidienne*, another Hugo-hater, in unsigned articles, December 26 and 27, reported Hugo showed great patience for fortitude while Charles was flaying the wayward genius, then burst into vociferous applause of his "professions de foi littéraires," applause which many people took for "the enthusiasm of repentance." Thus did Nodier satisfy at the same time the Academy and the public. It was easier to attack an individual, especially an old friend, whom he had recently characterized as "one of the most inventive geniuses to appear in any literary epoch," in an essay entitled "Des types en littérature" in the *Revue de Paris,* 1830, than to confront the learned assembly and guests. If Charles was still showing some resentment here against Hugo for capturing the romantic movement, then the gesture was unworthy of him in his moment of glory. In essence, though no one mentioned it, Charles was making his *adieux aux romantiques*. By attacking their present outstanding representative and titular head, he gave notice that he was abdicating whatever position he still held among them for a snug seat in the Academy.

As Weiss had stated, only the disgruntled *Débats* struck a

dissonant note by denouncing Nodier's speech as "pretty bad, aimless . . . unworthy of its author"; his defense of romanticism was "feeble, his profession of faith timid and embarrassed, nothing new, nothing precise." He merely repeated such clichés as "innovations approved by taste, etc., etc. A man of Nodier's literary stature should not have to repeat anyone else's sayings." By contrast, his friend Dr. Veron took personal charge of granting Nodier a brief accolade in the *Album* of the *Revue de Paris* for December 31 where he printed both speeches and saw in the choice of Nodier "a new sap of life and youth circulating in the old academic body."

In any event, Charles was installed as comfortably as possible in the chair numbered 25 where he had been preceded by C. de L'Estoile, three dukes of Coislin, Surian, D'Alembert, Choiseul-Gouffier, Portalis, Laujon, Etienne (first election), and Laya. He was to be followed by Mérimée and L. de Loménie—curious that Charles should be immediately preceded and followed by three men who disliked him, reason enough to explode "le bon Nodier" legend—Taine, Albert Sorel, Maurice Donnay, and Marcel Pagnol. He could now frequent the weekly meetings every Thursday, make speeches, hand out prizes for virtue, take part in the election of other immortals, and work on the dictionary.

In the interim, while waiting to be named *rapporteur* of the Academy's dictionary, Charles thought fit to continue his articles on linguistics and lexicology in the pages of *Le Temps*. But first he had the painful duty of signaling the passing of the man who had probably done most for him, whom he had come to regard as a substitute father and with whom he had kept up a regular correspondence, his old friend and patron, Jean De Bry, in an appropriate and moving obituary for *Le Temps*, January 6. The old regicide had lived just long enough to witness the honoring of his former protégé at the December 26 meeting of the Academy.

Aside from the articles mentioned above and the continuation of the *Souvenirs de la Révolution et de l'Empire* in the pages of the *Revue de Paris,* which we may assume were mostly written before his election, Charles published very little in the year of 1834, his time being largely taken up by the Academy and matters devolving from his nomination. In this category may be placed his omnibus edition of Roger's *Oeuvres diverses* (poetry, plays, comic operas). Was this repayment for Roger's vote? And Charles was soon initiated into Academy intrigues and how they were manipulated when he found himself—and his vote—absorbed by the powerful Jouy faction. Despite his gratitude to Népomucène Lemercier, whose vote, according to that gentleman's daughter, assured Nodier's election, Charles could not support his candidate—Lemercier also fancied himself a kingmaker—as we learn in a letter from Mademoiselle Lemercier to her father, dated September 28, 1834. "I find that Mr. Reynouard was in a terrible hurry to cast his vote with someone else rather than with you; and where is Mr. Nodier's gratitude for his appointment which you assured?"[33] Apparently Charles had more reasons to believe that Jouy, rather than Lemercier, had "assured" his election, for his vote went to Jouy's candidate, Eugene Scribe. This was exactly the situation that prevailed when Victor Hugo entered the lists two years later.

Gustave Simon has related in detail—basing his remarks on the notes the poet had left for a proposed third volume of the autobiographical *Victor Hugo raconté par un témoin de sa vie* —how he was baffled in his first attempt to join the Academy.[34] Though Lemercier normally formed, with Jouy and Jay, part of a classic triumvirate against romanticists, he had lately struck out for himself, as we saw above, and seemed to desire a clique of his own making which would sponsor members of the new school. In this intention he approached Hugo with the news of minister Laîné's death and suggested he ask for his seat. When Hugo temporized, Lemercier became very persuasive and insisted election to the Academy would aid the poet, whom he knew to be an orator, politically; that it was much easier for an academician to reach the senate, for instance, than a writer, no matter how famous. Hugo acquiesced and began his visits, *comme de juste,* with Chateaubriand.

Hugo's next visit was to the Arsenal, where he knew from long experience that Charles received his friends at five o'clock, preferably in his wife's room. Nodier greeted him with open arms and a friendly smile; but when he learned the purpose of his visit, his face changed. "You won't be elected," he said bluntly. "I know that," answered Hugo, "but I will have the support of the important members; besides, very few are elected the first time." Then after a pause, "I see that I cannot count on your vote." "To speak frankly," resumed Nodier, "since 1833 you have been following a tack I cannot condone. *Lucrezia Borgia!* I don't criticize this as literature, a poor hack like me doesn't judge a genius like you; but this play shocks my religious sense. You have affronted Catholicism, which is sacred to me, you have besmirched a pope." When Hugo tried to defend his position in that play, Nodier blurted out, "I am an oldtimer. Perhaps I have been left behind by you fellows, but I cannot follow you." "So you refuse?" "I'd give my vote on my knees to the author of *Notre Dame de Paris,* but I withhold it from the author of *Lucrezia Borgia.*" "Well, sir, the author of *Lucrezia Borgia* forbids the author of *Notre Dame de Paris* to ask you for it," and Hugo retired in a huff.

Next day he learned from their mutual friend Jal that Nodier's objection to *Lucrezia Borgia* was a pretext. Nodier had promised his vote to those who had secured his own election, Jouy and company, and they were voting for Dupaty. Moreover, and this Hugo could not know, Charles owed his appointment as *rapporteur du dictionnaire* to these same conservative republicans, so that he was doubly enmeshed in their cabal. In spite of the warning of Articles 15 and 16, which specifically state that an academician must not engage his vote before an election and that anyone having thus engaged his vote will not be admitted to election, Charles had not kept his vote free. When Hugo asked Jal why Nodier had not told him the truth instead of uttering all that nonsense about *Lucrezia Borgia,* he showed he did not comprehend him. Nodier could not bring himself to expose grubby reasons of commitment, might as well say financial, which preempted his vote in favor of a mediocre candidate and against a friend who had called him brother and once admired him as a guide and teacher. This stand was unworthy of Nodier as we have come to know him. Unfortunately, it was to be followed by other equally questionable acts which mar his image as pilot of a major literary movement.

VII

The Last Years

ON LEAVING the Academy one Thursday afternoon in the summer of 1834 Charles felt he had got a touch of the cholera. He took to his bed (he was to stay there over a month) from whence he wrote a witty letter about his symptoms to an unidentified friend. Repeated attacks in the following spring (which kept him in bed for three months) and winter, forced him to refer to more competent authority. In December, 1835, his ailment was finally diagnosed as chronic nephritis. Though this was not exactly correct, it showed the malady had so far progressed that doctors were at last able to identify the area of the disease that was to carry him off. From this point on Charles led the life of a valetudinarian. He was ordered to curtail his activities, especially those inducing excitement and fatigue. He was persuaded to forego his daily bookhunting expeditions along the quays between the hours of six and seven. Weiss, who had been returning to Paris every September or October since 1822, upon learning that his old friend was very ill came less often. Charles was rarely seen at their favorite haunts, the Café des Variétés, the Café Lamblin, the Café du Châtelet, the Palais Royal, and their usual restaurant, *Le Boeuf à la Mode*.

Worse yet, Nodier had to give up his beloved *mélodrames*, the nightly performances at the Gaieté, the Ambigu, the Porte Saint-Martin, the Variétés and the Séraphin, where he had been fascinated by the *ombres chinoises*. The inveterate theatergoer—he was reported to have seen *Le Boeuf enragé* a hundred times—missed most of all, perhaps, the antics of his favorite actor, Deburau, at the Funambules. And what about the Sunday dinners with Pixerécourt, Nodier's bitterest competitor for books, whom he called "the Corneille of the Boulevards" because of his fantastically successful melodramas, whom he met again at the famous lunches of the

227

Bibliophiles Français (Aimé Martin, Monmerqué, Labouderie), where Nodier's word was law? And the weekly visits to the great bookbinder, Thouvenin, the sessions at the bookstores, Crozet's and the latter's brother-in-law, Techener's, which seemed most animated when Nodier was present? These, though drastically reduced, did not have to be altogether eliminated and Charles would go on delighting with his sallies the bookloving gentry of Paris, Count Montaran, the Marquis de Ganay and de Chateau-Giron, Paul Lacroix, and the ubiquitous Pixerécourt. Did he not suggest just recently to the bookseller, J. J. Techener, the printing of a magazine intended strictly for bibliophiles? Of course he knew he would be involved in its publication, at least in an advisory capacity, but it was two years before his name was officially associated with the editorship of *Le Bulletin du Bibliophile*. In fact, considering the wretched condition of his health, it is quite amazing the number of articles, stories, prefaces, etc., he managed to contribute—not to mention a voluminous correspondence—in the last eight years of his life.

Toward the end of May, 1835, feeling much better and eager to get away from the fatiguing contemplation of the overwhelming backlog of work that had piled up during his illness, Charles took Désirée on a long-overdue holiday to Belgium. After a hectic week in Brussels, where, to their surprise, they were fêted at official dinners and receptions given in their honor, the Nodiers went to Malines where Charles was awakened the following morning by the music of the Light Horse Regimental Band. From there Charles wrote to Baron Taylor, June 5, to tell him, though he had suffered a recurrence of his illness and was in some pain, he had thoroughly loved Brussels, Taylor's birthplace, where "he enjoyed much less incognito than at Paris" and where the publisher Adolph Haumann had literally overwhelmed him with "politesses."

The newspapers, having got wind of Nodier's presence in Belgium, published his itinerary, so the rest of the trip was really the triumphal progress of a celebrity across the little country, a refreshing experience for him. No wonder he called his three-week visit to Belgium the sojourn of a successful actor on tour. Faithful Weiss reported to his diary, June 24, 1835, "Fallot [assistant librarian at the Institute] tells me that Nodier's trip to Belgium is a series of ovations and triumphs. In many towns he was offered the wine of honor and everywhere he was welcomed and fêted as he deserves." Nodier's *Une Corbeille de rognures,* published on leaves of different colors, was brought out the following year by Hennebert in Tournay to commemorate Charles' visit. In the *Revue de Bruxelles* for December, 1837, there appeared over his name a truncated version of *La Légende de soeur Béatrix* —about the first third of it, stopping just short of the story of Sister Beatrice—entitled "Notre-Dame-des-Epines-Fleuries. After Nodier's death, Baron Frederick de Reiffenberg, whom Charles had gone to see about books at Louvain in 1835, printed a regular *faire-part* complete with black border and cross over grave in the pages of the first volume of *Le Bibliophile Belge* (1845), though Charles had been dead more than a year. As editor of this newly founded periodical, in emulation of its elder sister, Nodier's *Bulletin du Bibliophile,* Reiffenberg added five pages recalling his friend's visit nine years earlier.

On June 17, 1835, he was back in France. Unable to travel by any but the easiest of stages, Charles arrived in Paris June 21. But he found he was to go out again in August to represent the Academy, along with Roger and Michaud, at the unveiling of a statue to Cuvier in Montbéliard.

In the interim he had been appointed *rapporteur* of the dictionary of the Academy, and suddenly he reversed his former stand on that work. In the first of four articles published in *Le Temps* on this subject, August 25, 1835, Nodier admitted that he may have been somewhat caustic in his past criticism of the *Dictionnaire,* since the perfect dictionary of the living language, does not and really cannot exist, and (as he will state in a later article) nothing is easier to criticize than a dictionary. What were the objections to the first edition in 1694? Critics reproached it for having "disdained etymology, for not having kept abreast of industrial and scientific nomenclatures, and for not drawing examples from the established writers of the time." These had been essentially his own objections to *all* editions.

Nodier next took up these points one by one to refute them. Etymology, which was a popular science in the seventeenth century, may be summed up in the works of Ménage; who, though he really had a place in the Academy, "since he was a man of great learning, was really a very bad etymologist; he would have drawn this illustrious company into grave error, if it had had faith in his judgment." So the Academy did well not to listen to him and to leave to a later age the study of etymology. It showed wisdom too in not including the jargons of industry and science: "If [the Academy] had followed Furetière's sketchy plan, its dictionary would have fallen into that class of books which are outdated before they leave the press and it would be as little consulted as Furetière's own dictionary." Nomenclature changes too fast and specialized lexicons are always available to those concerned. As to the last point, the failure of the first edition to base itself on writers who made authority in the language, none of these gentlemen was in existence when the Academy began its dictionary, so how could it have quoted them? Conclusion:

> The Academy therefore acted with perfect wisdom in setting aside from its plan etymologies, which were still to be found, scientific nomenclature, which will always have to be renewed, and quotations from classic authors, impossible in a language which was only twenty years old and of which the Academy represented the principal authority.

The three abovementioned objections must be taken into consideration by any good dictionary, but the time was not ripe for the Academy to entertain them. "The Academy had the duty to compose the *Dictionary* of the usual language, to clarify it by sensible definitions and familiar examples correctly expressed; the Academy did just that." According to Nodier, if it had done otherwise, the *Dictionnaire* would have been as dead as the etymologies of Court de Gébelin and the nomenclatures of Tournefort and Macquer.

In a follow-up article of September 22 Nodier focused his

attention on the sixth edition, the one he had flayed so mercilessly four years before. Now he found that many improvements were to be noted, though in the main the 1831 version followed the plan of the first. Thus, "innumerable additions prescribed by usage and confirmed by the authority of the most recent good writers, more exact definitions, usually clearer and occasionally more correct, a multitude of forgotten acceptations restored to their normal place," gave the sixth edition a really classic advantage over all the others. He went out of his way to point out that he had nothing to do with this edition, which he praised as "the literary charter, the grammatical Bible of the nation." In a third article, entitled "Des satires publiées à l'occasion du premier Dictionnaire de l'Académie" (October 2), he reviewed Saint-Evremond's *Comédie des académistes* (1646), which he called an insipid farce. He doubted (along with Voltaire!) that Saint-Evremond wrote the *Conversation du Maréchal d'Hocquincourt et du Père Canaye*. "Médiocre," disposes of the next satire in point of time, Ménage's *Requête des dictionnaires* (1652). As for Furetière's first *Factum contre quelques-uns* (1685), he rated this a masterpiece of diplomacy and stated that Furetière was entirely justified in questioning the Academy's right to monopolize the field of lexicography. Nodier admitted that Furetière's second *Factum* of the following year was vitriolic and harsh, but he had been expelled from its membership and there was some justification for descending to personalities. The third *Factum* by the same author (1688) Nodier classed as "a fine polemic and a treasure-house of sallies"; only the attack on La Fontaine contained in it was unjustified in his estimation. Chastein's *L'Apothéose du dictionnaire de l'Académie* (1696) included some excellent "remarques critiques" which the Academy used to advantage; his *Enterrement du dictionnaire de l'Académie* (1697) contained judicious "remarques grammaticales." Finally, in a fourth article (January 28, 1836) Nodier again praised the sixth edition for containing "thousands of truths," lauded its Préface and the man responsible for it, the perpetual secretary of the Academy, Villemain. Later in the year, Charles wrote an "Introduction nécessaire" to Paul Ackermann's *Vocabulaire de la langue française extrait de la dernière édition du dictionnaire de l'Académie Française* in which he praised the Academy for not creating signs to explain pronunciation.

The above paragraphs offer a lesson in the ephemeral nature of literary judgments; that which seemed black may be seen to be white, depending on whether one is in or out. Nodier here displayed versatility in using the same names, Ménage, Furetière, Court de Gébelin, to splash mud against or to whitewash the walls of the Academy, as needed. An observer who was constantly on the alert quietly but firmly condemned this time-serving tendency in Nodier's manner when he wrote shortly thereafter, "*Le Temps* contains an article by Nodier, 'De la dignité des avocats et de l'indignité des bibliothécaires' [February 20, 1836]. In this article, entirely too learned to my mind, larded as it is with Latin quotations which have nothing to do here, Nodier very wittily pokes fun at the lawyers' mannerisms and pretensions. But he will be reproached for having seized this occasion to compliment Mr. Dupin at the very moment when it seems likely that gentleman will be called to administer, at least indirectly, the affairs of France. When Nodier dedicated I no longer remember which one of his works [*Souvenirs, épisodes et portraits pour servir à l'histoire de la Révolution et de l'Empire,* 1831] to Mr. Laffitte in disgrace [he had just lost his cabinet post and gone bankrupt] there was dignity in that act. But there is none in showering praise on a man in favor whose public character is anything but estimable." (Weiss, *Journal,* February 22, 1836). First the transformation of the attacks on the *Dictionnaire* into a rosary of lauds, then the pats on the backs of Villemain and Dupin, the very men who had looked sour at his reception, all this was Charles' way of expressing thanks for having been named *rapporteur.*

And now let the reader contemplate two estimates of Charles' reformed behavior, both written by women who knew him intimately. The first is taken from Madame Ancelot's *Salons de Paris, foyers éteints* (1858, p. 124). "As he came to love people less he praised them more, as if to fill up with words the measure of affection he had withdrawn from them; since he did not wish to be shaken in his convictions, it followed that he must perforce praise those of others." The second gem is drawn from the biography written by his daughter, Marie Nodier-Mennessier, *Charles Nodier, épisodes et souvenirs de sa vie* (1867, p. 29). "It was when the maturity of reflection and the fatigue of living led him to accept everyone's opinions that he almost never agreed with anyone."

Though he had become very domestic in his attitude toward the Academy (and its dictionary, once he had taken possession of it), he could still show his claws on occasion to the run-of-the-mill academicians. At a session of the Academy on pronunciation—Nodier was presiding—he had just explained the rule requiring that a *t* placed between two *i*'s be pronounced as a *c*, "making allowances for the exceptions, of course." And with that he was about to turn the page when the voice of Dupaty barked out dogmatically, "There aren't any exceptions; the rule is absolute." "Do you affirm it?" returned Nodier wearily; then, fixing his prey with half-closed eyes, he drawls gently, "Alors, faites-moi *l'amicié* de répéter ça; je retrancherai la *moicié* de mon observation, et vous prendrez en *picié* mon ignorance."

Despite his determination to serve everyone, Charles' eminent position in the Academy cost him more friends than it gained. "Since I had the misfortune," he wrote in the introduction to *La Bibliographie des fous* (November, 1835) "of making irreconcilable enemies of the two or three great men I praised to the skies but did not have the strength to maintain in that exalted position (leading them to conclude that I did not praise them enough) I have taken a solemn oath never to speak of contemporaries again." Aside from the rebuff offered Hugo in that year (1836) he noted the cooling of another friend of more than twenty years standing, Aimé Martin, who was also seeking, unsuccessfully, a seat in the Academy. Unable to explain his many failures, for the reasons given below Martin decided that Nodier must be the obstacle blocking his election. In confidence he told François Grille—an envious scribbler who secretly detested Nodier—that he (Martin) and Nodier were constantly competing for the same things: a seat in the Academy, books at Techener's or at Crozet's, in short, their careers ran parallel courses. "Nodier could not stand being bested out of an Elzevir or a Gryphius that he coveted," Martin was reported to have said, "and, while feigning to joke about it, he held a grudge against the successful buyer that went deep though it was suppressed." "You will have the book," he would say quietly, "but you won't get my vote."[1] Later, this same Grille had the gall to write to Nodier to ask him why he wouldn't vote for Martin (November 15, 1842). During this period, Martin must have had somewhat the same idea, for we find Charles explaining to him that his election does not depend solely on friend Nodier.

"My stupidity has not prevented me from becoming an academician and I daresay there's nothing new about that. When I entered the Academy *with the firm intention of subordinating myself to all* [italics added] I did not make a secret of the fact that all my desires regarding future candidates were summed up in you, Ballanche, and Victor Hugo." So Aimé Martin's seat was assured and it was only a question of time; but Charles could not tell him *when* he would be elected; that was beyond his control. "When you have become a member, you will understand," Charles concluded, assuring him that if it lay in his power to do something about it, he would; meantime he would go on voting for Martin every time his name came up.[2] Needless to add, Aimé Martin was never elected, but it would be difficult to put the blame on Charles; the other two gentlemen "who summed up all his desires" were: Victor Hugo in 1841 and Ballanche in 1842.

Nodier took cognizance of the emergence of another enemy in the opening pages of his wearisome "Voyage pittoresque dans le Paraguay Roux," published in the *Revue de Paris* (February, 1836), where he cited "le bel ouvrage" of the young bibliographer, J. M. Quérard [*La France littéraire ou dictionnaire bibliographique,* 1834] "where he speaks so ill of me." Again in 1834, the orientalist and converted Jew, "Baron" Ferdinand Eckstein, who had been living and working in France since the Restoration, gave an appreciation of Charles' "Notions élémentaires de linguistique" in *L'Investigateur* (September), the official organ of the Historical Institute. This article Sainte-Beuve termed "severe," but it was worse than that. Eckstein accused Nodier of being a dilettante who had not kept abreast of "le mouvement des sciences" and flatly disagreed with his pivotal points concerning the universal language and the perfect alphabet. Nodier acknowledged with characteristic aplomb and disarming candor in two supplements to the "Notions" published in *Le Temps,* November 8 and 10, 1834. In the first he admitted that Eckstein's was one of the best articles he had ever read in a magazine, and in the second he excused his ignorance by saying that Eckstein was too learned to understand his simplicity and that he was too simple to understand the orientalist's great learning. Nodier then retired from the combat with the weak contention that the origin of language was lost in mystery, so why argue? (!) It seems Eckstein accepted the invitation to disengage the contest hardly begun, for nothing further came from that quarter on the subject; which was perhaps best for the subject, since neither one knew what he was talking about. Nodier was, after all, a dilettante and the "Baron" was an *arriviste* intellectual with a bad case of undigested Hegel. In this negative sense, we must admit Charles had the best of it.

On the debit side, too, must be placed a series of tiresome satires against industrial and scientific progress that Nodier published at this time in the *Revue de Paris.* Later grouped under the pretentious heading, "Fantaisies du dériseur sensé," these pieces bore the separate titles "Hurlubleu," "Grand Manifafa d'Hurlubière, ou la perfectibilité, histoire progressive," "Léviathan-le-Long," "Archikan des Patagons de l'île savante, ou la perfectibilité, pour faire suite à Hurlubleu" (1833) and "Voyage pittoresque et industriel dans le Paraguay Roux et la palingénésie australe" (1836). It is astounding that anyone so lucid in charting the new movement in literature against the backdrop of social change after the great revolution could have been so blind to the advance of science and industry. As Weiss, who was rarely wrong, put it, "Nodier has not understood what is wonderful about this century; he has not made an ensemble of all his works. Nothing of his will remain." (*Journal,* October 3, 1833.)

Nodier had always been weak in science; "il n'avait pas

la tête savante," to paraphrase one of his own expressions. More than forty years earlier Girod de Chantrans experienced great difficulty in showing Charles the simplest rudiments of algebra; his pupil had thrown up a wall of resistance even to the commonest notions of arithmetic: "I am ready to believe that two and two make four," he would say, "but how can you prove it to me?" At Novillars he had been equally impervious to elementary physics and was stumped by problems that any secondary-school freshman could solve with ease. Later, the experimental science of chemistry gave him no end of trouble. His ability as a botanist and entomologist, on the other hand, may be traced to his amazingly retentive memory; he excelled in them because they demanded of him no more than the art of bibliography: they appealed to his genius for classification. For the rest, he preferred knowledge of the intuitive sort and rightly dedicated his life to literature. But it is hard to understand why the man who had paved the way for the new literature should have opposed the new travel by rail, lighting by gas, mutual education, technical and scientific terms desperately needed to explain recent achievements in science and industry. We have already seen that Nodier resisted the introduction of the "jargons" of science and industry into the Academy's dictionary with such fanatical fury as to induce a reluctance on the part of that organ to include new terms. Indeed, a century later, Emile Picard could still deplore the "excessive prudence" the dictionary exercised in admitting new scientific and technical words, "which sufficient usage would seem to have consecrated."[3]

His action in this respect was shortsighted and boneheaded, as was his tenacious clinging to ancient orthography—*françois* for *français*, *sentimens* for *sentiments*, and terminating all imperfect and conditional tenses with *oit* and *oient* instead of *ait* and *aient*—which went back to pre-Voltaire days. His daughter Marie affected this silly spelling to the end of her life, and the editors of the *Bulletin du Bibliophile* were so impressed with this nonsense that they did not abandon it until 1865! If language is made by common usage, as Charles contended so often and with so much justice, then why oppose so stubbornly and so stupidly movement and change in language, which are, after all, signs of life? If romantic literature, as he justly maintained, was the reflection of the contemporary social ethos, then why should writers portray it in the language that was current two hundred years before? Is not a language that is properly embellished by terms reflecting scientific discoveries and new techniques the only valid instrument of the interpreters of an age?

He was happier when his satire fell upon changes in literary fashions, as in this paragraph from the opening pages of his short story, *Paul, ou la ressemblance* (1836):

This great epic traveler of antiquity [Ulysses] whose tales I love so well would be quite surprised if he had to relate his immortal fable today. He would be told that his Circe is nothing more than Levaillant's Narina, or Bougainville's Oberea. His sirens are seals or sea cows; Charybdis and Scylla, rocks; Polyphemus a blind, man-eating Patagonian. Oh, the happy influence of discoveries and progress!

Literature suffers when imagination falters and poetry is dismissed; but this is hardly a reason to condemn discoveries which may open new vistas for the imagination to ponder.

One of the basic elements in Nodier's makeup encouraging him to oppose change sprang from the superstitious nature of his beliefs. He was never a very religious man, but he was impressed with the hobgoblin stories the Nodiers' superannuated maid Denise told him when he was a boy, and as time went on he added all the common and uncommon superstitions he heard of or read about. These strange beliefs he carried to his grave, and whenever a black cat crossed his path, or he spilled salt, or he was thirteenth at table, or—since he was an entomologist—the dread *blaps mortis aga* fell at his feet or fluttered through the open window onto his coverlet, he was sure something disastrous would result. It was usually with great glee that he pointed out the coincidences (which he did not consider coincidences, but cause and effect) which seemed to justify his apprehensions.

We were first introduced to this side of Nodier's preoccupations in his essay, "De quelques phénomènes du sommeil," published in the *Revue de Paris* in January 1831. There, in speaking of the popular interpretation of dreams, he commented, "That is perhaps mere superstition, as I am ready to admit; but may I be so bold as to ask, what local truth is not traceable to superstition and what universal superstition does not contain a truth?" But this subject received its fullest expression in *M. de la Mettrie, Revue de Paris,* September, 1831, where that philosopher, in an imagined conversation with the author, undertakes a brilliant defense of world superstitions as based on logical motives, the origins of which have been either lost or forgotten. Throughout the dialogue, La Mettrie makes a consistent plea for superstitious acts and gestures as being merely emblems or symbols, the outward signs of deep-rooted distress or imminent danger, and that all superstitions, when diligently traced back to their origin, may be shown to have a history as ancient as that of man himself. It was this gift of the clairvoyant philosopher that fascinated Nodier.

Then Charles returned to the horror tale à la Edgar Allan Poe with the *Histoire d'Hélène Gillet* (extra-sensory perception), *Mademoiselle de Marsan* (illuminist contacts) and *L'Amour et le grimoire* (diabolism), 1832. These are not without a touch of the macabre, but it was not until *Un domestique de M. le Marquis de Louvois*, subtitled *Paul ou la ressemblance,* and *M. Cazotte* (1836) that the occult began to reappear in his tales with compelling force. In the first of these stories the Virgin Mary appears to the grieving mother of Paul as the *dea ex machina* who indicates to her the continuing existence of Paul and bids her send her husband into the mountains to seek him. Though this develops as a simple case of striking identity, thus keeping the tale within the bounds of hard logic, and though the marquis' servant refused to assume Paul's brilliant prospects, which nullifies the supernatural intervention of the Virgin Mary, Nodier manages a plea in favor of belief in the occult through the mouth of Paul's father. When his wife acquaints him with her vision, he says, "I hesitated [going to the mountain] because the company of enlightened people and constant reading had cured me of popular prejudices. Is this a great benefit? It must be, since philosophers are so eager to have everyone share it."

In *M. Cazotte*, a fragment (Weiss was broken-hearted when he learned Nodier would not finish it), the hero is about to expose a grand divination concerning unknown details of the assassination of Henry IV through the powers of Madame Lebrun (Marion Delorme) when the story is abruptly put off because of the lateness of the hour. In the ghost story, *Inès de las Sierras* (1837), the rational solution is not given until the end, à la Anne Radcliff, whom most critics agree Nodier seems to be following here. (Might there not have been a Spanish influence as well in this typical fusion of the natural with the supernatural?) But in *La Légende de Soeur Béatrix* (1837) Nodier does nothing to spoil the miracle that unfolds in the naive tradition of medieval lore. In this little prose poem Notre-Dame-des-Epines-Fleuries carries on the custodial duties of the chapel dedicated to her worship as a humble substitute for the wayward Beatrice, who has run off with Raymond. Sixteen years later, when Beatrice, abandoned by her lover and bearing the marks of crime and debauchery, returns to the chapel as a penitent, the Virgin climbs back onto her altar and Beatrice, miraculously resuming her youth and purity (a sign her transgressions have been forgiven), goes on with her duties as before. Thanks to the complicity of her patroness, Beatrice's long absence has gone unnoticed and she dies a centenarian and a saint.

At the same time that he was propounding his faith in popular superstitions, Nodier was moving toward a *mystique* of popular art which made him the first mythographer and a precursor of modern anthropology. Ultimately it led him to an aesthetic theory not far removed from Tolstoi's later expression of it in *What is Art?* According to this thesis, art sprang pure from the common people where it had been implanted, like the universal language—in which he also believed—by the divine will. This heritage should therefore be collected by writers with reverent fingers, unsullied, unsophisticated and unchanged. These fables, myths, legends, and popular tales were to be transmitted to posterity as a sacred legacy equal to the Ten Commandments, whose capsule-like wisdom they reflected in a variety of imaginative forms. It was this mission of preserving and encouraging artistic manifestations of the anonymous mass that took the place of religion in Nodier's last years.

A quarter of a century earlier, Charles was urging the Slovenes in Illyria to gather and preserve their folklore before it was too late. In the Introduction to the *Voyages pittoresques et romantiques* (1820) he dedicated himself and his colleagues in that work to a similar task, but he saw it in clearer focus. "We will not scorn local legends and fairy tales," he explained. "These are perhaps prejudices, but the mythology of the ancients was also composed of prejudices and those enchanting lies became the common property of all peoples. It is thanks to their prestige that the glory of ancient Greece and Rome was perpetuated across the centuries and that an empire, more solid than the one resulting from might and conquest, was preserved to these ancient mistresses of the earth."

Was he not saying, in effect, that all that was left of the glory of Greece was a body of legend which still had currency in world literature? Indeed, he continued, it is impossible to understand our own literature without a knowledge of this corpus of mythology. Although mythology of his day was poorer, he went on, it was not entirely without significance: Dante borrowed tableaux from it which later inspired Michelangelo; Shakespeare got his fairies and sorceresses there, and German literature was loaded with allusions to it. Nodier was keenly aware that too much Western European lore, ergo literature, had been lost, or at least neglected, because it was deemed crude and barbarous in comparison to the myths of the ancients. It was too early for evaluation; like the Gothic monuments, the myths of France had their *raison d'être*.

Nodier insisted again and again that he was only trying to recreate fairy tales and legends he had heard as a child and which had been handed down from time immemorial. The envious Grille said that Nodier could be seen occasionally at the Café Déhodenq, "surrounded by a crowd of unknown authors whom he advised and guided in return for their applause of his works."[4] This was a gross misrepresentation of what Nodier was trying to do: point out to young, unknown writers—now that the known authors had strayed away from him—the vast body of material that lay dormant in the *récits populaires*. "Let us hasten to listen to the delightful stories of the people," he said in the exordium to *La Légende de Soeur Béatrix*, "before they forget them, before they become ashamed of them and, like Eve made shy by her nakedness, cover their chaste poetry with a veil." As Emile Ripert said, Nodier was inviting them to glorify in literature these tales which sprang from the very soul of the people, not only because time was short and the tales would soon disappear forever, but also because the early years of the nineteenth century offered a unique literary opportunity for this sort of task.[5]

Not the least of his merits in this respect was his ceaseless defense of the various *patois* spoken by the common people in many provinces of France and held in contempt by cultivated Frenchmen. In that age of budding nationalism there were movements afoot to suppress local dialects in an effort to unify the language by having them declared unconstitutional! Nodier's indignation knew no bounds when he read the outrageous plan to sweep away the dialects of southern France by legislation proposed by the Cahors Committee. Earlier, he had burst into eloquent sarcasm against the harebrained reforms of the conventionists Barrère and the Abbé Grégoire to "uniform" the language.[6] As Ripert stated, Nodier had already found the impassioned tones of the later Mistral in defending his beloved *patois*.

Charles was practically alone at the time, among literate Frenchmen, in considering dialects living languages capable of producing great literature. His correspondence shows how closely he followed the legal battles in which the survival of dialects was involved. Nodier also encouraged and assisted the barber-poet of Agen, Jasmin. Charles invited him to the Arsenal and helped him find a publisher for his poems in the Languedoc dialect.[7] Finally, Jules Corbelet, in *Glossaire étymologique et comparatif du patois picard* (1851), and Pierquin de Gembloux, *Histoire littéraire, philologique et bibli-*

ographique des patois (1858), both cite Nodier, whose ideas they are carrying out, as the inspirer of their work on the *patois*.[8] This is one facet of Nodier's multiple activity that has evoked no controversy.

Cécile L. (Adèle Hugo), in a brilliant article for *L'Evénement* published January 9, 1849, said that Charles was always hailing unsung heroes and discovering new geniuses that nobody ever heard of, then or later. Such was apparently the case of the young peasant he picked up in a café somewhere and brought home to delight the guests of the Arsenal. Faced with a large company, the "poet" suddenly went dumb, looked down at his shoes, and nothing was to be got from him for the rest of the evening. Had Charles endowed him with his own wit in private conversation or was the rustic really so shy?

To this we have no ready answer, except that Nodier must have encountered many such disillusionments in his efforts to reach the heart of the people, for the most part inarticulate in their own behalf. Such was seemingly not the case in the unusual experiment carried out, at Nodier's instigation, by the philosopher, Ballanche. Charles, who for a time was engrossed in Ballanche's theory of palingenesis, challenged him to harangue a group of workingmen outside the Arsenal to prove his ideas were easy to grasp and would not be above the comprehension of the man in the street. Together they faced the mob and began a discussion which ended to everyone's high satisfaction. Let Ballanche tell it. "Can you believe that I was drawn into a discussion provoked by Nodier in which I was led to expound my historical system, founded on the Christian dogma of the fall and the rehabilitation [of man], and that I was perfectly understood?"[9]

Another of Nodier's "discoveries" that worked out to everyone's advantage was the eccentric polyglot Hungarian, Menteli, whom he brought to the Arsenal when he took over the library in 1824. According to Weiss' *Journal*, January 6, 1837, Menteli occupied a sort of hovel there (*un bouge*) and fed on roots and bread purchased from the soldiers in a barracks nearby. Toward the end of 1836, while drawing his weekly supply of water, he fell into the Seine and drowned. He was reputed to have spoken all the languages of Europe and Asia, though no one knew where he had learned them, and had aided Nodier materially in classifying all the undecipherable manuscripts. Charles marked his passing with a notice inserted in *Le Temps*, January 1, 1837.

Every year Weiss sent a crop of promising young men from Franche-Comté to be guided and aided in the busy capital by the master of the Arsenal. More often than not, Nodier was able to find them suitable employment. But one candidate who came from there in 1837, without Weiss' blessing, caused Charles a little moment of embarrassment. It was young Rodet, the fruit of Nodier's philandering with *la dame du comptoir* at Lons nineteen years earlier when he was supposed to have been tending to business in Quintigny, accompanied by his mother. Madame Rodet decided it was time for her son, now a strapping boy of 18, to enter a career; since his father had made such a success in literature, why not make him a writer? When Charles got over the shock of this untimely apparition, he opposed Madame Rodet's plans for her son with all the arguments at his command. "Well, what shall I do with my son?" she asked in despair. Désirée, who was present at the interview, cut in, "What else but a café owner!" This flash of down-to-earth wit seems to have saved a sticky situation and provided the Arsenal habitués with merry conversation for many days thereafter.

Not content with exalting the heroism of humble folk in his short stories—the blind Gervais in *Les Aveugles de Chamounay*, Paul in *Un Domestique du Marquis de Louvois*, George in *Lydie* and the saintly *Lidivine* and her grandson—Charles reduced his own life to the simplicity and humility of his protagonists. Cécile L. has described, in the article quoted earlier, how the stove-pipe "impudently" crossed the magnificent salon of the Arsenal. The potbellied stove it served was used by the master to warm his cabbage soup, which lent an odor of poverty to the elegant mansion. When the gay youngsters came no more to the Arsenal and the bookhunting expeditions had to be abandoned, Nodier could be seen of an evening on the Vincennes road dragging his weary body to a wretched cabaret in Saint-Mandé where he feasted on peasant bread and ate the humble offerings of the place with pewter forks and spoons. "He made himself, as much as lay within him, child, people, the man in the street," she tells us. He observed faithfully all the domestic traditional eating: the Twelfth Night cake (whoever gets the bean is king, though he break a tooth on it), the Easter ham, doughnuts at carnival time, and the birthday and name-day feasts.

Perhaps, without realizing it, Charles was illustrating another facet of French romanticism, observed early in 1826 by Cyprien Desmarais in his *Essai sur les classiques et les romantiques*. Desmarais was convinced contemporary literature could make itself romantic simply by becoming "naive et populaire." In the preface to *Les Quatre Talismans* (1838) Nodier dedicated the story "to that class of society which has, according to me, understood best its obligations and which could get the most out of life, if it realized all its advantages; I mean the working class." The fable of the four brothers which follows amply develops this thesis. A one-eyed genie grants talismans of riches, beauty, and wisdom, in that order, to the first three brothers who abandon the youngest to his fate. Having exhausted his supply of talismans, the genie awards the fourth brother, Ebid, a set of tools. Douban, the rich man, succeeds only in attracting envy and robbers and is finally reduced to beggary. Mahoud, the seducer, is driven from place to place by jealous husbands and ends by marrying the ugliest woman in all the world, who beats him, then destroys the amulet that made him so desirable to women and throws him out to beg. Pirouz, the wise man, has practiced medicine so successfully that he is called as a consultant in a hopeless case, to cure the king of Egypt who is not ill but bored; since his talisman tells him nothing of the king's malady, he cannot help him and is condemned to death, but at this point a doctor of the court, who had been observing Pirouz's many successes among the people and guessing some secret power lay behind his ability to diagnose, offers to take Pirouz as a subject for vivisection. Once in the doctor's laboratory, Pirouz is persuaded to give up his amulet in exchange for his freedom, and he too is forced to beg. Now all three brothers, as frequently happens in such fables, in their quest for alms are attracted to the home of *Le Bienfaisant*, who is known for his generosity. Who should this be but brother Ebid, who dutifully learned to use the tools the genie gave him, became an industrious workman, made a splendid marriage, and is enjoying a comfortable old age. The moral is given in the last line: "We will easily agree that of all the talismans which promise happiness to the vain ambitions of men, none is surer than work."

Offering work as a solution of man's fate is an old story. Voltaire's well-known admonition in *Candide* is "Cultivons nos jardins!" But in Nodier the lesson was not the result of disillusionment and cynicism; it was rather his growing conviction that the minds of simple people are the repository of unfathomable intuitions, and the lower the social scale the more sacred that trust. Hence the power of divination, of prophecy, and of extrasensory perception on the part of simpletons and madmen in Nodier's stories. He deemed them purer vessels for receiving, reflecting, and preserving a host of supernatural events which they could not understand and therefore could not spoil. "I understood then," he says in speaking of the simple-minded *Baptiste Montauban* (1833) "that he was an idiot or, in the language of the country, *un innocent*"; and he comments, "Ours is a funny world where two elect beings, namely the inoffensive one and the one who prefers to live alone, are repulsed with scorn in every corner of civilization, like poor children who have died without the benefit of baptism!" Nodier had pointed out earlier ("De quelques phénomènes du sommeil") that the ancients had only one word to designate the two concepts of *solitary* and *idiot*.

Probably the best of his short stories on this theme was *Jean-François les bas-bleus*, which first appeared in *Les Cent-et-une nouvelles nouvelles des cent-et-un* (1823), but which he placed immediately after *Baptiste Montauban* (1833) in the eleventh volume of his *Works* subtitled *Contes en prose et en vers* (1837), thereby stressing that *Jean-François les bas-bleus* marked a further development of his ideas. There are many points of similarity between the two idiots, Jean-François and Baptiste. Both show signs of early brilliance in scholarship and are intended for the priesthood by honest but poor parents; both are extremely obedient sons; both are crossed in love, become confused and take refuge in silence rather than disoblige their parents and both become the butt of children and wags as the town idiots. Here the similarity ends; Nodier endowed his countryman Jean-François with extrasensory perception. The simpleton Baptiste has a strange power over birds and animals, it is true, but he is no visionary. He talks volubly and sweetly only in the presence of non-human beings; otherwise he remains silent. Whenever he speaks, he makes sense. Jean-François, on the other hand, carries on a continuous muttering with unseen interlocutors somewhere in space and can be drawn into conversations of an intellectual nature only. Now and then he seems to be listening to a voice from afar as his eyes take on a fixed expression of inspiration. While in this trance he notes the exact moment of the beheading of Marie Antoinette in Paris, one hundred leagues away from Besançon. Later, when he sees his former sweetheart, her mother, and her brother guillotined in a similar vision, he drops dead in the street. Fantastic? So was America before Columbus, says Nodier.

Though *La Neuvaine de la chandeleur* (1838) has overtones of extrasensory perception—the hero and the heroine live in different cities yet see each other in a vision before they become acquainted—the story has a disappointing close: Charles thought fit to revert to the death-before-marriage theme of novels he wrote around 1818 or 1819. Not so *Lydie ou la résurrection* (1839), the last of his short stories in this vein. Varying the formula, he has George, the husband, die in a fire while trying to save his children, leaving Lydie, his widow, hopelessly mad. But every night, as she relates to a traveler, in her sleep she sees George in a sort of paradise for the resuscitated until such time as she will join him there forever. When the traveler asks her if she has this "dream" every evening, she answers with some surprise, "Do you call that a dream, like the others? Oh, don't become alarmed, I shall not hold it against you. The living can judge only by

their senses, which are shrouded in impenetrable darkness."
The traveler thanks her for the consolation he has derived
from her vision:

Where I saw only an enigma impossible to solve without
great effort and sacrifice, you have taught me that the
solution of this imposing mystery belongs to those who
know how to love and suffer. Fear of suffering made me
afraid of loving. I did not know that by avoiding the rig-
orous trials of the heart out of a pusillanimous doubt of
my strength that I was altering in me the most vital principle of my immortality, the only one that can obtain for
us an eternal recompense and permit us to share in the
eternal joys. Your words have relit the torch of active
charity that I was striving to quench in my breast. I am
going back among men to aid them in their troubles, or
at least to weep with them when I am helpless to assist
them. I am going to take up my share of the calamities
that are part and parcel of our transitory existence; let
there accumulate on my bowed head all those I can spare
others too. If I have any regrets, the greatest must be the
blind negligence of this duty for so long, thanks to a false
philosophy; a duty too easy to perform once man decides
to be worthy of his destiny.There can be no real misfortune for a love that leans on hope and faith.

After his long conversation with Lydie, the tourist is told
by his guide that it is too late to visit the Château de Chillon.
Whereupon the traveler cries out petulantly, "What do I care
about the Château de Chillon and the remains of the Middle
Ages and for that matter all the poetic souvenirs, even the
marvels of nature I was going to admire in the Alps! My
friends are saddened by my absence, my mother is old and
infirm, I have left a sick servant at home, the oldest of our
neighbors has lost his cow, the money I am squandering
on pleasure here is lacking in twenty homes in my village;
tomorrow I shall take the road that leads back to the Juras."
So here too an all-important lesson was learned from a de-
ranged mystic, who was privileged to live a good part of her

earthly life in the other world. As Professor Castex has stated, "Nodier's fantastic stories, begun under the sign of anxiety, conclude in a myth to the glory of evangelical wisdom."[10]

His health was failing rapidly. At the end of 1836 he announced to Weiss that a cataract had formed on his left eye and he could use his right eye only with the aid of powerful glasses. He had gone completely deaf in his right ear and the hearing of his left ear was impaired. For some time now he trembled violently when he wrote. As Cécile L. tells us in the article previously quoted, "Action became repulsive to him, he hated responsibility and seemed to take pleasure in being ill." Though he was only in his fifty-seventh year, he looked seventy-five; his better than average frame, always slightly stooped, was pronouncedly bent as he walked with a laborious, dragging motion. Ironically, the man who all his life had tried to make himself four to eight years younger, was practically reduced to producing documents now to prove his actual age.

In the late thirties and early forties Charles was more in bed than out. Such energy as he could muster was devoted to the Thursday meetings of the Academy—often the only sortie of the week for him—writing articles, prefaces, and keeping up with his correspondence. Occasional articles, signed with a new pseudonym, Dr. Néophobus, against progress, the metric system, neologisms, the new nomenclature Thierry had found for the carolingian and merovingian kings of France, greeted the reader in the pages of the *Revue de Paris*. A rare review or a notice contributed to *L'Artiste* or *Le Bulletin du Bibliophile* completed the leaven of magazine writing for this period. The keepsake albums of the day carried some short stories by Nodier. Thus *Le Génie bonhomme* appeared in four languages in the *Veillées de Famille* (1837), *L'Amateur de livres* in *Les Français Peints Par Eux-Mêmes* (Volume III, 1841), *Un renard pris au piège* and *Tablettes de la giraffe du Jardin des Plantes* in *Scènes de la Vie Privée et Publique des Animaux* (1842). Charles had returned to his first love, books. With or without benefit of another alias, Mr. Oldbook, he compiled *notes littéraires et bibliographiques* for the libraries of his friends, Pixerécourt (1838), Crozet (1841),

Sampayo (1842), and for himself, *Description raisonnée d'une jolie collection de livres* (1844).

But the preface-seekers were Charles' busiest clients. Any book advertising a foreword by Charles Nodier was bound to be a success in the trade, or so the authors and publishers thought. One grateful author spoke poetically of "the white marble staircase you fashioned to lead into the humble dwelling I had built." Friends, acquaintances, friends of friends, sisters and wives of famous writers, people he had not seen in thirty years, all begged the favor of a preface. Nodier grew so tired of these importunities that he refused as many as he could by letter; but he did this so gently, so artfully, and so diplomatically that even these were eagerly printed in lieu of prefaces by fame-starved authors! Here is one he wrote in answer to George Duval's request, prompted by his publisher, for a preface to his *Souvenirs de la Terreur* (1841):

Your publisher knows that I keep a preface-shop for my friends' benefit and that I have not the courage to refuse anyone. What he does not realize is that smart people universally laugh at this innocent bit of charlatanism which my extreme docility has led me to abet in spite of myself. An ingenious artist pictured me the other day in a charming caricature as a manufacturer of forewords, words for any and all occasions in and out of season (*avant-propos, à tout propos et hors de propos*). A criticism I find most just and which I accept with almost grateful acknowledgment, but of which I don't want you to suffer the consequences.

So in response to the publisher's request Nodier was sending this letter: "Let him publish this; everyone will know what I think of your book." He did; Nodier's letter appeared as an "Introduction historique." In another, caught between the desire to please and the need for telling the truth, Charles indicated with great delicacy that he had not seen the author in many years, that he had only met him briefly and was a little surprised that he broke his long silence merely to ask a favor. This letter to the publisher Spachmann was nonetheless used as a preface to A. S. Saint-Valry's novel, *Madame de Mably* (1837).

Contrary to his confession that he did not have the heart to refuse anyone, Nodier could and did refuse, when the occasion demanded in letters which could not be used as prefaces. The following, undated and addressed no further than "mon cher ami," may be taken as a prime example:

My dear friend,

Although I do not know what good one of my prefaces can do, or rather, being persuaded of the utter uselessness of these preliminary lucubrations, in all other circumstances I would have acceded with pleasure to your publisher's request that I sign the foreword to your book. The esteem in which I hold you personally, the friendship which has bound us for so many years would have made this task pleasant and easy; but the illness which grips me warns me that I have only one preface left to write, namely the account I owe to the Sovereign Judge of all men for the useless days and the wasted paper.

I would say to you, then, as Ovid to his book, go without me to the town, my friend. Pity me for not being able to contribute to the success of your work by a cooperation which might turn out to be compromising, and please believe that I wish for its success with a fervor and an impatience which I never had for my own.

Yours,
Charles Nodier[11]

His reputation as an authority on the language and as a master of style spread so far that letters came from distant quarters asking him to settle disputes concerning correct usage, proper gender, and points of grammar. He once gave French grammar a slight lump to allow an *employé de la marine* to get back into the good graces of his commanding officer; on another he was sent an enormous fish (*un énorme brochet de la Brenne*) by a graceful loser.

Sieges of bedridden helplessness alternated with recurrent attacks of hypoglycemia when he ventured out. In his capacity as director of the Academy in 1839 Nodier was invited to Passy to preside at the funeral of a fellow-member, his old friend, Michaud. His letter of September 30 to Lebrun asks him to find a substitute. "I have never been to a funeral and

my old friend's would be more painful to me than any other.
I am in any case in such poor health today and am so grieved
by the blow which has struck the Academy that I beg you
to entrust this task, which unfortunately my duty calls me
to fulfill, to another of our colleagues." Lebrun excused him
and presided at the obsequies of Michaud, assisted by Chateaubriand.[12] This was an unpleasant event Charles was perhaps glad to miss; but he also wrote many letters refusing
invitations to dinner from Balzac, Dumas, Hugo, and others
because of ill health.

In the January, 1842, issue of the *Bulletin du Bibliophile*
Techener announced that Nodier had suffered "une grave in-
disposition." In that year Charles was belatedly promoted to
officer of the Legion of Honor, but he derived little pleasure
from this accolade and had scant opportunity to show off his
rosette, confined to his bed as he was most of this year and
the next. "I will be carried in a litter to the Academy to vote
for you," Charles told Vigny after the poet's third unsuccessful
attempt. When Balzac came to the Arsenal to solicit his vote,
Nodier said, "I'll do better than give you my vote, my friend,
I'll leave you my seat." Marie, who met the pale and visibly
shaken novelist as he left the interview, said this was the first
indication the family had that her father was dying. "What
shall I do? I fainted in the street yesterday and they brought
me home more dead than alive," he wrote to the Duchess
d'Orléans' secretary, Asseline, at the time he was ghost-
writing her husband's *Journal de l'expédition des Portes de
Fers* (c. 1843). "I was unable to go to the Academy today.
If I feel strong enough to go out tomorrow, I shall certainly
make an effort to come; but if I don't, will they excuse me?"[13]

Montrond, chancing to meet Nodier during his last illness,
could hardly recognize this wizened, emaciated shell as his
old friend. He was so taken aback that he could not suppress
an exclamation of astonishment: "My God, my poor friend,
how ugly our mistresses have grown!" and Weiss, who, after
many delays and postponements finally reached Paris again
in the spring of 1843, amazed Nodier with his beaming good
health: "How sound you still are!" Charles wrote to his
friend after they parted. "You will have thirty or forty years
to carry on my memory in Besançon." Weiss was so im-

pressed with Nodier's condition that he left Paris secretly minutes after Charles' pathetic "See you next Thursday!" But Nodier was not fooled: "I learned only today, Sunday, that you left last Thursday, though I suspected you had already made your plans. We are both certain 'next Thursday' will never come for us on this earth." *Le bon Weiss* was to survive Nodier twenty-two years.

On December 6, 1843, he insisted on going to the Hôtel de Ville to vote for Alexandre Thierry, who was running for municipal councillor. He would not be dissuaded from performing what he considered to be his civic duty. On his return, he fainted on the stairs of the Arsenal and had to be carried to his bed; he never left it. From the moment he was obliged to assume the horizontal position, which he acknowledged with satisfaction was still "the best of all," Nodier was prepared for the end. "Thoughts of dying did not frighten him," wrote Cécile L., who was at his bedside during the agony. "He looked upon death as the repose of a tired man." After the new year, Sainte-Beuve reported in the *Chroniques parisiennes* (January 3) that Nodier was "gravement malade"; five days later, he was glad to announce, "We learn with pleasure the news that Nodier's health is better; his numerous friends hope to possess for a long time to come his talent and his heart which will be dearer to them than ever." But this was only a momentary respite.

Until the last moment, the Arsenal stairway was crowded with people. Even Louis Philippe sent daily to be informed of his health, which caused Charles to comment, "Who would have thought that they [the king and queen] would be concerned about a poor devil like me?" When his condition became critical, he expressed the desire to see a priest so he could make his last confession. Immediately members of the family wanted to summon a high prelate from Notre Dame, but Charles would not hear of it; the simple *curé* of the Church of Saint Paul and Saint Louis in the Rue Antoine nearby was good enough.

On Friday evening, January 26, Nodier's mind became confused and he rattled on in delirious, disconnected sentences, among which someone grasped, "Read Tacitus and Fénelon to improve your style." No one knew to whom this was di-

rected. Was he still giving advice to young writers, or was he
remembering a childhood lesson by his father, the professor of
Latin and rhetoric? The eclipse of his faculties was only momentary; complete lucidity returned in the morning. He asked
for a glass of water and when he had drunk, Marie, who had
brought it to him, asked if it was good. "Yes, like all things
that come to me from you," he answered. She buried her face
in his pillow to hide her emotions. He then asked after the
health of his grandchildren (Marie's daughters, Berthe, eleven,
Thècle, five, Marie, two, and her son, Emmanuel, eight) and,
upon receiving a favorable report, bid them all please go back
to bed. After saying goodbye to his wife and daughter, he
consoled them and gently asked that they remember him.
"What is the date?" Someone said it was January 27. "Good,"
he replied, "you will remember the date." A few minutes later
he muttered, "Oh! it's incredible how much you have to suffer
to die." Then he turned and faced his beloved Elzevirs and,
though he could no longer see them, lovingly stroked the back-
spines of some volumes bound for him by Dérôme. Upon
which he heaved a great sigh and died. It was seven o'clock.

Balzac wrote to Madame Hanska in St. Petersburg on
March 2: "Nodier died as he had lived, with grace and goodwill, with all his wit, sensitivity, and in full possession of all
his faculties, in short, and as a practicing Catholic; he was
shriven and received the last sacrament. He died calmly, one
might even say joyfully. Five minutes before the end he asked
after the health of his grandchildren and said, 'No illnesses?
Then all is well.' He wanted to be shrouded in his daughter's
wedding veil. [This is confirmed by Nodier's poem, *Change-
ment de domicile* (1834):

> . . . pour linceul,
> Le voile nuptial de Marie, et serrée
> Sur mon coeur, une écharpe au nom de Désirée;
> Et puis, dans me deux mains, leurs rubans, leurs cheveux,
> Leurs bouquets, leurs chansons,—Voilà ce que je veux.

Vodoz thinks this wish was carried out.[14]] Mass was said in
his room, to which he listened with true devotion. In fine, he
was proper, gay, charming, and gracious right up to the last
moment. He let me know that he was deeply moved by my

letter [in which Balzac informed him of his withdrawal as candidate for a seat in the Academy] and regretted dying before he could repair the injustice shown me by the Academy; that he had always wanted me to succeed him and that he still hoped I would."[15]

The funeral took place at noon the following Monday, January 29th, from the same church of Saint Paul and Saint Louis, which was hardly big enough to contain the immense throng of friends and dignitaries who attended. Villemain, Etienne, Victor Hugo, and Lebrun were the pallbearers. Villemain, the same gentleman who had looked so unhappy at Charles' reception into the Academy ten years earlier, was "most profoundly affected," *L'Echo du Jura* reported in its account of the funeral published on Saturday, February 3. On the way to the cemetery, Grenier traveled in the same carriage as Hetzel, who had published many of Nodier's books, Tony Johannot, who had illustrated some of them, and Balzac. Grenier recalled that the latter "spoke all the way to Père Lachaise of Nodier in glowing terms, appreciating the man and the writer with rare sagacity and perfect justice. He expounded to us his celebrated theory concerning the marshals of French literature, in whose ranks he did not hesitate to place the man whose bier we were following."[16] Was this the eulogy Balzac had prepared in case he succeeded Nodier? In subsequent remarks, Grenier added that Balzac was rather bitter about his own misunderstood genius; which would seem to indicate that he had given up hope of occupying any but the famous forty-first seat.

At the graveside there were the usual speeches, first by Etienne, representing the Academy, who recalled Nodier's indefatigable efforts on the famous dictionary, another by Caix, on behalf of the Arsenal librarians, and one by Baron Taylor, who spoke for Nodier's friends. At the conclusion of the last speech, a young man in overalls stepped forward from a group of workingmen and laid a wreath on the catafalque, inscribed "in the name of the working classes." A fitting gesture on the part of that heretofore mute segment of society Nodier had represented so well in his last orientation. Fittingly too, in his last repose Nodier faces Balzac's tomb, and on his left lies Gérard de Nerval.

Notes to Chapters

NOTES TO CHAPTER ONE

1. Charles Weiss, Lettre à Mérimée, 26 mai, 1844. MS in the Bibliothèque de Louvenjoul, D557, Folios 411-12.

2. George Lenôtre, *La Compagnie de Jéhu*, 1931, p. 250, quoted in Maurice Billey, "Un magistrat révolutionnaire. Le père de Charles Nodier," *Bulletin des Sociétés Savantes de Franche-Comté*, No. 2, 1955, p. 159. Billey's 40-page article provides all the known facts regarding Antoine Nodier's tenure on the bench.

3. Dr. Benassis, "Charles Nodier ou l'onirique," *Revue Thérapeutique des Alcaloïdes*, 49:12, May 1941.

4. Anonymous newspaper articles, "Sur Charles Nodier," in *Le Patriote Jurassien*, which appeared from February 21 to March 13, 1844, after Nodier's death and presumably written by his cousin, Dr. Dumont.

5. See Georges Gazier, "La Jeunesse de Charles Nodier," *RHL* 29:433-51 (1922), where a good deal of this correspondence is reproduced. Also Emile Monot, "En l'honneur de Charles Nodier," *Le Vieux Lons*, VI, 99-127 (1913). Six letters from Charles Nodier to Jean Joseph Goy.

6. A. Estignard, *Correspondance inédite de Charles Nodier*, Moniteur Universel, 1876. Lettre IV, p. 8.

7. Quoted in Léonce Pingaud, *La Jeunesse de Charles Nodier*, Champion, 1914, p. 246.

8. Besançon Municipal Library, MS 1416, Correspondance de Charles Nodier, 185 letters, Folio 2, letter from Nodier to Weiss, Paris, 11 nivôse, an IX.

9. A. Viatte, *Les Sources occultes du romantisme*, Charpentier, 1928 (2 vols.), II, 154.

10 Estignard, *op. cit.*, Lettre XIII.

11. In his *Louis David, son école et son temps, souvenirs*, 1855. Also, "Les barbus d'à présent et les barbus de 1800," which appeared in Vol. VII of *Cent-un*, 1832. Nodier made a feeble attempt to answer this last in an article entitled "Les Barbus," which appeared in *Le Temps*, October 5, 1832.

12. Estignard, *op. cit.*, Lettre VI.

13. Jean Larat, *La Tradition de l'exotisme dans l'oeuvre de Charles Nodier*, Champion, 1923, p. 99.

14. Pingaud, *op. cit.*, p. 249.

15. Archives Nationales, MS F⁷6457, Folio 9.

16. Nodier, *Mélanges tirés d'une petite bibliothèque*, 1829, p. 74, note 2. Allen was an Elizabethan Jesuit who noted that all Catholic

missionaries who had been persecuted by the Crown were potential regicides (1587). See P. Quennell, *Shakespeare*, p. 67 (1963).

17. Archives Nationales, MS F⁷6457, Folio 4. Also in Pierre de Vaissière, Nodier conspirateur, *Le Correspondant* (October 25, 1896). Reprinted by De Soye et fils, 23 pp., and F. Baldensperger, "Un interrogatoire de Charles Nodier, Paris, an XII," *RHL* 12:503-07 (1905).

NOTES TO CHAPTER TWO

1. Archives Nationales, Paris F⁷6457, Affaires politiques, an V, 1830. BP 9691-9740. Dossier 9740 entitled "Charles Nodier," Folio 19. Letter dated 8 ventôse, an 13 (February 26, 1805).

2. *Ibid.*, Folio 62. All the documents relating to this conspiracy are to be found in the second half of the dossier 9740 headed "Conspiration projétée dans les départements du Doubs et du Jura," Folios 60-86. The archives of the Doubs department have been thoroughly examined by Marius Dargaud for documents relating to this case. His findings were published in "Nodier mémorialiste," *Revue des Sciences Humaines*, pp. 273-81 (August-September, 1951). The reader interested in this conspiracy may also consult with profit Ernest Hauterive, *La Police secrète du premier empire*, Perrin, 1908, pp. 350-51, number 1091, "Anarchistes." Léclanché later published an absurd denial of the whole plot entitled *La Vérité, ou l'antidote de la conspiration de Mont-sous-Vaudrey* (c. 1810).

3. Auguste Dusillet, "Discours," in *Bulletin de l'Académie des Sciences, Belles-Lettres et Arts de Besançon*, séance publique du 28 janvier, 1846, pp. 3-5.

4. Billey, *op. cit.*, p. 161.

5. Camille Aymonnier, "Charles Nodier linguiste," *Pays Comtois*, 107: 227-33 (August, 1937). Yanette Delétang-Tardif, "Je visite les soleils . . . ," *Cahiers du Sud*, 32: 358-63 (1950). A. Richard Oliver, "Nodier's criticism of the *Dictionnaire de l'Académie Française*," *Modern Language Journal*, 41: 20-25 (January 1957). Jean Richer, *Le roi de Bohème ou les tentations du langage*, Club Français du Livre, 1950.

6. Estignard, *op. cit.*, Lettre XXIX.

7. Nodier later predicted the invention and use of Esperanto. He envisaged "the establishment of a known language like algebra, which will certainly not be supple nor eloquent nor poetic, but whose construction may be very exact; it will be very easy to teach and extremely convenient to use in the few applications to which it will have to be limited: namely the most basic communications of everyday life." Nodier, *Mélanges tirés d'une petite bibliothèque*, LI, "De différents systèmes d'orthographe et de prononciation," pp. 405-06 (1829).

8. Archives Nationales, Charles Nodier, Folios 54-58.

9. See this whole correspondence between Roujoux and Weiss in Gazier, *op. cit., RHL,* 29: 433-45 (1922).

10. Ida Saint-Elme, *Mémoires d'une contemporaine,* Ladvocat, 1828 (8 vols.), IV, 382.

11. Charles Nodier, *Statistique illyrienne,* Ljubljana, Edition "Satura," 1933. Introduction by Janko Tavzes, p. xv.

12. Louis Madelin, *Fouché,* Plon-Nourrit, 1901 (2 vols.), II, 247.

13. Ljubljana, Municipal Archives, F^5, no. 1.

14. In *Le Journal des Débats,* February 4 and 21, 1814, under the title "Littérature Slave"; in *Mélanges de littérature et de critique,* 1820, II, 353-71; in *Annales Romantiques,* 1827-28, pp. 112-18 (abbreviated version) and in *Dictionnaire de la conversation et de la lecture,* 1836, under the heading "Langue et littérature illyriennes," the beginning and the end of the article being slightly altered to conform to the needs of the dictionary.

15. Georges Lefebvre, *Napoléon,* Presses Universitaires de France, 3rd ed., 1947, p. 291.

16. Quoted in Michel Salomon, *Charles Nodier et le Groupe Romantique,* Perrin, 1908, p. 61.

17. Bibliothèque Municipale de Besançon, MS 1416, Folio 151.

18. Quoted in Augustin Thierry, *Les grandes mystifications littéraires,* pp. 162-63.

19. An interesting parallel could be drawn between Nodier's *Histoire* and his friend Bonneville's *Les Jésuites chassés de la maçonnerie et leur poignard brisé par les maçons,* London, 1788 (2 vols.). Bonneville was not a mason, yet he tried to show their organization being infiltrated by the Jesuits, just as Nodier, who had never been in the army, supposed a vast underground opposed to Napoleon penetrating the emperor's most faithful units. Note too the use of classical pseudonyms in both works: Spartacus, the very name used by Nodier to cover the identity of General Moreau, is here used to cloak Adam Weishaupt, who started the legend of Jesuit infiltration and began the Illuminist sect. Nodier owed his introduction to German literature to Bonneville; might not this influence have spread to other areas?

NOTES TO CHAPTER THREE

1. See my article, "Charles Nodier's Cult of Shakespeare as a Facet of French Romanticism," *Orbis Litterarum,* Tome XVII, Fascicules 3-4, 1962. (Copenhagen)

2. *Victor Hugo raconté par un témoin de sa vie,* Librairie Internationale, 1864, II, 394-96.

3. Charles Nodier, *Statistique illyrienne,* France Dobrovoljc, ed., Ljubljana, Edition Satura, 1933.

4. See Eunice Morgan Schenck's excellent thesis, *La part de Charles Nodier dans la formation des idées romantiques de Victor Hugo jusqu'à la préface de Cromwell*, Champion, 1914, p. 27, where some of these articles are reproduced.

5. Jean Larat, *op. cit.*, pp. 193-94.

6. Madame de Stael, *Germany*, London, Murray, 1813 (3 vols.), II, 394.

NOTES TO CHAPTER FOUR

1. Nodier, *Correspondance inédite*, Lettre à Kératry (1838?), in *BBB* 49: 298, 1849.

2. Estignard, *op. cit.*, Lettre LXVIII.

3. Dr. L. Baudin, "Etude médico-littéraire: Charles Nodier médecin et malade," Besançon, Josquin, 1902. Extracted from the *Proceedings of the Académie de Besançon*.

4. There is also the similarity of this hero to Karl Moor of Schiller's *Die Räuber*. Another possible source of *Jean Sbogar*, as pointed out in *Victor Hugo par un témoin* . . . , I, 36, was the real life story of Michael Pezza, better known as Fra Diavolo.

5. Nodier, *Oeuvres*, I:202.

6. Chapter I, "Euloge Schneider ou la Terreur en Alsace," *Revue de Paris*, 1829.

7. Nodier, "Cours d'Aimé Martin," December 20, 1813.

8. Nodier, "Littérature slave," February 4 and 21; "Cours de littérature dramatique, Schlegel," March 4; "Rançon de Du Guesclin," March 20, 1814.

9. Jacob (Paul Lacroix), "Recherches sur la vie littéraire de Charles Nodier," *BBB* 68: 97 (1868).

10. Estignard, *op. cit.*, Lettre XII, where he quotes from Gleizes' letter explaining this symbol to Nodier.

11. Pingaud, *op. cit.*, p. 130.

12. See Marcel Ruff's masterful essay entitled "Maturin et les romantiques français," in a new edition of Nodier and Taylor's *Bertram*, Corti, 1955, pp. 7-66. Ruff studies the impact of this play and of the novel *Melmoth* on Hugo, Balzac, Vigny, Delacroix, and Baudelaire.

13. Pingaud, *op. cit.*, p. 131.

14. Madame Ancelot, *Les salons de Paris*, Tardieu, 1858, p. 124.

15. Of course they were not, but only modern scholarship has discovered that the rule of the unities Scaliger and the later neoclassicists in France thought they saw in Aristotle's *Poetics* was based on an elaborated interpretation of the text.

16. Chateaubriand, *Mémoires d'outre-tombe*, Levaillant ed., Flammarion, 1950 (4 vols.), III: 210 and note 17.

17. Bibliothèque de l'Arsenal, MS 13.990, folio 17. Nodier also wrote

to Chateaubriand on his behalf at this time (1825). The reader may see this letter in the *Bulletin* of the *Société Chateaubriand*, nouvelle série, No. 3, 1959, p. 29, where it was published by M. Pierre Clarac.

18. Amédée Pichot, *Voyage historique et littéraire en Angleterre et en Ecosse*, Ladvocat et Gosselin, 1825 (3 vols.), III: 292-96.

19. Nodier, *Promenade de Dieppe aux montagnes d'Ecosse*, Barba, 1821, pp. 54-55.

20. *Oeuvres de Lord Byron*, quatrième édition par A. P[ichot] précédée d'une notice sur Lord Byron par M. Charles Nodier, Paris, Ladvocat, 1822-25 (8 vols.). My quotes are drawn from Ladvocat's 1824 reprint of Pichot's *Essai sur le génie et le caractère de Lord Byron*, précédé d'une notice préliminaire par M. Charles Nodier, pp. 1-16.

21. Schenck, *op. cit.*, p. 59.

22. Lamartine, *Oeuvres*, Bosquet, 1826 (2 vols.), préface, I:X-XVII.

NOTES TO CHAPTER FIVE

1. Maurice Constantin-Weyer, *L'aventure vécue de Dumas père*, 1944, p. 98.

2. For this information I am indebted in part to Edmond Biré, *Victor Hugo avant 1830*, 1883, p. 293-94, and to Schenck, *op. cit.*, p. 79.

3. Hugo, *Oeuvres complètes*, Hetzel edition, I:8.

4. Georg Brandes, *Main Currents in Nineteenth Century Literature*, 1901-05, IV:33-34.

5. Hugo, *Choses vues, nouvelle série, A Reims*, pp. 5 and 20 respectively.

6. E. Henriot, *Les Romantiques*, 1954, p. 68.

7. Nodier manuscript in the Bibliothèque Nationale, NAF 24.010. Folios 316-32, five letters to Monsieur le Comte, July 8-30, 1825.

8. *Victor Hugo raconté*, etc., II:110-11.

9. Pingaud, *op. cit.*, p. 215.

10. *Ibid.*, p. 135.

11. *Annales Romantiques*, 1827-28, pp. 187-201 and 187 note.

12. René Bray, *Chronologie du romantisme*, 1932, p. 149.

13. Quoted in Ernest Dupuy, *Alfred de Vigny*, 1912, I:192.

14. Helen Maxwell King, *Les doctrines littéraires de la Quotidienne*, 1920, p. 144 and note 7.

15. Gustave Simon, "Charles Nodier, lettres inédites à Victor Hugo," in *RM* 177: 336-37 (1927).

16. Schenck, *op. cit.*, pp. 61-75.

17. René Canat, *L'Hellénisme des romantiques*, 1951, I:181, and Léon Séché, *Le Cénacle de La Muse Française*, 1908, p. 236 note 1.

18. Nodier, *Oeuvres*, X:ix.

19. Bray, *op. cit.*, p. 155.

20. Bray, *op. cit.*, p. 170.

21. *Mercure du XIXe Siècle,* XIX:30-33.

22. Christian A. E. Jensen, *L'Evolution du romantisme, l'année 1826,* 1959, p. 189.

23. Estignard, *op. cit.,* Lettre XCI, March, 1827.

24. Hugo, *Correspondance,* I:444-45.

25. André Billy, *Sainte-Beuve, sa vie et son temps,* 1952, I:64.

26. Estignard, *op. cit.,* Lettre XCVIII.

27. *Lettres de Charles Weiss à Charles Nodier,* publiées par Léonce Pingaud, Champion, 1889, Lettre XXXVI, 10 février, 1829, p. 60.

28. Hugo, *Correspondance,* I:459-60.

29. Sainte-Beuve, *Nouveaux Lundis,* article on Charles Magnin, V:455.

30. Edmond Eggli, *Schiller et le romantisme français,* 1927, I:491. In fact, he sees *Jean Sbogar,* dramatized version, as forming a transition piece between *Robert, chef des brigands,* La Martelière's adaptation of Schiller's *Robbers,* and *Hernani.* I:492.

31. Valentine de Lamartine, *Lettres à Lamartine,* 1892, pp. 93-94.

32. Hugo, *Correspondance,* I:501.

33. *Ibid.,* I:514.

34. *Victor Hugo raconté,* etc., p. 377.

35. Simon, *op. cit., RM* 178:13

36. Hugo, *Correspondance,* I:576.

37. Pingaud, "Le 'Moi' romantique," in *RHL* XXV:194, 1918.

38. Paul Souday, *Les Romantiques à l'Académie,* 1928. Discours de Sainte-Beuve et Réponse de Victor Hugo.

39. Michel Salomon, "Le salon de l'Arsenal d'après des documents inédits," *Revue de Paris,* September 15, 1906, p. 321. Hugo's letter to Cailleux dated March 1, 1845.

40. Bibliophile Jacob, "Charles Nodier et le romantique," in *BBB* XV:1132 (1862).

NOTES TO CHAPTER SIX

1. Unpublished letters, Archives de l'Académie Française, Fauteuil 25.

2. Published in Charavay, *L'Amateur d'Autographes,* Vol. IV, 1868, 5-6.

3. G. Simon, *loc. cit., pp.* 332-34.

4. *BBB* 47:203-04.

5. Estignard, *op. cit.,* Lettre XCII, pp. 196-97.

6. Besides his essay mentioned above, Chapter II, note 5, *cf.* his article, "Charles Nodier dériseur sensé," *Mercure de France* 315:92-97 (1952).

7. Letter of May 5, 1830, published by Jules Marsan in his review of Larat's *La tradition de l'exotisme dans l'oeuvre de Charles Nodier, RLC* IV:359-60 (1924).

8. Letter of May 22, 1830, and notes. *BBB* 58:819-21.

9. Copy of letter to Jules Mennessier, July, 1830, in the Arsenal Library, MS 13.004, Folio 73.

10. Letter to Jean De Bry, September 28, 1830, in Charavay, *op. cit.*, II:132. 1864-65.

11. Edouard Turquety, "Une causerie de Charles Nodier," *BBB* 66:161-73.

12. Nodier, *Souvenirs*, etc., 1831, I, "Préliminaires," XXII.

13. Gazier, "Nodier à l'Arsenal d'après les carnets de voyages de son ami Charles Weiss." *RHL* 31:421 (1924).

14. Nodier, *Souvenirs*, XXXIV.

15. Jacob, "Charles Nodier et Jean De Bry," *BBB* 64:880.

16. *Ibid.*, 869.

17. Nodier, "De la littérature pendant la Révolution. Eloquence de la Tribune. La Gironde." *Revue de Paris*. V:7-8 (1829). See also his "Quelques observations pour servir à l'histoire de la nouvelle école littéraire," *Revue de Paris*, VII:142-43 (1829).

18. Nodier, "Des types en littérature," *Revue de Paris*, XVIII:196 (1830).

19. Nodier, "Miscellanées," *Revue de Paris*, 21:145 (1830) and 24:18 (March, 1831).

20. *Lettres à Lamartine, 1815-1865*, Calmann-Levy, 1892, p. 139.

21. Paul Fabre de Commentry, *Etude de littérature médicale. Charles Nodier naturaliste et médecin; sa théorie du choléra; sa dernière maladie.* Imprimerie du centre médicale, Montluçon, 1891, p. 9. He reproduces most of Charles' letter to Weiss from Metz, which may be found in its entirety in Estignard, *op. cit.*, pp. 249-52.

22. Nodier, Letter to Dr. Koreff, April 4, 1832, in *BBB* 60:1732.

23. Weiss, Letter to Mérimée dated June 12, 1844, in Bibliothèque de Louvenjoul, MS D557, Folios 424-25.

24. Gazier, *loc. cit.*, p. 429.

25. Most recently by André Lebois, *Un bréviaire de compagnonnage. La Fée aux miettes de Charles Nodier*, Archives des Lettres Modernes, No. 40, 1961 (40 pages); and Antoine Fongaro, "A-t-on lu la *Fée aux Miettes?*" in *Revue des Sciences Humaines*, fasicule 107, juillet-septembre, 1962, pp. 439-52.

26. Pingaud, *Lettres de Weiss à Nodier*, Champion, 1889, p. 104.

27. René Doumic, "Comment on devient académicien," in *Trois siècles de l'Académie Française*, p. 62.

28. Letter published by Bibliophile Jacob, Charles Nodier et Jean De Bry, *BBB* 64:882-83.

29. Nodier, Letter to Amanton (unpublished) in the Arsenal Library, MS 14.038.

30. Published by Bibliophile Jacob in "Charles Nodier et le romantique," *BBB* 62:1137.

31. Unpublished MS in Victor Cousin Library. MS 241, Vol. XXVIII, five letters to Victor Cousin, 1830-42.

32. Weiss, *Journal*, extracts published by Eugène Tavernier in *Les Gaudes*, Vols. VIII and IX, August 1, 1908-October, 1913.

33. Maurice Souriau, *Népomucène Lemercier et ses correspondants*, p. 270.

34. Gustave Simon, "Mémoires inédits, Une élection à l'Académie Française en 1836." In *Le Temps*, December 14, 1913.

NOTES TO CHAPTER SEVEN

1. Quoted in *BBB* 58:821-22.

2. Nodier, Letter of November 9, 1836, *ibid.*, 825.

3. Emile Picard, "Quelques savants à l'Académie Française," in *Trois siècles de l'Académie Française*, p. 398.

4. François Grille, *Miettes littéraires*, 1853, III:284.

5. Emile Ripert, *La renaissance provençale*, 1917, p. 111.

6. Nodier, "Comment les patois furent détruits en France," *BBB* February, 1835. (Separate pamphlet to accompany No. 14) and "La Convention et la grammaire," originally published in *Drapeau Blanc*, August 27, 1819, as "Le Génie de la Révolution considéré dans l'éducation."

7. Nodier "Les Papillotes du perruquier d'Agen," *BBB*, October, 1835. (To accompany No. 20.)

8. Jean Larat, *op. cit.*, p. 210.

9. Quoted in Viatte, *op. cit.*, p. 230.

10. In his *Le Conte fantastique en France de Nodier à Maupassant*, 1951, p. 167.

11. Unpublished Arsenal MS 13.004, Folio 70.

12. Papiers Lebrun, MS in the Bibliothèque Mazarine, Carton 6, Liasse 1, Folios 37-38. (Unpublished.)

13. Four letters of Charles Nodier in the possession of Adolphe Asseline's great-granddaughter, Madame Madeleine Pourpoint.

14. Jules Vodoz, *La Fée aux miettes. Essai sur le rôle du subconscient dans l'oeuvre de Charles Nodier*, 1925, p. 314, note 4.

15. Balzac, *Correspondance 1819-1850*, Lévy, 1876 (2 vols.), II:86-87.

16. Edouard Grenier, Charles Nodier et Musset, in *Revue Bleue* 50:304 (1892). Elsewhere Balzac, though he dedicated *La Rabouilleuse* to Nodier and used to call him "un grand musicien littéraire," was less generous: Larat, *op. cit.*, p. 431, wrote that Balzac thought Nodier a *dilettante ennuyé* and only regretted his death because then he could not obtain his vote, and Professor Castex has pointed out in a recent article, "Balzac et Charles Nodier," in *L'Année Balzacienne* (1962) that the great novelist mentioned Nodier in a letter to Alphonse Levasseur "with considerable disdain as a literary loafer" (p. 198) and that he was put out because "Nodier, in his capacity as a critic, had not made more of Balzac's novels (which would have helped the latter no end) in spite of the fact that he had made several advances to Nodier on this subject" (p. 209).

Index